IMPROVING TEACHING

Effective teaching makes a huge difference to students' knowledge, and their life chances. But improving teaching is extremely difficult – many changes within schools have little impact on classroom practice. This new book from bestselling author, Harry Fletcher-Wood, shows how leaders can design and deliver effective professional development and help teachers make lasting improvements. Addressing common barriers, including lack of focus and time pressure, it synthesises key ideas and shows how they can be implemented step-by-step.

Blending research and experience, the book offers practical tools to help teacher educators refine their practice and solve the critical challenges they face, including:

- Designing a coherent programme
- Leading effective training
- Coaching teachers to improve
- Supporting teachers to adopt new habits
- Leading change within the school
- Evaluating impact

Each challenge is addressed through bitesize steps, illustrated with worked examples. Suggested actions, reflection questions and checklists help the reader put new ideas into practice immediately. Readable, evidence-informed and easy-to-apply, *Improving Teaching* is an essential guide for anyone helping teachers to get better.

Harry Fletcher-Wood is a former history teacher and head of professional development. He has worked on developing expert teachers at Teach First and Ambition Institute, and is currently Director of Training at Steplab, leading their Certificate programme for teacher educators. Harry co-led the Education Endowment Foundation's systematic review of professional development.

IMPROVING TEACHING

A Guide to Effective Professional Development

Harry Fletcher-Wood

Routledge
Taylor & Francis Group
LONDON AND NEW YORK

Designed cover image: © Getty Images

First published 2026
by Routledge
4 Park Square, Milton Park, Abingdon, Oxon OX14 4RN

and by Routledge
605 Third Avenue, New York, NY 10158

Routledge is an imprint of the Taylor & Francis Group, an informa business

British Library Cataloguing-in-Publication Data
Names: Fletcher-Wood, Harry author
Title: Improving teaching : a step-by-step guide to effective professional development / Harry Fletcher-Wood.
Description: Abingdon, Oxon ; New York, NY : Routledge, 2026. | Includes bibliographical references and index.
Identifiers: LCCN 2026007243 (print) | LCCN 2026007244 (ebook) | ISBN 9781032574943 hardback | ISBN 9781032574936 paperback | ISBN 9781003439622 ebook
Subjects: LCSH: Effective teaching | Teaching–Methodology | Teaching–Vocational guidance
Classification: LCC LB1025.3 .F588 2026 (print) | LCC LB1025.3 (ebook)
LC record available at https://lccn.loc.gov/2026007243
LC ebook record available at https://lccn.loc.gov/2026007244

ISBN: 978-1-032-57494-3 (hbk)
ISBN: 978-1-032-57493-6 (pbk)
ISBN: 978-1-003-43962-2 (ebk)

DOI: 10.4324/9781003439622

Typeset in Interstate
by Apex CoVantage, LLC

For Doug Lemov and Dylan Wiliam

CONTENTS

ACKNOWLEDGEMENTS

I developed the core themes in this book for the Ambition Institute Teacher Education Fellowship. I'm grateful to the wonderful school leaders who participated - especially the Pilot Cohort: Ben Bignall, Lucy Blewett, Jen Calvert, Josh Goodrich and Emma McCrea. Thank you particularly to the Fellows who have kindly shared their work as case studies: Claire Couves, Lucy Davies, Alex Douglas, John Kirkman and Lucy Newman.

My understanding of the evidence around teacher development has been shaped by two collaborative projects with Sam Sims, examining weaknesses in existing studies and testing a better model. Intensely smart, hard-working and generous, Sam has taught me a huge amount, and been huge fun to work with. Sarah Cottinghatt and Alison O'Mara-Eves also played a key role in the latter project. I enjoyed working with James Zuccollo and his colleagues at the Education Policy Institute on an earlier meta-analysis of professional development programmes.

Over a decade ago, Doug Lemov and Brent Maddin humbly and generously taught me how to make deliberate practice work. My touchstone for training design remains the work of Doug, Colleen Driggs, Jen Kim, Erica Woolway, Katie Yezzi, and the Teach Like a Champion team. My understanding of how practice works and, in particular, how to evaluate it, grew enormously through working with Brent, Liam Honigsberg, Kaycee Salmacia, and Teacher Squared. The influence of both teams on Chapter 2 will be clear to anyone who has worked with them.

Josh Goodrich has taught me an enormous amount about instructional coaching, initially on the Teacher Education Fellowship, latterly at Steplab. He has an unerring instinct for what's needed to make changes work for teachers - and for making work fun. Developing the Steplab Certificate programmes has pushed my thinking about implementation - particular thanks to Rachel Sewell and Ania Townsend. Thank you also to Steve Allen for permission to share Farnborough Spencer Academy's coaching experience as a case study.

At Ambition Institute, Peps McCrea offered invaluable advice which helped me overcome key challenges in course design. Jen Barker shared wisdom and friendship, for two jobs in a row. The Fellowship, and the Institute for Teaching, would not have come into existence without the vision and determination of Marie Hamer and Matt Hood.

Earlier still, thank you to Sarah Jones, who saw my interest in teacher development before I did, and gave me the chance to pursue it. And to Dylan Wiliam, who has shaped the thinking of a generation of teachers and leaders - and has been invariably encouraging and generous in his support.

A few kind readers offered feedback on early drafts of this book: Bob Arnold, Brad Johnson, Gary Seal, Helen Riddle and Finola Wilson. I received valuable feedback from Routledge's anonymous review panel. Annamarie Kino, Ashley Johnstone, and Lucia Schmid patiently steered the book through the publishing process.

The journey would not have been complete, or joyful, without the company of Loren, Daniel, Christopher, and Benjamin.

Introduction

Introduction: Chapter map

It's hard to teach well
It's hard to help teachers teach well

This matters:

- **Access to effective teaching matters**
- **Every teacher can improve**

But we're not very good at improving teaching:

- We focus on structural changes which have limited impact on classrooms
- Improvement plateaus for most teachers after a couple of years
- Teachers are sceptical about professional development

This book draws on three experiences:

- Leading professional development in a school, learning through trial and error
- Leading research to establish what makes professional development effective
- Leading courses for teacher educators, testing these ideas across contexts

This book is a practical guide for anyone trying to improve teaching

The book is designed around two big goals:

Helping teachers improve, by establishing:

1) How we can build a coherent professional development programme
2) How we can lead effective training
3) How we can coach individual teachers
4) How we can help teachers change

Improving teaching across the school, by deciding:

5) How we can choose a focus for improvement
6) How we can lead change
7) How we can evaluate our impact

The book is imperfect – tell me what you learn

DOI: 10.4324/9781003439622-1

The challenge

If you ask teacher educators the biggest challenge they face,[1] some point to student activity in lessons:

- "Students are not completing enough work/producing high-quality work in lesson."
- "Students with special educational needs have a poor experience in lessons, and are not learning much."
- "Students are passive in the classroom."
- "Students' books are disorganised and include little work."

Some highlight weaknesses in teaching:

- "Teachers don't manage behaviour well in lessons."
- "Teachers are not always as effective as they could be."
- "Teachers apply the science of learning incoherently."
- "Teachers have inconsistent mental models of effective pedagogy."
- "Teachers ask closed questions, and don't follow up to encourage effective discussion."

Others look at the school as a whole:

- "We can't be sure that lessons are consistently ensuring high-quality learning outcomes."
- "There isn't enough consistently effective teaching happening across the school."

While others point to professional development, and its impact:

- "Teachers' practice is not improving."
- "Professional development does not transfer to the classroom: teachers are motivated during the session, but don't use the strategies they learn."
- "Teachers are not developing skills/habits as quickly or as consistently as needed."
- "Teachers think they are good enough already."

Their words suggest two crucial challenges facing anyone trying to improve teaching:

1) It's hard to teach well.
2) It's hard to help teachers improve.

This book tries to show how we can solve them.

> *It's hard to improve teaching – this book tries to show how we can do it.*

Why improve teaching?

It's really hard to teach well. If I were choosing a teacher for my child, I would want someone who could build relationships well and manage the classroom effectively. I'd hope they knew their stuff and could teach it inspiringly. I'd want my child to learn a lot - and have fun doing it. This is a demanding job description, and we haven't even considered sport, inclusion, trips, communicating effectively with parents, or the 1001 other things we ask of teachers. Few humans can do all these things well. Super as teachers are, schools aren't staffed by superheroes. There's always room for improvement.

Improvement - increasing teaching effectiveness - matters. Students with more effective teachers learn more.[2] These teachers boost grades *and* make a lasting difference to students' lives.[3] Ideally, every student would have access to "more effective" teachers. But improving teaching matters most for the students who need it most: poorer students are more likely to have unqualified teachers, less experienced teachers, and teachers who aren't subject experts.[4] If we can improve teaching, we can improve students' lives.

Improving teaching means working with a rich mix of people. On average, one in ten of our colleagues will be new to the profession.[5] They'll work alongside experienced colleagues who are set in their ways, colleagues who've seen it all before and view innovation with understandable cynicism, and colleagues who would love to get better, but have spent all night up with their own kids. Some teachers will be struggling with behaviour, others with new subjects or curricula, some with planning, others with marking. A few may be enthusiastic geeks who we can hope will take on our role one day. Every one of them, every one of us, can improve. *If* we can find a way to help them.

Teaching is hard. Improving teaching matters. Every teacher can improve - if we can find a way to help them.

Dead ends in improving teaching

In the last fifteen years, there have been many policies intended to improve schools:

- Changing school structures: encouraging schools to become academies, academies to form trusts, anyone to create free schools;
- Changing entry criteria: discouraging teachers with third-class degrees from becoming teachers; raising and lowering teacher bursaries in different subjects;
- Increasing pressure on teachers: more observations, performance-related pay;
- Changing the curriculum, exams, and inspection frameworks.

There isn't scope to discuss the pros and cons of each. What matters is how little most have influenced the classroom. Take academisation - making schools independent of the local council. The first academies were dramatically different from the schools they replaced, as new leaders, new buildings, and new money created wholly new environments. But academisation now means a new name (perhaps), a new uniform (perhaps), and a new leader (perhaps). Schools make changes like this all the time: new programmes, structures, job titles. They're obvious, noisy, and time-consuming. But *tinkering with structures rarely changes what really matters: teachers' and students' classroom habits*. If we want students to learn more, we must change how teachers plan, call on students, and give feedback - and how students focus, contribute, and persevere.[6] Some of these policies have helped, raising expectations and creating impressive schools and trusts. Others have proved distracting. What matters most - but what is often neglected, as though it were beyond the reach of policy-makers - is improving classroom practice.

Tinkering with structures rarely does what matters most: influence teachers' and students' classroom practice.

Is professional development helping?

Structural changes can create an environment which supports professional development. But this isn't enough to ensure teachers improve: they need help, guidance, and encouragement to change. Providing this help is tricky. Every school has some kind of professional development programme. But these programmes rarely improve teaching. This might be because:

- Professional development means a handful of sessions listening to speakers in the hall. Little connects these sessions to day-to-day practice: speakers' suggestions are soon forgotten.
- Schools lack an agreed model of effective teaching, or a shared set of priorities. Leaders and teachers may disagree about how to improve, causing discontent or paralysis. Or teachers may be pulled in different directions by leaders with conflicting priorities.
- Teachers receive feedback which is vague, excessive, or unhelpful. They come to treat observations and meetings as chores to prepare and perform for - not chances to improve.
- Teachers become sceptical and cynical about professional development. They'd rather be marking or planning - so they opt out when they can, disengage when they can't.

We can use two bodies of evidence to test whether professional development really improves teaching. First, we can look at teacher growth: how much more do students learn with an experienced teacher, as opposed to a novice? Teacher effectiveness jumps initially - then stagnates. The initial jump makes sense: think back to everything you struggled with in your first week of teaching. Think how fast you learned. Within two or three years however, teacher growth stagnates. Teachers still get better - but much, much more slowly.[7] Indeed, in an average year, three in ten teachers improve, five stay the same - and two get worse.[8] If most teachers don't get better most years, professional development can't be making much of a difference.

Second, we can ask teachers. Most say that professional development isn't doing much good. Only four in ten believe what their school does improves teaching.[9] What if professional development stopped - *for five years*? Most teachers are unconcerned. Out of ten:

- Two say it's no problem: they'll get better anyway.
- Two say it makes no difference: they wouldn't have changed anyway.
- Four expect their growth to be slightly worse.
- Just two expect to be significantly worse.[10]

The influence this has on teachers' priorities is best illustrated by an imagined choice between perks including free food, unlimited photocopying, or an extra free hour each week. Half of teachers choose the extra hour; 17% the free food. Just 7% want three days' professional development *of their choice*.[11] When food is more tempting than help to improve, we - teacher educators - have a problem. Believing that, "Things are different in our school" is tempting - but perhaps unrealistic. Most senior leaders believe their school's professional development is working. Most classroom teachers disagree.[12] Teachers' perceptions mirror the evidence around teacher growth: most professional development isn't helping.

Most existing professional development isn't helping teachers improve.

Attempting to improve teaching

Over the last decade, I've worked on this challenge in three different ways. Each informs this book.

As a head of teaching and learning...

In 2012, as I joined a new school, I was invited to lead professional development. Someone had to do it, and apparently I'd shown particular interest in teaching and learning at interview. I built the programme from scratch. This meant setting goals, leading sessions, establishing teacher learning communities and, later, introducing instructional coaching. It proved hard! I was excited, my colleagues were enthusiastic, but I lacked a template, or a mentor. Much of my learning came through trial and error. For example, seeing the limited impact of early sessions, I learned to focus less on the underlying research and more on supporting teacher implementation. Meanwhile, I struggled to protect professional development time: briefings overran, middle leaders missed sessions, heads of department used the time to order stock. Most importantly, teaching didn't improve as fast as I'd have liked.

Later, working with other heads of teaching and learning, I learned how common these experiences are. Teacher educators are often appointed because they're teaching enthusiasts. Enthusiasm helps, but it doesn't make you an effective teacher educator. It's easy to feel like an imposter when you're meant to "develop" older, wiser, and more effective colleagues. Teacher educators do often get a blank slate. There's usually an existing programme, but they're appointed to design - to imagine - something better. There's rarely a roadmap. Professional development is always under pressure from more urgent tasks: pupil incidents, parental calls, marking. It's constrained by policies the teacher educator struggles to influence, like timetabling and performance management. I've lived these challenges: I've tried to write a book which both addresses them and reflects schools' realities.

As a researcher...

Seeking to become a better teacher educator, I dug into the evidence around teacher development. Three research projects transformed my thinking. First, Sam Sims and I tested the consensus around effective professional development. This consensus was well-established, widely accepted, and informed national teacher development standards. But we found significant weaknesses in the evidence and the theory underpinning it.[13] Second, James Zuccollo and I conducted a meta-analysis of teacher professional development programmes.[14] Closely studying programme design and implementation proved eye-opening. Some programmes adopted questionable goals: discouraging teacher intervention, for example, leaving students to work things out themselves (and baffled).[15] Other programmes were undone by their implementation: student logins didn't work,[16] busy teachers dropped out,[17] programmes didn't align with schools' needs.[18] Third, I worked with Sam Sims again on a systematic review of teacher professional development. We developed and tested a new model to explain what makes a programme successful, finding compelling evidence for it.[19]

The book reflects this research. My goal is helping teacher educators, so rather than recapitulating the technical intricacies, I've shown how our findings apply in practice. (If you really want to interrogate the process, each paper is freely available online.) The results of our systematic review guide my suggestions for designing professional development in Chapters 2 and 3. I address the barriers which have hampered past programmes through the implementation strategies discussed in Chapters 4 and 6. We now have research showing what makes teacher development effective. Evaluations of past programmes record hundreds of successes and failures from which we can learn. I've spent years making sense of this evidence: I've tried to synthesise it in this book, and make it usable for teacher educators.

As a course leader...

Building on this research and experience, I've created two development programmes for teacher educators. First, I designed and led the Fellowship in Teacher Education at Ambition Institute, from its inception to its fifth cohort. I began by examining the evidence around developing teacher educators. This proved limited! So I looked for outside inspiration, from medical training in the UK, and from teacher development organisations as far afield as Singapore and the USA. Meanwhile, I interviewed teacher educators, trying to understand the pressures they faced and the help they needed. Designing in the abstract can only take you so far: I tested my ideas through a pilot programme. Working with that pilot group, and then another four cohorts of brilliant teacher educators, pushed my thinking and refined the programme's underlying ideas and practical tools. More recently, I designed the Certificate in Professional Development Leadership at Steplab. The goal was similar - better teacher development. But the programme benefits from focusing on specific models of improvement - and from Steplab's platform and resources. In all, I've spent over a decade working with, and learning from, hundreds of teacher educators.

These teacher educators have rigorously tested almost everything in this book. They've applied its principles as coaches, senior leaders, headteachers, teacher trainers, and across groups of schools. They've adapted the tools to work in small, rural primary schools, big, struggling secondary schools, ambitious, growing trusts, and established teacher training providers. They've overcome uncertainty, lack of time, and shifting, competing priorities. The teacher educators I've worked with have acted as a jury. They've sorted the promising, the powerful, and the possible from the idealistic, the impractical, and the impossible. In this book, I've tried to share the approaches which have worked for them, across a range of schools. Hopefully, this means they will work for you too.

What does the book do?

I began by saying that improving teaching is difficult, and important. Next, I suggested that much professional development doesn't help. This book aims to help teacher educators overcome these challenges. I then described how I've worked on them, through practice, research, and teaching teacher educators. This book turns my learning from these experiences into practical guidance. It shares the strategies I've used, and taught others to use. It breaks each strategy into steps, offering guidance and models for each. And it tries to share the insights I've gained along the way. The book offers teacher educators a toolkit to improve teaching.

This book offers a toolkit for teacher educators to improve teaching, based on my learning from practice, research, and teaching teacher educators.

Who is the book for?

If you want to help teachers get better, this book is for you. It's primarily addressed to leaders improving teaching in schools. But wherever you work, you can use its strategies. All problems in education are fractal.[20] A teacher must inspire students, promote thinking, and ensure learning. A leader faces identical challenges. Effective teacher learning considers working memory, promotes independent practice, and supports habit change. This applies whether you're coaching a trainee, supporting a department, training the whole school, or planning learning across fifty schools. For simplicity, each chapter describes how these principles apply to a school's professional development programme. But they work just as well in coaching conversations, departments, and groups of schools. At the end of each chapter, I suggest ways they could be applied by an individual teacher, a middle leader, and a leader working across schools. In Chapter 8, I explore these challenges further. The most immediately relevant elements of the book will change, as your role changes, and as your teacher development programme evolves. We can't do everything at once: building an effective programme takes years. But whatever your title and wherever you work, if you're trying to improve teaching, I hope this book will help.

If you want to help teachers improve, this book is for you.

How is the book organised?

This book is shaped around the challenges teacher educators face. Part I looks at helping teachers improve. We consider:

1) How we can build a coherent professional development programme
2) How we can lead effective training
3) How we can coach individual teachers
4) How we can help teachers change

This should help you design and lead effective professional development sessions. But teacher educators are drawn into a bigger question: how can the school support ongoing teacher improvement? In Part II, we consider:

5) How we can choose a focus for improvement
6) How we can lead change
7) How we can evaluate our impact

Each chapter tackles one of these challenges. The chapters build on one another: it's easier to design an effective training session with a coherent model of teaching, for example. But if a particular challenge is on your mind, start there (the introduction concludes with an overview of the book to help you choose where). Each chapter follows a similar structure: I introduce the goal, show what success looks like, and explain how to pursue it, with worked examples of each step. Each chapter begins with a map, to aid navigation, and concludes with practical guidance, including a case study, checklist, and suggested next steps. In the final chapter, I address wider questions which teacher educators frequently ask, and share suggestions to address specific challenges.

The book offers a practical guide to address seven key challenges: Part I looks at leading teacher development; Part II looks at how the school can promote teacher improvement.

A note on language

The words we use to describe teacher development attract controversy with remarkable ease. For example, I've heard the term, "professional development" criticised. Apparently, "professional development and learning" is better, although I'm not sure how we can develop without learning. The word "training" is often described as unprofessional and demeaning - although I understand that pilots, surgeons, and astronauts happily undergo training. I'm not always convinced that these debates help us improve teaching, but to avoid ambiguity, here are a few terms I'll use throughout:

- Professional development - activity designed to improve teaching. As we'll see, this ends up being quite far reaching.

- Teacher educator - anyone helping teachers improve. This this may include coaches, mentors, heads of teaching and learning, headteachers, and trust leaders.
- Session - any period of time dedicated to professional development.
- Training - what happens during sessions.

Let's focus on substance, not semantics.

Coda

This book shares what I've learned. It is, no doubt, imperfect, due to the limits of my experience, the errors in my judgement, and my failure to communicate effectively. That's why I'm always curious to know what you make of it: how you use it, what you learn, and how you can improve upon it. Please let me know.

I'm still learning - please help!

Where should I start?

The chart below summarises the book. Each chapter builds on the previous ones, but if a particular issue is on your mind, you may want to start there.

Chapter 8 includes a survey checking teachers' perceptions of professional development provision - this might also help you choose priorities.

Improving Teaching: an overview

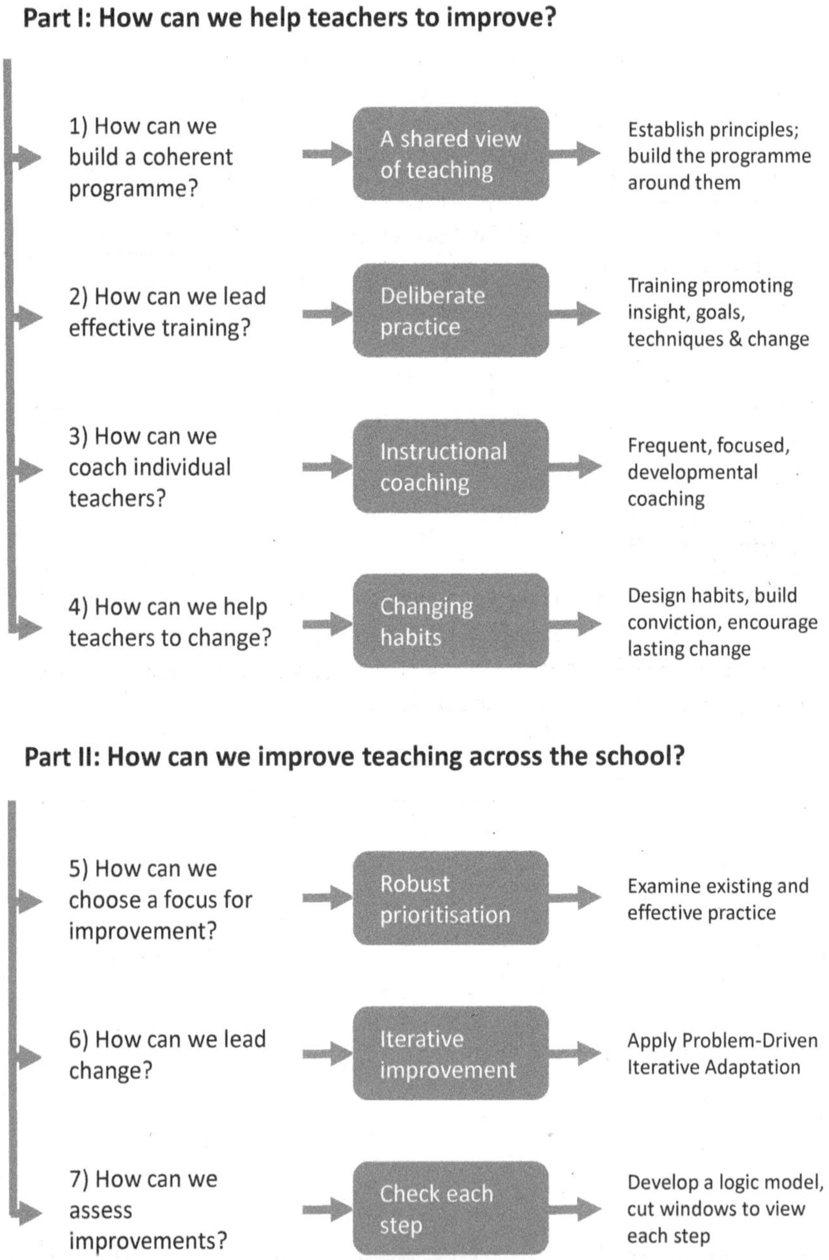

Part I

How can we help teachers improve?

Part I looks at how teacher educators can help teachers get better. We examine four challenges:

- In Chapter 1, we consider how to build a coherent teacher development programme. An effective programme draws on a shared understanding of effective teaching. How can we build this shared understanding?
- In Chapter 2, we look at helping teachers gain new skills. It's hard to design an effective training session: we must introduce an idea or skill, enlist teachers' enthusiasm, help teachers master it, and prepare them to apply it. We examine ways to design and run a session which achieves these goals.
- In Chapter 3, we look at observing lessons, and coaching teachers to improve. What should we look for when observing teaching? How can we ensure feedback conversations help?
- Chapter 4 looks at helping teachers make lasting changes. Teachers are busy; change is hard. How can we make it easier to get going, and keep going?

This division helps us consider one challenge at a time – but it's artificial. A teacher educator may draw on ideas from all four chapters in a single interaction. For example, during a coaching meeting, we would apply ideas from Chapter 3, on coaching. But our approach reflects our model of teaching (Chapter 1) and would seek to support change (Chapter 4). The examples within each chapter go some way towards showing how ideas in different chapters can be integrated successfully. In Part II, we turn to building teacher improvement into the school's work. We'll look at how we can apply the strategies described in Part I to create lasting change in schools.

DOI: 10.4324/9781003439622-2

1 How can we build a coherent professional development programme?

Chapter map

An effective teacher development programme is founded on a shared view of teaching and learning

↓

The science of learning offers a powerful source of coherence, because:

- Teachers need to know how learning happens
- The science of learning guides the teacher development process
- The science of learning is here to stay

Step 1: Establish the principles of learning for ourselves

a) Establish what we know, and need to know
b) Deepen our knowledge
c) Articulate what we know

Or, use an existing model

Step 2: Articulate and exemplify the principles and practices

a) Formulate the principles
b) Organise the principles memorably
c) Collate examples

Step 3: Build the teacher development programme on these principles

a) Ensure staff know and can use the principles
b) Shape professional development using the principles
c) Evaluate progress and refine the principles

Step 4: Support subject specificity

↓

We can then plan training (Chapter 2), coach individuals (Chapter 3), support teachers to change (Chapter 4), and improve teaching across the school (Part II).

DOI: 10.4324/9781003439622-3

When we take on responsibility for teacher professional development, we're not just committing to organising a few training sessions. Planning sessions may be our first concern (if it's your biggest concern currently, you may want to skip to Chapter 2). But our underlying task is creating a programme which offers every teacher the learning and support they need in order to improve. In this chapter, we'll first look at why this matters, by contrasting scattered training activities with a coherent programme. The chapter then guides you to choose organising principles and apply them to your programme. We'll look at the science of learning as a potential source of coherence, a glue to hold different elements together. Then, we'll examine three steps which take us from a blank page to a coherent programme: establishing principles of learning, articulating and exemplifying them, and building a programme around them. With these foundations in place, we can decide and communicate what we want to improve, how we plan to improve, and what action is needed.

The goal of this chapter is to help you build a coherent professional development programme using the science of learning.

Why does building a coherent programme matter?

Let's contrast two ways to approach professional development. We'll call the first "unfocused". Lots of professional development takes place, but sessions jump from one topic to another. One example is the approach many schools used to take to supporting newly-qualified teachers. Each week, a different member of staff presents on their area of expertise: week one, Mehal on modelling; week two, Maria on using technology; week three, Michael on autism. This approach has advantages: it covers a range of topics, draws on a breadth of expertise, and it's easy for those presenting. But it's not a programme: it's a series of isolated sessions. This means it lacks coherence: each presenter shares their approach - but Mehal's vision of great teaching contrasts almost entirely with Maria's. Teachers are left to make sense of these conflicting messages. Moreover, there's no underlying plan to help teachers connect ideas, revisit the most important ones, and build a meaningful model of teaching.

This example is a convenient illustration; it's something readers may have experienced. It also reflects the way many schools approach professional development as a whole. For example, we may see:

- Training jumping between topics: literacy one term, questioning the next, emotional climate the one after;
- Different elements pulling in different directions: whole-school training on behaviour, coaching focused on feedback, inquiry groups studying whatever interests them;
- Three different leaders responsible for coaching, initial teacher training and whole-school professional development - each pursuing slightly different goals.

Some elements may be effective. Every element could be effective, in its own terms. But we make it hard for teachers to improve if each new session brings a new topic, a new goal, and perhaps even a new way of looking at teaching. Changing teaching practice requires sustained, focused effort and support. An unfocused approach undermines this.

Let's compare an unfocused approach with a coherent professional development programme. Two differences stand out. First, decisions about teaching and learning are guided, not by individual preferences, but by an agreed core of principles and practices. These principles might include modelling, giving usable feedback, and supporting students to meet the highest expectations. This agreed core is used everywhere. We find it in lesson planning and observation feedback, idle discussion, and leadership team meetings. (Teachers are also encouraged to innovate and experiment, sticking to the principles, but adapting the practices to suit their needs.) Second, professional development isn't an assortment of scattered efforts - it's a coherent programme. Different elements align to pursue common goals (goals drawn from the agreed core). Let's say the current goal is better modelling. We might see whole-school training introduce the principles, departments adapt the practices to fit their subjects, and coaches offer individual feedback on the results.

These two features - a shared view of good teaching and a coherent programme - make improving teaching much easier. Teachers still enjoy a range of influences, with training and feedback from different colleagues, each with their own slant and style. But these influences sit within a common framework: they no longer pull in different directions. This makes goals and expectations clearer. Professional development sessions echo and reinforce each other, rather than sitting in isolation (or contradicting one another). This means teachers get many chances to make sense of, test, adapt, and adopt new ideas. We can picture the effect this coherent programme has. Faced with multiple, conflicting, half-remembered improvement suggestions, most teachers will let them slide, and get on with their job. By offering clear goals and focused, ongoing support instead, we should increase teachers' motivation and their ability to change. A coherent programme makes teacher improvement far more likely.

> *An effective teacher development programme coherently pursues goals rooted in a shared view of teaching and learning.*

What makes a programme coherent?

If it is to be coherent, we need something to hold our programme together, some guiding purpose. In the short term, we could build a programme around a specific goal: improving behaviour, for example. But we need some kind of lasting framework. Our preferences and beliefs won't suffice. Valuable as they are, we need a source of coherence which works no matter who you are, who you teach, what you teach, and where you teach. The best source of this coherence is the science of learning, for three reasons.

The core task for teacher development is teaching teachers how learners learn

Students learn better when new learning builds on prior knowledge, when they meaningfully process new ideas, and when they revisit key points. They learn better when teaching reflects how learning happens. Mechanics need to know how engines work, medics need to know how the body functions, and teachers need to know how learning happens. The most important thing a school's professional development programme can do is help teachers understand and apply the science of learning.

Over the last decade, the science of learning has gained far greater attention in schools and in teacher training. But it remains a professional development priority, for two reasons. First, many teachers still haven't encountered or grasped key ideas. For example, fewer than four in ten teachers report having *heard* of Ebbinghaus's forgetting curve (which illustrates how fast learners forget new information).[1] More than eight in ten teachers have heard of cognitive load theory. But, given a list of possible types of cognitive load, only two thirds correctly selected intrinsic and extraneous. Almost half chose incorrect options, including live, static, imposed and overload - or said they didn't know at all.[2] Universal teacher understanding of the science of learning remains a distant goal.

The second reason for prioritising the science of learning is that introducing the principles is easy - applying them consistently and effectively is hard. Minimising unwanted cognitive load sounds fairly simple. Minimising unwanted cognitive load - while faithfully portraying complex ideas, appropriately challenging students with a range of prior knowledge, covering the curriculum quickly enough, and maintaining student motivation, sounds almost as complicated as it is. Teacher educators often set out to cover the science of learning in a half term, before moving on to something harder. But teachers have to absorb the principles, adapt them to their subject, phase and teaching style, and adopt new habits. This takes far longer. So, what teacher educators set out to cover swiftly becomes instead an ongoing focus for professional development. **Teaching teachers to understand and apply the science of learning is a huge task, never finished: it should be at the core of our teacher development programme.**

> *To teach effectively, teachers must apply the science of learning - this makes it a lasting, meaningful focus for teacher development.*

The science of learning guides the teacher development process

Focusing on the science of learning has an added benefit: it shapes the *process* of teacher development. First, it informs training design. Teaching teachers is not so different to teaching students. Teachers, like students, form misconceptions, forget things, and need to think about the meaning of new ideas. The science of learning helps us plan training which addresses these challenges. Second, it creates common ground across subjects and phases. Effective teaching looks different in drama, maths, and early years - but all successful teachers encourage meaningful processing, tackle misconceptions, and revisit key points. Third, by creating common ground, the science of learning helps us develop a shared understanding and common language around effective teaching. This common language makes it far easier to recognise, discuss, and learn from good practice.[3] So, **the science of learning guides how we teach teachers, providing a unifying focus for school improvement**.

The science of learning helps us take a coherent approach to the process of teacher development.

The science of learning is here to stay

Some claim that the science of learning is a fad.[4] Is this a fair criticism? To answer, I'll draw on Michael Young's work on establishing what we should teach. Young contrasted a curriculum based on a fixed set of facts with a curriculum which reflects the findings of a research community (such as historians, or chemists).[5] Venerating a handful of facts is clearly limiting. Instead, we want to share the key findings of a specific research community: scholars studying how people learn. This distinction allows us to identify how fixed a curriculum for teachers should be (and how faddish this is). Much of what we teach - the underlying principles of learning - is established fact. For example, Ebbinghaus's discovery of the forgetting curve (how fast people forget new information) dates from 1880. His findings were replicated by researchers in 2015.[6] That people forget new information quickly is a crucial insight: we'll want to teach it for the foreseeable future. Equally, when research moves on, what we teach should change too. For example, there's currently extensive academic debate about growth mindset. Researchers disagree about basic questions. Does it help students? Which students? When and how?[7] As researchers learn more, what we tell teachers will change. **We are sharing the established insights of a research community (and updating what we teach when the research moves on). This provides a clear rationale for our teacher development programme.**

The science of learning offers a durable source of coherence.

The science of learning is the framework, not the whole

The science of learning underpins teacher development - but it's not the whole programme. Teachers need to know how students learn and *how they can best teach their students specific topics*. Some strategies have been rigorously tested by researchers - but only in a few subjects and contexts. For example, researchers have established that working memory is limited, and breaking down new ideas can help. They've rarely researched how best to break down the ideas for tomorrow's lesson. So, the science of learning tells us what's needed, offering general principles. We need to help teachers apply these principles, drawing on craft wisdom and subject expertise to make subject and lesson-specific decisions. We also need to draw on other disciplines, like behavioural science, to look at how best to manage behaviour. **The science of learning offers a framework: effective teacher development builds on this framework.**

The science of learning offers a framework - we must go beyond it to address behaviour, and teachers' subject and lesson-specific needs.

Drawing these ideas together, applying the science of learning is at the core of effective teaching. Helping teachers do this should therefore be at the core of our professional development programme. The science of learning guides our planning of teacher development, and unifies our school improvement efforts. It makes our programme coherent. Next, we'll look at how we go about this: by establishing underlying principles, articulating and exemplifying them, and building a teacher development programme around them.

The science of learning provides core principles for teaching and for teacher development - and so, the basis of our programme.

How do we build a coherent professional development programme?

We need, first, an agreed core of teaching principles and practices. We can begin by establishing a set of learning principles for ourselves. We then need to articulate and exemplify them effectively. (Alternatively, we can adopt an existing set of principles - I've offered an example on page 26.) This done, we can shape the professional development programme around the principles. Each step can be taken individually, or as a group. Working as a group has several advantages, including gaining a range of perspectives and building a team of advocates for the approach (we discuss this further in Chapter 8). For simplicity, I have described the steps to take - not the group activities we might use in taking them. You can take each step yourself, or guide a group through them.

Step 1 - Develop an agreed core: establish the principles of learning for ourselves

We begin the work of building coherent professional development by ensuring we are clear in our own minds what kind of teaching we hope to see, and why.

What does Step 1 look like?

Paul has been involved in leading teaching and learning for a while, but he's conscious that his knowledge is rusty in some areas. He still uses some materials from his own initial training, and he want to make sure he's up to date. He begins by reading, or rereading, a few key texts. This proves useful immediately: he identifies ways to improve his own lesson planning process. He also invites any interested colleagues to join an informal weekly reading group. An enthusiastic team quickly emerges; members range from an assistant head to a second-year teacher. They read and discuss a chapter or a paper each week. They test the literature, identifying areas where multiple experts seem to concur, and sharing professional wisdom. They soon begin to develop a working document of the key things they've learned. By the end of term, this includes over a dozen pages of ideas, notes, observations, and references.

Step 1a) Establishing what we need to know, and what we already know

Imagine a novice teacher asking "How does learning happen?" Pause for a moment and write down how you would respond. Then, turn the page.

This question bothers me. First, because I managed to teach for many years without really considering it. I planned lessons using intuition, imitation, trial and error – but not an accurate understanding of how students learn. This is a trap we want our teachers to avoid. Second, because I still find it remarkably difficult to answer concisely and usefully, despite years of practice. How learning happens is just one of many reasonable teacher questions, such as:

1) What helps students pay attention?
2) What helps students understand new ideas?
3) What helps students remember new ideas?
4) What do we want students to understand and remember? When? Why?
5) How can a teacher get better independent work from students?
6) What can a teacher do when a student is distracted? Confused? Disillusioned?
7) How can a teacher identify whether a student is any of these things? How can a teacher pre-empt them?
8) What should a teacher do if one student is struggling? Five? Twenty-five?
9) How can a teacher help students organise ideas?
10) How often should a teacher revisit a new idea?
11) How can a teacher check understanding efficiently and effectively?
12) What kind of feedback helps students improve? How can a teacher sustainably provide it?
13) How can a teacher build a supportive culture of learning?

(These are the underlying questions. Teachers' actual questions tend to focus on a specific situation. For example, "Year 8 seem to ignore my feedback, what should I do?")

Each question presents similar difficulties. As experienced teachers, we know how to address them in the classroom. But our knowledge is usually tacit. We may not even be aware of how we are weaving teaching techniques together to keep a class focused or a discussion flowing. Even if we are, doing something well doesn't mean we can teach it to others. We might explain, "I get better independent work by modelling what I want students to do." This is true, but it's unlikely to be usable for less-experienced teachers. It leaves tacit how we select and introduce a model, how we help students spot the key features and apply them to their work. Our knowledge is also subject-specific. We reach for examples we're familiar with, but they may mean nothing to teachers of other subjects or ages. If we are to use the principles of learning as a base for our programme, we need to be able to explain them clearly. We need to take our tacit, subject-specific knowledge and make it explicit and meaningful to others.

Teacher educators need to be able to articulate how learning happens: this means making tacit, subject-specific knowledge explicit and meaningful.

We can begin developing an agreed core by drafting initial answers to the questions above. This is a first step towards codifying principles of learning to use within the school. It also helps us check our knowledge, our skill in sharing this knowledge, and areas we need to revise. (As with every step, this can be done individually or collectively.)

Action 1a) Write your answers to the questions above. Ask a colleague to review your answers. Use their feedback to identify the questions which proved hardest to answer clearly, and which you would like to review.

Step 1b) Deepening our knowledge

Step 1a established what we need to know about, and the gaps in our existing knowledge. Let's now consider the depth of knowledge required. We must articulate the principles of learning compellingly in training, coaching, and leadership team meetings. This requires a deep understanding of the principles, the evidence (and its limits), and the practical implications for teachers. We must also bring this knowledge to life. To do so, we will need rich and varied examples and non-examples. Take a single teaching technique, like varying practice: mixing up the content and form of questions. (This is an example of a desirable difficulty: it makes learning harder initially, but improves retention subsequently.)[8] We must be able to:

- Explain why varying practice helps;
- Show how to do it (and what to avoid);
- Suggest ways to maintain student motivation when varying practice (since students will find lessons harder initially);
- Tailor our advice to different contexts: it may be easier with a confident class, and work better in maths than in history.

This is far harder than simply varying practice in our own teaching! It requires us to deepen our knowledge of student learning.

Teacher educators need extensive knowledge: what to do, how to do it, and why - across subjects.

A book about teacher development can't also cover the intricacies of student learning. Instead, it can suggest ways to refresh our knowledge by reading or rereading a few key texts. (If you're pressed for time, or want suggested answers, I've shared how I would describe learning on page 26.) This list includes the most valuable and readable books, and my own efforts to answer these questions.

Who?	*What?*	*Why?*
Craig Barton	How I wish I'd taught maths	Not just for maths teachers! A very clear summary of a wide variety of evidence and its practical applications.
Harry Fletcher-Wood	Responsive teaching	A practical synthesis of the evidence from the science of learning and formative assessment, applied to lesson planning, checking understanding, and feedback.

(Continued)

Who?	*What?*	*Why?*
Harry Fletcher-Wood	Habits of success	Shows how behavioural science can be applied to motivate students and manage behaviour.
Doug Lemov	Teach like a champion	The best breakdown of successful teaching practice available.
Graham Nuthall	The hidden lives of learners	Nuthall got closer to student learning than anyone before or since. Worthwhile ideas on every page.
Dylan Wiliam	Embedded formative assessment	Oldie but goldie: lots of good advice about how to understand what students have learned, and meet their needs.
Daniel Willingham	Why don't students like school?	A succinct, clear, memorable summary of the science of learning in usable form.

You could also look at Education Endowment Foundation guidance reports (these include both subject-specific reports on science, literacy or maths, and reports on topics, such as feedback).

Action 1b) Read or reread as many of the texts above as you can make time for. Look for answers to the questions you found hardest in Step 1a. Note key points you'd want teachers to grasp for each question.

Step 1c) Articulating what we know

Having reread and refreshed our memory, we can revise our answers to the questions posed in Step 1a. The next paragraph is an example of what an answer might look like to the first question: what helps students to pay attention?

> There are innumerable draws on students' attention: sights, sounds, physical impressions, emotions. Students may attend to any of these instead of learning. Teachers need to address or remove possible distractions: shut the windows on the sounds of the playground, clean last lesson's names from the whiteboard, prevent off-task discussion. Teaching techniques can help. For example, teachers can use unobtrusive non-verbal and individual reminders to keep students on task without distracting the class. Attention informs lesson planning too. There's a place for collaborative tasks, but activities which demand sustained individual thought are best conducted in silence to help students attend to them. Longer term, we want to help students build habits of attention. They should get used to always writing in a focused way when asked to do so, for example. We can also help students learn to manage their attention themselves. If they are doing homework, they can pre-empt distractions: leave their phone in another room, shut the door, get comfortable.

Reviewing this paragraph, we might first notice that it draws on ideas from a wide range of disciplines. These include psychology, behavioural science, the science of habit (around how to sustain attention), and perhaps even neuroscience (how the brain perceives stimuli). But this research is leavened by the wisdom of practice: the answer includes teaching techniques which should work (cleaning the whiteboard), but haven't been, and perhaps couldn't be, rigorously tested by researchers. Our goal is to organise knowledge useably for teachers - not write an academic paper. As we conclude Step 1, we should be confident in our own minds about the principles of learning. This is the foundation for Step 2: sharing these principles with our colleagues.

Establishing principles of learning in our own minds is the foundation for sharing them with our colleagues.

Action 1c) Write or rewrite your answers to the questions in Step 1a. (This would be a particularly good task to do as a teaching and learning or leadership team.) Review your answers. Are they clear? Are there any remaining knowledge gaps?

Step 2 - Develop an agreed core: articulate and exemplify the principles and practices

Some teachers will be as eager as you are to dig into the evidence. Some will instead prioritise marking, pastoral care, leading sports teams, or caring for their own children. That's fine. Our goal isn't to get every teacher reading educational research - it's to ensure every teacher knows, and can apply, the crucial insights. The job of teacher educators and enthusiasts is to do the digging, then make what they find usable for their colleagues. So, we need to take the answers we've established in Step 1 and shape them into something teachers can easily grasp and use. To do that, we'll take three sub-steps:

- Formulating principles;
- Organising them succinctly and memorably;
- Collating a range of examples.

This may be an iterative process: trying to organise the principles succinctly could lead us to refine how we formulate them, for example.

Is it worth going through this process from scratch? We might think it unnecessary: how students learn is, as we've seen, fairly well established. Is it worth spending a term or more reinventing this body of evidence? Done well, this can deepen leaders' and teachers' understanding of, and investment in, the principles. But if you're looking to skip this step (or want a model), I've shared a set of principles on page 26.

What does Step 2 look like?

After a term reading, Paul's teaching and learning team begins trying to codify their knowledge. They review the notes they took while reading, and turn the mass of ideas into a few clear principles, including, "Plan around prior knowledge", and "Frequently monitor student understanding." The team shares the document with a few colleagues for early feedback. This elicits concern that there are too many principles, and they are too specific. The team responds by cutting the document down, and merging some of the principles. For example, "Frequently check student understanding" and, "Establish what students have understood at the end of the lesson", are closely related. The team unites them in a single heading: "Check student understanding several times a lesson." Then they look to make the principles more succinct. For each principle, they choose a single word and subheading: in this case, "Check: assess student understanding frequently." Having settled the principles, each group member contributes a handful of examples. The team includes teachers from across the school, so the document soon has examples from a range of subjects and age groups. They then test the document again: each team member presents it to their department for feedback. This done, and after a few final tweaks, they are ready to launch it to the whole school.

Step 2a) Formulating the principles

Through Step 1, we have acquired and collated a body of knowledge. But it's not yet in a usable form. We must organise the principles memorably if they are to guide teaching and professional development. We may have recorded a loosely-connected set of ideas; for example, that students often have misconceptions, that they persist unless/until they are tackled, that teachers may miss them, and so on. This is all true, but it's hard for teachers to recall or use scores of isolated ideas. We need to synthesise them into a few key principles: here, the principle might be to elicit and address student misconceptions.

So, in Step 2a, we'll distil everything from Step 1 into no more than 20 principles. (Fewer would be better, but we'll whittle them down in Step 2b.) At this stage, we should formulate universals: for example, feedback should be concise, precise, and usable. We may think of exceptions (sometimes, delaying feedback can help students learn too, for example). We can note these now, and deal with them later. As an underlying structure, we could organise the principles within the fundamental challenges teachers face:[9]

1) Securing students' attention;
2) Presenting key ideas effectively;
3) Ensuring students think hard about key ideas;
4) Assessing student understanding and give feedback;
5) Consolidating student learning – helping them organise and recall key ideas.

We might wish to identify at least three or four principles to address each challenge. There is an example set of principles (further refined) below, on page 26.

Teacher educators need to synthesise the body of knowledge they have collated into succinct and usable principles.

Action 2a) Review your answers from Step 1. Formulate 10-20 principles which represent that body of knowledge and tackle the fundamental challenges teachers face.

Step 2b) Organising the principles succinctly and memorably

School policies often used to be written as an unstructured mass of bullet points. The result was a confusing laundry list, which began something like this:

- Start each lesson with a settling activity while you take the register.
- Consider the individual needs of each student in planning learning activities.
- Use pair talk where appropriate.
- It is essential that all students get the opportunity to participate.

And went on for another page and a half. It appeared that ideas had been jotted down in the order they had occurred to the writer. Such lists proved neither memorable nor usable. Unmemorable, because we need a structure to remember multiple items; unusable, because no one was going to try to plan a lesson using this list. If we want our principles to guide teaching and learning, we need to offer something better.

We can make our principles more memorable and usable by:

1) **Encapsulating effective teaching and learning in a handful of principles.** Step 1 may have left us with 50 ideas; Step 2a cut that down to 20. This is still too many to be memorable: we need to encapsulate the key ideas in four to seven principles.[10] Let's say the principles we chose in Step 2a include challenging students, praising effort, and supporting students who are struggling. We can now combine these into one principle: create a positive emotional climate which challenges and supports students. In training, we can look separately at how to challenge, praise, and support students. But in our overall model they form a single principle.
2) **Naming each principle succinctly.** "Create a positive emotional climate which challenges and supports students" is thorough, but it doesn't trip off the tongue. We want succinct names for each principle: ideally just two or three words. In this case, we might say, "Positive emotional climate" or, "Challenge and support" or just, "Climate". This makes it easier for teachers to recall and refer to the principles.
3) **Organising the principles memorably.** An organising structure makes the principles memorable. We could use alliteration, a mnemonic, or a visual design. In writing *Habits of Success*, for example, I developed a five-step model for helping people form habits. Stuck in a hospital waiting room, I spent an hour trying multiple synonyms for each step. This allowed me to create a mnemonic, using the word SIMPLIFy (Specify a powerful habit, Inspire and Motivate students to begin, PLan change, Follow up). It's contrived and imperfect. But it's much more memorable than having no structure at all. For example, we might choose an alliterative structure:

    - **Consider** prior learning
    - **Connect** students to new ideas
    - **Create** a model
    - **Challenge** students to apply what they've learned
    - **Check** what students have understood

Teachers are much more likely to remember five Cs than they are five unconnected words.

This turns an array of ideas and potential actions into a memorable, usable model to guide teachers' thinking and professional development provision.

Teacher educators need to make key ideas usable by encapsulating them in a few key principles, naming them succinctly, and organising them memorably.

Action 2b) Encapsulate the key ideas from Step 2a in a handful of principles, name them succinctly, and organise them memorably.

Principles of learning

Creating a set of principles deepens teacher educators' understanding of learning and how best to communicate about it. It can also increase teachers' enthusiasm and understanding. But we don't have to work from scratch. The principles of learning hold true no matter where, what, or who we're teaching. Below, I've shared a set of principles you could use as a model (or simply adopt), drawn from a curriculum for teacher learning I created with a group of teacher educators.[11] Here, I've shared only the principles and their implications. The curriculum also includes examples, training activities and questions to check teachers' understanding. (It's available free – the link is in the references.)

1. Help students attend to learning

Principle 1: People can only consciously attend to a handful of stimuli at a time.

People experience thousands of potential stimuli each moment, but they can only consciously attend to a handful.	So	Teachers must ensure that students focus on what is to be learned and overcome competing demands on their attention.

2. Find out what students already know

Principle 2: Prior knowledge determines what students can learn

Students make sense of new information by reference to what they already know.	So	Teachers can help students to commit new information to long-term memory by connecting it to existing knowledge.

3. Help students focus on key ideas

Principle 3: Working memory capacity is limited

The site of conscious thinking - working memory - is limited in both capacity and duration. When students' working memories are overloaded, they are unable to retain or process some of the information they have been presented with. Individual students' working memory capacity differs, but there is no known way to increase working memory capacity. However, the more relevant prior knowledge students have, the less working memory will be required for a new idea, and the more easily they can process new information (Principle 2).	So	Teachers must ensure students focus on a few ideas, processes or pieces of information at a time.

4. Help students commit information to long-term memory

Principle 4a: Memory is the residue of thought

Students transfer information into their long-term memories when they think hard about its meaning.	So	Teachers must plan to ensure students think hard about the meaning of what is to be learned.

Principle 4b: Students may commit incomplete or incorrect ideas to their long-term memories

Students may hold misconceptions already or form new ones as they learn: if they maintain these misconceptions, these are what they are likely to recall.	So	Teachers need to identify what students are thinking and have understood during the lesson, without waiting for students to articulate their misconceptions.

5. Help students remember what they learn

Principle 5: Forgetting is inevitable

Learning is a persistent change in long-term memory, not just a temporary increase in student performance. Introducing students to an idea once is very unlikely to be enough for them to recall it after a month, a year, or beyond.	So	Teachers can make students' knowledge more secure by giving them practice in using and retrieving this information once their memories of an idea are beginning to fade. Retrieval practice increases recall more than restudying material, particularly if it is: - Varied: students practise different tasks, rather than one task at a time, increasing the number of cues helping students recall the idea, and increasing its usefulness. - Spaced (for verbal materials): increasing delays between practice episodes, especially if students answer correctly.

6. Help students use their knowledge flexibly

Principle 6: Information can be organised in increasingly sophisticated mental models

Students' knowledge of a concept extends and deepens when they practise it in new situations and contexts. Organisation and practice build a mental model, a framework which organises knowledge and makes it usable to students. This helps students transfer learning to new contexts and think critically about what they know.	So	Teachers can help students apply their knowledge by encouraging them to make links between ideas and to apply them in a variety of situations. Teachers can also help them by showing them how.

Step 2c) Collate examples

Abstract principles are poor guides. We can tell teachers to check students' understanding - but most teachers already check students' understanding. Their approach may be powerful and insightful, however - or cursory and ineffective: "Any questions?" If the principles are to guide teacher action, we must bring them to life, conveying what they look like in practice, through concrete examples (and non-examples). To illustrate the principle that teachers should ensure students focus on a few ideas at a time, in our set of principles, we offered:[12]

- Non-example: the practical requires unfamiliar equipment, so the teacher demonstrates how to set it up and explains how to conduct the experiment.
- Example: the teacher demonstrates how to set the equipment up in stages, asking students to complete each stage after the demonstration. Once all students have the equipment set up, the teacher explains how to conduct the experiment.

We wanted the non-example to reflect a reasonable approach (rather than a cartoon in which the teacher offers no guidance at all). The example then illustrates what closer adherence to the principle looks like, and how it helps. By offering multiple examples for each principle, we can portray the underlying goals more clearly, and show how they apply across a range of subjects and contexts. Here's another illustration of ensuring student focus, with younger children:

- Non-example: after modelling how to add one more to a given number while on the carpet, the teacher asks the students to go to their tables. They then ask two children to give out the maths books and tell all students to rule the margin, write the date and title. The children then begin to practise adding one more.
- Example: Before modelling how to add one more to a given number on the carpet, the teacher ensures that the children already have their maths book, have ruled the margin,

written the date and title. Once the teacher has modelled the process on the carpet, the children begin practising adding one more at their tables immediately.

Collating a range of examples completes our development of an agreed core approach to teaching and learning. The examples should make each principle's underlying meaning clearer and more usable. They should also reflect the range of contexts our teachers face, and the range of practice we want to encourage. We can use hypotheticals, or real examples from our colleagues' classrooms (demonstrating that the principles can be pursued successfully in our school). If we are working through these steps with a team, they can help with either approach.

Teacher educators need to bring the principles to life by collating a range of examples and non-examples.

Action 2c) Collate examples and non-examples for each principle. Develop a variety of examples which reflect the range of subjects and students your teachers work with.

Step 3 – Build the teacher development programme on these principles

Having developed a set of principles, we now need to put them to use. They should guide both thinking about teaching and learning and our approach to professional development.

What does Step 3 look like?

Paul wants to ensure his colleagues understand and use the principles the teaching and learning team has developed. He begins with formal launches: first with the leadership team, then heads of department, then the whole staff. He includes the principles in every policy and document and on every wall space he can find. Whenever he can, Paul reiterates key points: in briefings, emails, meetings and training sessions. Sometimes, he wonders whether he's overdoing it. But he keeps going, because he knows that adopting new language and ideas takes time, and that his colleagues face many competing pressures. The teaching and learning team offers a lot of support. Increasingly, they lead sessions, offer examples, and tackle misconceptions. In due course, Paul begins to see the effects: he hears the principles being discussed spontaneously, and sees the practices being used.

Meanwhile, Paul starts to reshape the professional development programme around the principles. After some debate, the leadership team agrees to focus on challenge and support next year. They are concerned some students aren't being challenged enough, and, when challenge is introduced, that the scaffolding students need isn't always provided. Paul reviews the professional development activities planned for the year with the teaching and learning team. They decide to use whole-school sessions to introduce and model key ideas, department time for co-planning, and coaching to support teachers to change. They also identify activities to cut: for example, individual pedagogy projects take a lot of time, and don't help teachers plan or problem-solve collaboratively. The teaching and learning team continues to read and learn together - and agrees to review the principles and their impact later in the year.

Step 3a) Ensure staff know and can use the principles

We want to achieve a shared language and understanding of effective teaching. We should see the principles used in planning and policies, lesson feedback and discussion - everywhere. This may prove tricky: a third of teachers say their school lacks this shared language.[13] Our work testing the principles (described in Step 2) has prepared the ground. Now, we must launch them to the whole school. First, we need to get leaders on board: we rely on them to encourage and reinforce the key ideas (we discuss this challenge in Chapter 8). We can treat the launch as a professional development session. This means explaining and modelling the principles, checking and clarifying understanding, and planning and practising application (approaches described in Chapter 2). Next, we can do something similar for middle leaders and coaches, then staff. Finally, we need to ensure that any document staff regularly use reflects the principles, including lesson plans, PowerPoint templates, observation proformas and performance management documents.

All of this is a start - but it's not enough. Just as a single lesson won't change students' thinking; a training session and a poster won't change teachers' thinking. We need to over-communicate, reinforcing the key ideas at every opportunity. Most obviously, we can use professional development sessions. We don't have to start from scratch every time. Instead, we can connect each session's goal to the underlying principles, and the overall model. For example, we might say:

> Today we're looking at using exit tickets. These are a powerful technique to achieve our principle of frequent checks for understanding. Exit tickets build on our work last term refining learning objectives: we can only create a meaningful exit ticket if we have a clear objective. We'll build on exit tickets when we look at ongoing classroom assessment.

Alongside sessions, we can create opportunities to revisit key ideas in existing routines, like briefings and bulletins. We could focus on one principle each term, for example, and share an example of a colleague's great practice each week. A morning reminder encourages teachers to consider the principles during lessons later on. Finally, we need to listen for and ask about teachers' use of the principles. We'll know we're getting somewhere when we hear staff talking about the principles unprompted.

To ensure staff understand and apply the principles, teacher educators need to over-communicate them, integrating them into the school's work.

Action 3a) Launch the principles, teaching them to leaders and staff. Then over-communicate them, referring to them at every opportunity and building them into everything the school does.

Step 3b) Shape professional development using the principles

We can now use our principles to shape the professional development programme. (This is an initial discussion of that goal – Part II addresses the process of developing a programme in detail.) Our aim is coherence (rather than the unfocused approach we discussed at the start of the chapter). We could choose one goal for the whole school: everyone works on improving student focus, for example. If the basics are in place however, we might instead invite departments or individuals to choose goals. These disparate efforts remain coherent because everyone is working within a shared model. Let's say science choose planning, English assessment, and maths feedback. These are three steps in a sequence of learning (we don't have science choosing discovery learning and maths direct instruction, for example). Let's say maths, art, and Spanish all choose feedback. We have agreed principles of effective feedback: teachers try to apply them to their subject. We've overcome the conflicting messages and priorities which unfocused professional development creates. Staff enjoy clear goals and expectations and, hopefully, recognise the underlying coherence.

How can we create a coherent programme?

- First, we **set goals**. We may set a shared goal for the whole school: we all need to use retrieval practice better. Or we may set a direction and invite departments or teachers to choose how to pursue it. For example, if we wish to increase student independence, teachers might choose between improving independent practice, feedback, or homework. (We look at how to identify priorities in Chapter 5.)
- Second, we **audit** our professional development provision. We look at each activity and ask, how does this help achieve our goals? What do breakfast briefings, reading groups, coaching, department time, and external courses contribute? We may find that breakfast briefings teach the principles, but external courses are authorised based on funding, not goals. We should establish both what each activity contributes now and how it could contribute, if tweaked.
- Third, we **align activities to our goals.** We could allocate "roles" to each activity. For example, department time should help teachers design independent practice tasks; coaching should help teachers use them. We may tweak activities to fit the goals: if staff are desperate to keep doing action research projects, we can adapt them to focus on our priorities. Seeking alignment also helps us reject activities: an external course may look interesting, but if it doesn't contribute to our goals, we can't authorise it.

We can then carefully communicate these decisions and the rationale behind them. Having set goals, we design training to achieve them: we look at how to do this in the next chapter.

Teacher educators need to set goals chosen from the principles, and align professional development activities to pursue these goals.

Action 3b) Set goals - or choose who will set goals, and how. Audit professional development provision to see how it does, or could, pursue these goals. Align professional development activities to the goals.

Step 3c) Evaluate progress and refine the principles

Our underlying goal is for all staff to apply the principles effectively in their work. So the principles offer a yardstick against which we can measure progress. Hopefully, we will see staff gain greater knowledge and understanding of the principles. We should also see the principles better applied in classrooms. (We examine how to evaluate professional development in detail in Chapter 7.) We will also want to evaluate and refine the principles themselves. As we use them, we should better understand learning and how best to teach teachers about it. Each year, we can review the principles, the examples, and the supports we provide teachers. (We look at iterating our approach to school improvement in Chapter 6.)

Teacher educators can evaluate progress towards applying the principles - and can refine the principles themselves.

Action 3c) Assess whether staff understand the principles, and their progress in applying them. Iterate and refine the principles themselves.

Step 4 - Support subject-specificity

When we establish shared principles, we look for common ground across subjects and phases. This common ground is extensive. No matter what students are learning, teachers need to select goals, show models, check understanding, and offer feedback. No matter what students are learning, a good goal, model, or piece of feedback has similar characteristics (an effective model clearly demonstrates the success criteria, for example). At the next level of detail, however, subject-specificity is crucial. What is a reasonable goal for a particular lesson? Which practice activity best meets that goal? What are the success criteria, and which model reveals them best? These questions are best answered by subject specialists working together.

So, in building a coherent programme, when and how should we promote subject-specificity? Initially, we need to ensure everyone grasps the principles. We can pursue this, while making our approach meaningful and usable for all staff, by weaving subject-specificity into Steps 1-3:

- As we develop shared principles (Step 2a), we need to check they make sense across subjects.
- We can ask departments to offer examples of the principles (Step 2c).
- When we share the principles with staff (Step 3a), we need to show how they apply in different subjects.
- We can plan professional development in which teachers work in subject or year teams (Step 3b).

Having achieved a shared understanding of the principles, we can also increasingly devolve decisions to departments. Middle leaders can choose goals, training, and support tailored to their team's needs. (We discuss how to support the strong middle leadership this requires in Chapter 8.)

Teacher educators should incorporate subject-specificity into every step of building a programme - and look to devolve decision-making to middle leaders.

Action 4) Review your plans for Steps 1-3, adding subject-/phase-specific support into every step. Once you've achieved a shared understanding, support middle leaders to choose next steps.

Case study

When John Kirkman joined Mossbourne Victoria Park Academy, it lacked a well-thought-out teacher development programme. Staff received coaching, but feedback was often vague and inconsistent. Teachers' understanding of learning was mixed: the pervading philosophy was "whatever works". This meant some teachers prioritised engagement over long-term learning, and it was hard for newer staff to develop quickly. Equally, there were some phenomenal teachers and GCSE results were very good (probably due to high behavioural expectations and catch-up interventions). So John needed to introduce change cautiously and consensually. In his first year, he wanted to create a document articulating a shared understanding of expert teaching. He planned to use this as a foundation for observations and professional development the following year. (His reflections, below, were written at the end of the first year.)

To make the creation of the document a success, John wanted to:

- *Ensure all staff were aligned to the theory of learning underpinning it;*
- *Involve staff from across the school in the drafting process;*
- *Pre-train staff in some of the pedagogy he hoped to include, so it felt familiar.*

He anticipated challenges in drawing on the expertise of successful colleagues and convincing sceptical teachers (especially leaders) that it would improve teaching. He was also concerned about how to make the document generic enough to work across subjects - but not so generic that it was useless. Here, he describes how he pursued these goals.

Align staff around an understanding of how we learn

I used the first 15 minutes of every extended leadership team meeting (of middle and senior leaders) to discuss reading set the week before, hear from heads of department about their subject pedagogy, or examine the different kinds of shared languages other schools used as part of their own teacher development. I selected a range of articles and book extracts linked to cognitive science. I focused initially on this group as they were the line managers of all other staff in the school. I thought that if I could align their thinking around this reading that they would likely become advocates for it. The (volunteer) teaching and learning committee, which started later on in the academic year, also completed the same reading.

Pre-train staff on pedagogy linked to understanding of how we learn

I wanted to ensure the very limited professional development time was spent on a coherent programme. This is where I relied heavily on the support of lead practitioners. These sessions focused on theory in the first half and then allowed departments time in the second half to work together to think about how they might transform this into practice in their own subject area.

Involve staff from across the academy in the writing and drafting of the shared language

I wanted the shared language to be owned by all staff at the academy, so wanted as many people as possible to be involved in its writing and construction. To do this, with the team of lead practitioners, I drafted the titles for each of the sections and decided on the overall title of the document - Eight Principles for Expert Teaching. We liked the word "principles" because it framed the document as a set of shared beliefs that the teaching staff should draw upon to help them make decisions in the classroom. I then spent the beginning of summer term putting together the document. I got lots of excellent feedback from staff - both in terms of the tone and style of the document and its content, most of which I acted upon. What has now been published feels like a co-constructed policy.

The first three principles were:

1) Plan from a sequenced curriculum
2) Create a climate for learning
3) Know your students

For each principle, the document sets out a description, a rationale, and implications for practice. The introduction to the first principle, plan from a sequenced curriculum, explains:

> The long-term sequenced curriculum is the vehicle with which teachers guide students to develop increasingly complex mental models within their subject disciplines. All lessons should be seen as episodes within a coherent whole, using teachers' knowledge of their subject and the students in their class to build their substantive and disciplinary knowledge and enhance their mastery of the subject.

The rationale for this principle begins:

> The ultimate aim of our teaching is to help students develop a set of subject-specific substantive and disciplinary knowledge that is stored in their long-term memory that is both flexible and durable.

The implications for this principle include that teachers should plan for misconceptions and sequence knowledge and activities to develop student understanding. Each implication includes specific guidance and prompt questions, such as "What future learning does success in this lesson support?"

The subsequent year, John wanted to ensure the document was used by staff and leaders. To achieve this, he planned to:

- Base the teaching professional development at the school around the principles themselves following a similar format to this year.
- Have a suggested focus each week for 10-minute department meeting professional development slots.
- Build the principles into the existing online observation platform and use the tags on it to link to the principles themselves so that I can spot expert practice and staff that need intervention and support at whole school level.
- Provide training to middle and senior leaders on how to use the principles.
- Reconvene the teaching and learning committee both to support with the above but also so that they can support me to review the principles so they can be refined for the following academic year.
- Use the teaching and learning committee to support the leading of professional development and teaching and learning briefings on Monday mornings.

Conclusion

A shared understanding of effective teaching and learning underpins our efforts to improve teaching. It allows us to align leaders, training, and coaching. It makes goals and expectations clear. This chapter is meant to help us move a step or two forward towards this: in clarifying a model of learning for you or for your colleagues, and in using that model to guide teaching and teacher development. With this in place, we can move on to design training and plan coaching – the subject of our next two chapters.

Next steps

Reflection questions

1) How coherent is your school's approach to teaching and learning? (Think about the messages and training staff receive - and the actions of leaders and staff.) How do you know?
2) How confident are you in:
   - Your knowledge of effective teaching and learning?
   - Articulating this knowledge?
   - Translating it to other subjects and phases?
3) What principles would you want all staff to understand and apply? How well do these principles apply across different phases and subjects?
4) What would it take for all leaders and staff understand and apply these principles?

Checklist

1) Establish the principles of learning for yourself/a small team
   a. Write your answers to the questions on page 19
   b. Reread key texts
   c. Review and revise your initial answers
2) Articulate and exemplify your answers
   a. Formulate a set of principles
   b. Organise the principles memorably
   c. Collate examples of the principles across subjects/phases
3) Use the principles to shape the teacher development programme
   a. Ensure staff know and can use the principles
   b. Shape professional development around the principles
   c. Review and refine the principles
4) Support subject-specificity

Getting started

If your school already has a set of principles, review them. If it doesn't, invite a group of volunteers to meet with you to begin developing them.

Success in different roles

You can apply the ideas in this chapter, whatever your role:

- **As a teacher. . .** if your school lacks a set of principles of learning, you can use Step 1 to establish principles for yourself. You could also begin working to develop shared principles with colleagues in the same subject or year team, or other interested colleagues. If your school has a set of principles, get to know them, find out how they were developed, and consider whether they could be improved.

- **As a middle leader. . .** if your school lacks shared principles of learning, you can use Steps 1 and 2 to develop these for your subject or phase, and apply them to your team's work improving teaching. You can also push for this process to happen whole-school.
- **As a leader working across schools. . .** you can encourage and support your schools to pursue this process individually. Or you could lead the process, following Steps 1-3, for your organisation.

2 How can we lead effective training?

Chapter map

Effective training prepares teachers to successfully apply new skills in the classroom.

↓

Effective training:
- Pursues four purposes (promoting insights, motivating goal-directed behaviour, teaching techniques and embedding change)
- Applies deliberate practice, breaking expert practice into specific skills

↓

Step 1: Choose a target skill

a) Choose a goal
b) Select a skill and success criteria

↓

Step 2: Design the practice activity

a) Focus practice on the target skill
b) Choose how teachers will practise
c) Clarify the task and teachers' roles

↓

Step 3: Prepare support to make practice shine

a) Select models
b) Plan teachers' preparation for practice
c) Prepare feedback

↓

Step 4: Ensure practice has a lasting impact

a) Plan progression
b) Promote insight
c) Track impact

↓

Step 5: Build a culture of practice

a) Build conviction
b) Make practice comfortable
c) Challenge colleagues

↓

We can then coach individuals (Chapter 3), support teachers to change (Chapter 4) and improve teaching across the school (Part II).

DOI: 10.4324/9781003439622-4

In Chapter 1, we established principles of teaching and learning. We know what we want teachers to do. The next step is helping teachers apply these principles in their classrooms. For this to happen, teachers must:

- Understand the principles
- Want to pursue them
- Know how to put the principles into practice
- Be ready to apply this knowledge in the classroom

In this chapter, we'll look at designing training sessions which achieve this. First, let's see how effective training can make a difference.

Why does effective training matter?

Consider two approaches to training. First, let's look at a common approach: discussion without practice. One learning principle at Gina's school is checking students' understanding frequently, and adapting teaching accordingly. Staff surveys and lesson observations suggest this isn't happening consistently. Gina plans a session to revisit the principle. First, she explains why checking understanding matters. Next, she shares example assessment tasks from different subjects. Finally, she invites staff to plan next steps with their departments.

The session goes well: teachers discuss thoughtfully and seem satisfied. But afterwards, little changes: few teachers check understanding more frequently. Those who do appear to struggle. For example, Gina sees Calvin use whiteboards to check whether students have grasped a key point. This reveals important gaps in student understanding - but he's unsure how to respond, and moves on with the lesson.

When the session ended, staff understood the principle, and were keen to act. But the session didn't prepare them to succeed. There are many components of an effective check for understanding: designing a task, gathering and analysing student responses, deciding what to do next. The session covered just one: what a good task looks like. It didn't touch on task design, analysis, or possible next steps. The session hinted at what staff should be doing, but didn't support them to act. Gina relied on teachers applying the principle while planning lessons. Some staff forgot. Some were too busy. Others tried, but got stuck, and - planning alone - couldn't get the advice they needed. Finally, the session didn't prepare teachers to make unfamiliar techniques work in the classroom. Attempting to introduce a change in the middle of a lesson is extremely demanding, as Calvin found. Superficially, the training was successful: staff learned something. Ultimately, it was ineffective: it didn't improve teaching.

Let's consider an alternative approach to training: deliberate practice. Gina chooses to focus the next session on just one component of checking for understanding, responding to incorrect answers. She explains and models the skill - but teachers spend most of the session preparing and practising their responses. Staff choose upcoming lessons, and identify likely student misconceptions and possible responses. Next, they practise. Teachers pose questions and their colleagues answer, correctly and incorrectly. Teachers practise evaluating each answer, deciding how to respond, then responding. After each round of practice, they review how effective the response was and how it could be improved. Teachers finish the session ready to apply the target skill in the classroom. After the session, Gina sees much better checking for understanding in lessons.

This approach works for several reasons. First, teachers have practised responding to answers they'll receive in future lessons. When these responses are needed, they should come more easily. Second, they have practised a process: predict student answers, plan responses, rehearse them. They're ready to apply this to their own lesson planning. Third, teachers could debate how long to spend addressing misconceptions for hours. Practice resolves this question. The discussion approach to training saw teachers talking about change - but left them to do the hard yards of implementation unaided. The deliberate practice approach supports teachers at every step: showing them what to do and how, then helping them practise until they are confident, comfortable, and ready to act. Effective training matters because it can make an immediate difference to teachers.

Effective training helps teachers master new skills through preparation and practice.

What makes a training session effective?

Two sources of evidence inform this approach to training design. First, we'll look at a recent systematic review of teacher professional development; second, we'll look at broader evidence for the deliberate practice approach. Finally, we'll see how common these approaches are, and the barriers they face.

Effective training pursues four purposes, using behaviour change mechanisms

A few years ago, the research consensus was that effective teacher development should be sustained and collaborative, subject-specific and practice-based, and supported by external expertise and teachers' buy-in.[1] Sam Sims and I were unconvinced: the underlying evidence was weak; some programmes adopted these features but proved ineffective.[2] We looked at over a hundred evaluations of professional development programmes to see what had made them effective. We were testing two possible explanations.[3]

Explanation 1 was that professional development can pursue four purposes:[4]

- Promoting insight: helping teachers grasp learning principles - for example, that working memory is limited;
- Motivating change: encouraging teachers to want to teach differently - for example, to reduce the burden on students' working memories;
- Teaching techniques: helping teachers master new skills - for example, introducing new ideas in stages;
- Embedding practice: supporting teachers to sustain changes until they become habits.

We suspected that a programme was more likely to succeed if it pursued all four. Teachers are unlikely to improve based on a new insight alone, for example. To improve student learning, they must also want to change, know how to change, and sustain that change. The results: across one hundred studies, programmes which pursued all four purposes increased student learning far more than programmes which pursued one, two, or three. **Effective professional development promotes insight, motivates change, teaches techniques, *and* embeds practice.**

Explanation 2 was that professional development succeeds if it uses specific techniques which help people change their behaviour. We looked at 14 techniques, such as setting goals, modelling change, and giving feedback. Each has been shown to help people change various behaviours, like exercising more, drinking less, and eating better. We suspected that the more of these techniques a programme used, the more likely teachers were to change. The results bore this out. Teachers may improve if we use a couple of mechanisms: showing them models and inviting them to set goals, for example. They are more likely to improve if we also rehearse the change, offer feedback, and plan next steps. (What we ask them to change matters. But, with a worthwhile goal, the more mechanisms we include, the better.) **Effective professional development uses mechanisms which help people change their behaviour.**

Effective training uses behaviour change mechanisms to promote insight, motivate goal-directed behaviour, teach techniques, and embed practice.

Effective training applies deliberate practice

How can a training session apply these mechanisms and pursue these purposes? Deliberate practice offers a promising model. People often practise purposefully: they try hard to improve.[5] Hard work alone, however, is rarely enough. Think of something you've mastered outside teaching. Perhaps you're a great cook, were a sports champion, or have a pilot's licence. What did you have to do to succeed?

I've asked hundreds of teacher educators this question. They've revealed a range of skills: from cooking to competitive swimming, piano playing to horse-riding. The ingredients of success they mention are strikingly similar. A cook may mention learning from a parent or a television chef, making favourite dishes many times, tasting them, and refining their approach. A basketball player may describe a coach demonstrating new skills, rehearsing them to perfection, then testing them in a game. The ingredients of effective training are identical, whether we're learning to cook, dance, fly, or teach.

The effective combination of these ingredients is called deliberate practice. Deliberate practice begins by breaking expert performance into specific skills. Then, it structures training to help people master those skills step by step, using mechanisms like models, rehearsal, and feedback.[6] We find this approach in effective training across domains. Medical training uses simulation and deliberate practice routinely (and very successfully).[7] In sport, players use deliberate practice; the best players use it the most.[8] Civil Rights protesters practised the intense self-control needed to maintain non-violent protests when faced with violence.[9]

Even Starbucks employees practise dealing with difficult customers, so they can respond effectively under pressure.[10] **Effective training uses deliberate practice to select skills and practise them to perfection.**

Effective training uses deliberate practice, specifying, modelling, rehearsing, and refining skills.

Effective approaches remain rare in teacher development

These approaches remain rare in teacher professional development. Our systematic review included over 100 programmes: just one in ten pursued all four purposes.[11] Researchers comparing training across professions found that teachers mostly practise *preparing* to teach.[12] They practise *planning* lessons or classroom management. They don't practise the skills needed to make a lesson plan succeed, like giving concise explanations and clear reminders. One teacher training programme reviewed the impact of this approach: they had been asking teachers to plan how they would handle classroom management challenges; teachers were left with "thoughtful, thorough classroom management blueprints - and chaotic classrooms".[13] When a job is difficult and important, professionals practise critical skills *before they need to use them*. This makes success more likely when they do use them. Teaching is difficult and important; teachers deserve effective preparation too.

This approach faces some scepticism. Advocates of deliberate practice overstated its power, claiming that - through practice alone - you or I could perform like Paganini or serve like Serena Williams.[14] Critics have shown that success rests on more than just practice.[15] Even they agree, however, that deliberate practice helps people improve dramatically.[16] An effective teacher enjoys talent, support, *and* deliberate practice.[17] As teacher educators, our influence over recruitment and school culture is limited. We can improve teacher development now.

Other critics have suggested that deliberate practice teaches rote skills, like shooting basketball hoops and reminding students to focus - not complex decision-making. But practising simple tasks helps us attend to complex ones:[18] a familiar entry routine lets us assess students' emotions as they arrive. Teachers can also practise complex tasks, testing how best to respond to an upset student as they arrive, for example. Finally, teachers may be sceptical because they have found practice uncomfortable or poorly-designed. We'll look at overcoming their doubts later in the chapter. Effective training remains rare; when we introduce it, we'll face scepticism. But **deliberate practice is the best bet we can make to improve teachers' skills.**

Deliberate practice remains rare: we must overcome understandable scepticism to introduce it successfully.

Drawing these ideas together, two strands of research guide our training design. First, a recent, systematic review of teacher professional development suggests we should use proven behaviour change mechanisms to promote insight, motivate goals, teach techniques, and embed practice. Second, deliberate practice offers a way to do this which works across professions. This approach is rare in teaching and faces some scepticism. It remains the most promising and best-evidenced way to design training that works.

Effective training uses deliberate practice to promote insights, motivate goals, teach techniques, and embed practice.

How do we plan an effective training session?

We'll look at five steps to plan an effective training session. First, setting goals and designing a practice activity. Next, making the practice activity effective and impactful. Finally, building a culture of practice. These steps allow us to create a deliberate practice session which addresses the purposes and uses the mechanisms we know to be effective.

Before we begin, three bits of context about following these steps:

- **We'll plan backwards**. When we plan a lesson, we plan backwards: we choose goals, then we decide how to achieve them. We'll do the same here: we'll choose a goal, then a practice activity, then the supports needed to make that activity work. I'll describe the steps *in the order we plan them* - not the order teachers will experience them. (Near the end of the chapter, I'll show how the steps we've planned come together as session.)
- **We can fit the steps into the time we have.** The steps cover the support needed for teachers to change their practice. We don't *have* to do everything in a single session. If our sessions are only 15 minutes, we might use one session to build teacher insight about why a change is needed. In the next, we can practise the change. That said, I prefer to cover every step every session. Each step provides momentum for the next. Splitting them across sessions makes it harder for one step to inform another, and delays teachers applying their learning. We can split steps between sessions where necessary, cover them in one session where possible.
- **We can take our time in learning to use the steps.** I first used practice in a training session in 2013. It took me about four years to go from this first, faltering attempt, to running sessions which attempted to do everything described below. There are still things I need to do better (like using timers and monitoring practice). So, I wouldn't suggest trying to do everything at once. Instead, each time you plan a session, pick the first step you want to improve. Work on it until you're ready to move on. Begin by trying to use practice. Then try to get it running smoothly. Then think about increasing its impact. Take the time you need to do each step well.

Take the time you need to make each step work.

Step 1 - Choose a target skill

Our first step is identifying what we want teachers to do better. Weaker training ranges freely over possible improvements. Effective training carefully selects the skill which matters most, ensuring teachers master it.

What does Step 1 look like?

We'll look at two examples in this chapter, to illustrate how deliberate practice can be used for a classroom skill - using non-verbal reminders to keep students on track - and for lesson preparation, through setting objectives.

This term, Daniel's school has prioritised ensuring behaviour promotes learning. Observations suggest low-level disruption is an ongoing issue. Teacher reminders to off-task students often distract others. Daniel wants to take several steps to help teachers identify and respond to distractions effectively. He begins with a skill which addresses much low-level disruption: using non-verbal reminders. Done well, these reminders should be subtle, should clearly show what the teacher wants, and should fit within teaching, rather than interrupting it.

Visiting the lessons of teachers in her department, Jen has become concerned that activities aren't always carefully-chosen. Her first instinct is to work on this. However, discussions with colleagues reveal an underlying issue. They struggle to explain exactly what they want students to take from the lesson: this makes choosing appropriate activities hard. Jen decides to begin at the beginning of lesson planning, focusing on setting objectives. She wants teachers to set objectives which are precise, ambitious, and achievable in a single lesson.

Step 1a) Choose a goal

We begin planning a training session by choosing a goal. We examine current practice against our principles of learning (discussed in Chapter 1), drawing on observations and surveys, conversations and anecdotes. Let's say one of our principles is ensuring student focus. Observations and surveys show that we're struggling to achieve this and suggest barriers. The goal we choose will address the most pressing barrier. We might aim for settled lesson starts, focused independent work, or respectful discussion. We can set a goal - and design training - to improve anything, from modelling the school's values to communicating effectively with parents. (We'll look at choosing school improvement priorities in Chapter 5.) Daniel's goal is improving behaviour by addressing low-level disruption; Jen's is improving planning by setting better objectives.

Effective training pursues an underlying goal which tackles a pressing issue.

Action 1a) Review current practice against your teaching and learning principles. Choose the most important change you'd like to see.

Step 1b) Select a skill and success criteria

A teacher integrates many skills to achieve a goal. Effective questioning, for example, requires a teacher to plan good questions, ensure student attention, pose questions in ways that promote student thinking, gather answers efficiently, evaluate those answers, and decide what to do next. We cannot practise all these skills at once. Our next planning step is choosing a single skill to focus on. (If teachers master this skill quickly, we can integrate it with other skills; we discuss this in Step 4a.)

First, we must identify the skills needed to achieve our goal. For example, to improve lesson planning, Jen thought about setting objectives and choosing activities. We can then select either the first, or the most immediately promising, skill needed to pursue our goal. We may focus particularly on skills teachers use frequently (such as calling for silence) or find unnatural (like asking a question then pausing to allow thought).[19] Jen was concerned teachers weren't ready to choose activities; she chose setting objectives as a prerequisite. Daniel chose an immediately promising skill: using non-verbal reminders.

Next, we identify success criteria for the skill: what does it look like when done well? For example, Jen is looking for objectives which are precise, ambitious, and achievable. Identifying these success criteria helps us plan explanations, models, and practice activities. Effective training relies on selecting specific skills to improve, and identifying the success criteria for each skill. One more example - to illustrate how far this approach applies. To help staff communicate better with parents, we identify skills like building rapport and showing understanding of parents' concerns. For the latter, success criteria might include listening without interrupting and summarising key points.

Effective training breaks the goal into skills and identifies the success criteria for each skill.

Step 1b) Select the skill you want teachers to master: the first or most promising step towards achieving your goal. Identify three or four success criteria: what should we see when the skill is done well?

Step 2 - Design the practice activity

Step 2 is designing a practice activity that helps teachers master the chosen skill. Careful planning is crucial. First, to ensure teachers welcome practice. Second, so that practice prepares them to apply the skill effectively in the classroom. I've discussed each sub-step in detail, because Step 2 is decisive. Getting these choices right is crucial if practice is to succeed. A reminder, also, that we're planning backwards. Our goal in Step 2 is to create an effective practice activity. In Step 3, we'll put in place the support, like models and feedback, needed to make it work.

What does Step 2 look like?

Daniel is designing practice to help teachers use gestures, smiles, and nods to remind students to focus. They will practise in pairs: one acting as the teacher, the other, the distracted student. Daniel wants to simplify the situation, to help the person teaching focus on using reminders, not the lesson's content. So instead of asking them to teach a real lesson, he prepares a text they can read to the student. He also wants teachers to experience success, so he will ask those playing distracted students to respond immediately to a clear reminder.

Jen is designing practice to help teachers set better objectives. She wants them to focus on objectives without worrying about gaps in their subject knowledge. So she chooses a relatively simple unit, which is coming up soon, and which everyone has taught previously. To ensure everyone benefits, she plans for colleagues to work individually, creating objectives for every lesson in the unit. They'll then review and refine the objectives in small groups.

Step 2a) Focus practice on the target skill

Teaching makes extreme cognitive demands on teachers. Consider Maddie Lampert's thoughts about a single decision: who should speak next? Richard is struggling to answer a question. Lampert suspects Catherine will be able to answer correctly:

> But what effect would that have on Richard? How would it affect Catherine if I did not let her continue? What effect would either course of action have on what the rest of the class could learn about the math, as well as what they could learn about Richard and about Catherine or about the racial and gender groups to which these students. . . belonged?[20]

Teachers face many such dilemmas, every lesson. Priorities conflict: a detailed explanation may lose students' attention; an enjoyable activity may obscure key ideas.[21] Decisions must be made almost immediately: an expectant audience allows little time for reflection. Teachers deal with these demands by forming habits. They come to handle recurring tasks, like managing disruption or settling students into lessons, almost automatically.[22]

This makes changing teaching while teaching extremely difficult. The lesson already absorbs the teacher: change diverts their attention, causing mistakes elsewhere. Teachers are swept along by existing habits, even when they mean to change. Lessons rarely allow space and time to teach effectively *and to change teaching at the same time*. We must create this space in training. To do so, **effective practice "deliberately *distorts* the setting in which participants will ultimately perform in order to focus on a specific skill under maximum concentration".**[23] This is perhaps the most important sentence in this chapter. Take Daniel's session on non-verbal reminders. In a lesson, a teacher must consider what they're saying, what to say next, whether students understand, the next task, who's distracted - and how to respond. Daniel strips these concerns away. He gives teachers a text to read so they don't have to choose what to say. They face a single student, so they don't have to spot who's distracted. They can focus on refining the target skill: using a clear, positive non-verbal reminder.

It's hard to teach effectively and improve teaching at the same time - training must create space to focus on a specific skill.

This is often misunderstood. Some teacher educators miss the focus on a single skill, equating deliberate practice with microteaching or role play.[24] But in microteaching and role play, teachers teach - rather than practising a specific skill in a simplified situation. They may gain fresh insights (in particular, about how hard teaching is!) but they are unlikely to master specific skills. Some teachers complain that practice "feels unrealistic". But true realism - practising multiple skills at lesson speed - is just as hard as teaching. We begin with simplified, unrealistic practice, so teachers can master a single skill. Skills are building blocks: having mastered one, teachers can practise another, combining them to move towards realism. For example, Daniel's teachers first practise giving non-verbal reminders in isolation, then practise spotting a distracted student *and* giving a reminder. (We can also add authenticity, *if* it doesn't distract from the target skill. For example, practising in a teacher's own classroom feels authentic, but doesn't change the focus.) Deliberate practice is deliberately unrealistic, to help teachers master specific skills.

Simplifying the classroom situation is central to deliberate practice.

In planning a lesson, the key question is what we want students to think about.[25] In planning training, the key question is what we want teachers to practise - and what we must strip away to make this possible. We've discussed a classroom management example (practising non-verbal reminders), but this applies to any skill. Take lesson planning. Just as classrooms are busy with tasks, decisions, and demands, lesson planning is busy, as teachers consider objectives, activities, and resources. To help teachers improve, we simplify this, focusing on one skill. For example, Jen asks them to practise setting objectives - and not the activities and resources those objectives require. Once teachers can set objectives well, she can focus on other lesson planning skills. The table below offers further examples. The first column shows the target skill; the remaining columns show ways to simplify reality to practise that skill.

If we want teachers to practise...	*We give them...*	*So they can focus on...*	*And not...*
Responding to interruptions	A text to read	Responding to the interruption	What they are teaching
Giving sanctions	A scenario which clearly merits a sanction	What to say	Whether to give a sanction
Deciding whether to give a sanction	A decision to make	Whether to give a sanction	What to say when giving a sanction
Writing exit tickets	Lesson objectives	Writing exit tickets which fit the objectives	Deciding the lesson's purpose
Reviewing exit tickets	Exit tickets with student answers	Reviewing the exit tickets	The purpose of the assessment
Modelling the school's values	A value to model and a situation in which to model it	Demonstrating and explaining the value	When and what to model

Would we normally expect teachers to write exit tickets without setting objectives? No. But if we want teachers to get better at writing exit tickets, we must let them focus on it. Writing objectives matters - we can focus on this in another session. Ensuring objectives and exit tickets correspond matters too - but teachers must master each skill individually if they are to do both together.

Effective training strips away concerns so teachers can focus on the target skill.

Action 2a) Simplify the situation: design a practice activity which strips away other concerns so teachers can focus on the target skill.

Step 2b) Choose how teachers will practise together

We have a practice activity in mind - we must now choose how teachers will work together. Usually, we want a format which allows teachers lots of time to practise, offers them feedback, and helps them refine the target skill. Most often, this means practising in pairs, threes, or fours. This creates a simple scenario, and gives each teacher many turns. For example, Daniel has teachers practise in pairs: one gives a non-verbal reminder, the other responds.

We might also use:

- **Quick-fire practice.** Let's say we're working on using a warm, supportive tone when giving a sanction. We can create a condensed practice task: practising a single sentence. A quick task creates time for teachers to practise many times, refining their approach, or to practise in a larger group and see the skill modelled many times. Practising at pace is also energising; it helps build a culture of practice (we'll discuss this in Step 5).
- **Individual practice.** Individual practice allows teachers to try a skill or a script they've prepared. It may help if they lack confidence (or if the session is remote or asynchronous). Working individually gives teachers lots of practice - everyone's practising at once. But it's hard for us to monitor, and teachers get no feedback. One way around this is asking teachers to film themselves practising.

- **Rehearsal.** Rehearsal - practising a lesson segment or scenario - is usually too realistic to allow improvement. Teachers are too busy to focus on a target skill, and rehearsal takes longer, giving teachers fewer chances to practise and improve. However, we might consider using it if teachers have practised many skills successfully, and we want to combine those skills, or model them to a larger group.

There's no perfect format for practice: our choice reflects the target skill and teachers' confidence, motivation, and expertise. What matters most is helping teachers focus on and refine the target skill. Switching between practice formats can maintain enthusiasm. We can also consider our ability to monitor practice, the feedback teachers will get, and the culture of practice we're building. (We discuss these further below.)

> *Effective practice gives teachers multiple chances to refine the target skill, in a format that suits their motivation and needs.*

Action 2b) Choose how teachers will practise. Consider the target skill, how much time each teacher will be able to practise, and their confidence, motivation, and expertise.

Step 2c) Clarify the task and teachers' roles

One barrier to practice is teacher uncertainty about what to do. Having chosen a focus and a format, clarifying details - like how long each teacher should practise - makes successful practice more likely. We can set everything out on a single slide for teachers to refer to while practising; Daniel's is below. Top right, it shows that teachers should be in groups of four. The left-hand side sets out the target skill, practice task, teachers' roles and timings. The right-hand side shows the success criteria and prompts for feedback. Teachers can check what they should be doing, how, and for how long, at any point. This pre-empts confusion and helps them focus on practice. We can clarify the task and roles further by modelling the practice activity - we discuss this below.

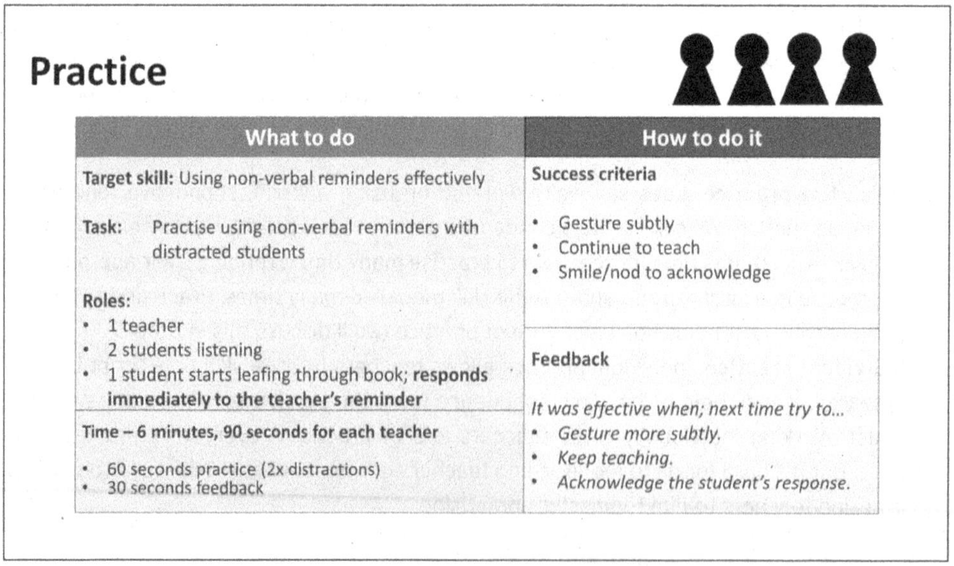

It's particularly important to specify how colleagues playing students should respond during practice. Invited to act as students, they may be tempted to reenact recent classroom conflicts. To ensure structured practice which allows teachers to master the target skill, we must clarify exactly what those playing students should and should not do. For example, when practising non-verbal reminders in fours, Daniel stipulates just one distracted student, and (in bold on the slide above) that they should respond immediately to a reminder. This helps teachers enjoy practice and master the target skill, before we choose to make things harder.

Effective practice is highly structured - teachers must know exactly what to do.

Action 2c) Set out exactly how the practice activity should run, so that teachers can check while they are practising. Specify how colleagues should respond to teachers' actions.

Step 3 - Prepare support to make practice shine

Having designed the activity, practice should happen. Continuing to plan backwards, we now want to ensure the activity runs smoothly and teachers practise successfully. Step 3 looks at the support we can prepare to make practice shine: models, preparation, and feedback.

What does Step 3 look like?

Daniel has planned practice to help teachers use non-verbal reminders. He now prepares the support teachers need to practise successfully. First, he selects models. He chooses two videos showing teachers using non-verbal reminders, in different classes and with different teaching styles. Daniel plans to highlight the success criteria they illustrate and the ways these criteria can be met. He will also model examples and non-examples himself. Next, he plans for teachers to prepare for practice, by skimming over the text they'll be reading while teaching, and choosing the gestures they'll use to regain students' attention. Finally, Daniel plans feedback: teachers will give one another feedback based on the success criteria, and he will offer group feedback about common issues - he anticipates emphasising the importance of subtle gestures.

Jen's teachers are practising setting lesson objectives. She plans two kinds of model: first, to illustrate the success criteria, she asks three colleagues to share examples of recent objectives. Jen will then model the process of creating an objective. To prepare for practice, teachers will review the unit plan for the lessons they'll focus on. They'll then set objectives individually; before sharing them with colleagues for feedback.

Step 3a) Select models

A teacher who sees a new skill modelled is much more likely to be able to apply it successfully.[26] We must choose models and decide how to introduce them. Our options include:

- **Video models.** Videos show teachers using the target skill in the classroom and integrating it with other skills. Creating a video library is time-consuming. I'd suggest starting with those available from Steplab or Teach Like a Champion.
- **Live models.** We can model the target skill ourselves. This requires careful planning, to ensure we demonstrate the success criteria clearly. By varying the model, we can illustrate each criterion: we might say the same sentence several times, for example, to show the impact of tone, pace, and expression.
- **Artefacts.** If our target skill relates to planning or assessment, we can share example lesson plans or resources.
- **Process models.** Just as we might work with students to improve a sentence on the board, we can show teachers how to draft and refine a lesson objective or explanation.
- **Practice models.** We can demonstrate the practice activity before teachers practise. This is particularly helpful when they are new to practice.

The more models we offer, the better. Two models are better than one. A video and a live model is better than one or the other. Modelling the skill and the practice is better than modelling the skill alone. This is because any single model is limited. First, each model reveals some aspects of the skill - and obscures others.[27] For example, a video of a charismatic teacher may show how energy and pace improve questioning, but hide the importance of planning questions. Second, a model shows the skill in one context: in one school, subject, and class. Teachers often focus on that context and struggle to see how the skill would work in their classroom. A second, contrasting model helps them recognise the common features - the success criteria - and the scope to adapt the skill to suit their teaching style. Finally, multiple models can illustrate the difference between doing the skill well and poorly. The more models we show, the easier we make it for teachers to grasp and apply the skill.

Having chosen models, we must plan how to introduce them. Models can be overwhelming: those watching may focus on the actions, words, or thoughts of the teacher or of the students. We must help them focus on the aspects of the target skill the model reveals. This means being explicit about what to look for and what to ignore. If the target skill is framing questions supportively, we might invite those watching to, "Ignore the teacher's movements, focus on their choice of words and tone." (Asking teachers to disregard superficial distractions, like uniforms and seating arrangements, helps overcome their uncertainty about videos from unfamiliar contexts.) We can also choose when to introduce a model: modelling the skill before teachers prepare to practise (discussed next) exerts a stronger influence than modelling after they prepare. The latter may be more appropriate for teachers with more experience of the skill. A careful introduction helps teachers grasp the crucial features of a model.

Effective training shows teachers what to do, using carefully-chosen and carefully-introduced models.

Action 3a) Choose multiple models which show teachers how to perform the target skill successfully. Plan how to introduce the models so teachers grasp the crucial features.

Step 3b) Plan teachers' preparation for practise

Teachers need to prepare - briefly and individually - before practice. For example:

Before practising...	*Teachers need to...*
Writing a succinct explanation	Review the idea they will be explaining
Emphasising key points while giving an explanation	Review the explanation script, marking where to pause and what to stress
Non-verbal reminders (Daniel's activity)	Read the text they will be 'teaching' and choose how to remind the distracted student

This preparation is psychological, as well as practical: it helps teachers think themselves into the situation. It's needed every time teachers practise (including between rounds of practice). We discuss preparation only briefly, because the activity we've designed dictates the preparation required. This shouldn't obscure its importance: preparation for practice is essential.

Effective training gives teachers time to prepare for practice.

Action 3b: Review the activity and identify what teachers need to prepare before practising. Allow time for individual preparation.

Step 3c) Prepare feedback

Feedback helps teachers refine their efforts and master the target skill. The success criteria we chose in Step 1b establish how to do the skill well - they shape our feedback. Where teachers are meeting the success criteria, we want them to keep going. Where they're not, we want to encourage change. So, effective feedback:

- Highlights one success criterion the teacher is meeting
- Suggests one criterion to work on
- Supports the teacher to apply the suggestion through further practice

For example, Daniel tells Lucy: "It was effective when you smiled to acknowledge the student was back on track. Next time, try gesturing more subtly to avoid distracting other students." This feedback is manageable, because it mentions just one strength and one suggestion. It helps Lucy refine the target skill by focusing on the success criteria. It encourages her to improve by using the feedback in another round of practice. Teachers may resist acting on feedback, preferring to discuss, reflect on, or disagree with it. But the best use (and best test) of feedback is to apply it. Having done so, they can debate it at leisure.

We can give teachers feedback during practice and highlight common issues to the group. But we can't see everything: most feedback comes from the colleagues teachers are practising with. How can we make this feedback effective? First, we ensure teachers grasp the success criteria, and so, what to look for, through models (Step 3a). Second, we offer guidance. For example, the slide we show during practice (repeated below) offers prompts and the success criteria. We can also demonstrate how to give and act on feedback while modelling the practice activity (Step 3a). Finally, we can monitor the feedback teachers give, and suggest ways to refine it.

Practice

What to do	How to do it
Target skill: Using non-verbal reminders effectively **Task:** Practise using non-verbal reminders with distracted students **Roles:** • 1 teacher • 2 students listening • 1 student starts leafing through book; **responds immediately to the teacher's reminder**	**Success criteria** • Gesture subtly • Continue to teach • Smile/nod to acknowledge
Time – 6 minutes, 90 seconds for each teacher • 60 seconds practice (2x distractions) • 30 seconds feedback	**Feedback** *It was effective when; next time try to…* • *Gesture more subtly.* • *Keep teaching.* • *Acknowledge the student's response.*

Effective training gives teachers feedback, guiding them to practise again, focusing on improving a single success criterion.

Action 3c) Plan guidance to help teachers give effective feedback, which highlights a single success criterion to improve. Plan time for teachers to apply feedback through subsequent rounds of practice.

Interlude

This is easily the longest and most demanding chapter in the book. Why is there so much to it? Designing and leading successful practice is extremely challenging. Almost every step is informed by mistakes I've made, or seen made. For example, in Step 2c, I emphasised the importance of specifying how those playing students should respond. Why? The first time I led practice in my school, a bored "student" threw his book across the room. I hadn't specified how he should respond. Not doing so undermined the session. I'm not going to recount every mis-step I've made. Unavoidably, you'll experience a few of them yourself. The chapter is long and intricate because there's a lot to get right. But if you've done everything so far, you already have a strong session. Now we're polishing it: it's downhill from here.

Step 4 - Ensure practice has a lasting impact

We've chosen a skill (Step 1) and designed an activity to practise it (Step 2). In Step 3, we added support to make practice work, through models, preparation, and feedback. We must now ensure this has a lasting impact. First, we'll build on teachers' success practising the target skill, ensuring improvements stick, and combining the target skill with others. We'll then look at helping teachers gain new insights into teaching. Finally, we'll explore ways to track how teachers are changing. In doing so, we move from planning an isolated session to ensuring lasting impact.

What does Step 4 look like?

Daniel's colleagues are practising non-verbal reminders. To use them effectively, teachers must monitor student behaviour and position themselves appropriately.[28] Daniel will mention this before practice and revisit these skills if he sees teachers struggling. If they practise reminders successfully, Daniel plans two ways to increase challenge and integrate other skills. First, he'll move practice from pairs to fours, challenging the teacher to spot who's off-task before giving a reminder. Then, he'll ask the distracted colleague to remain off-task after the first reminder, challenging the teacher to intervene more actively. To help teachers retain the skill, Daniel plans to practise non-verbal reminders briefly in two future sessions, on giving sanctions and effective explanations.

The main insight Daniel wants teachers to take from the session is that non-verbal reminders can be as effective as verbal reminders, but are less confrontational and distracting. He considers demonstrating this by verbally reminding colleagues to focus during practice - but decides not to test their goodwill. Instead, while everyone is working quietly, he'll give a thumbs up to one colleague and loudly ask a question to another. Then, he'll ask who noticed each, illustrating that gestures are much less likely to attract other students' attention.

During the session, Daniel plans to track teachers' growing skill in two ways. First, he'll circulate and check whether each teacher uses a non-verbal reminder. Second, he'll look at *how* they give reminders: how clear are they? How subtle? How well-integrated into teaching? After the session, he'll track its impact by checking the same things during lesson visits. He'll also look at whether teachers are choosing appropriate moments for non-verbal reminders. Do they miss opportunities to use them? Do they use non-verbal reminders when verbal ones might be better? The data Daniel collects will inform feedback during the session, and his planning of future sessions.

Jen's colleagues are practising setting lesson objectives. This requires a good grasp of the unit plan and underlying subject knowledge, so Jen chooses a unit they have all taught previously. She begins the session by briefly reviewing the unit's key ideas, and brings textbooks in case colleagues need further reminders. Jen is working towards helping teachers align activities with lesson objectives. If setting effective objectives proves easy, she will ask them to choose activities for one of the lessons.

Since objectives are always needed when practising planning, Jen can revisit this skill easily. Her next session is on choosing activities; she plans to begin by asking teachers to set objectives.

Jen hopes the session will help teachers see the objective as the core of the lesson. She wants them to grasp the difference between writing down things they hope to cover, and specifying a goal which determines how the lesson will be shaped. Her examples and non-examples should illustrate how focused an effective objective is. She plans one more prompt: at the end, she will ask colleagues how the session itself reflected its objectives.

Effective objectives are precise, ambitious, and achievable. Jen will look for precision while colleagues are writing objectives, since it's crucial, and easy to spot. (She'll invite them to reconcile ambition and achievability when they share their objectives with one another.) She then wants a quick, easy way to check whether colleagues are using the ideas from the session. Each week, she asks them to send her the objectives of a single lesson. Alongside her ongoing observations, this helps her track progress and plan the next session.

Step 4a) Plan progression

No skill is an island: each has prerequisites and logical next steps. Let's say our target skill is pausing after a question, then nominating a respondent, to ensure all students are thinking. Prerequisite skills include formulating meaningful questions and establishing silence so students can listen, think, and respond. Logical next steps include prompting students to answer and challenging them to refine their answers. In Step 2, we discussed focusing practice on the target skill. (For example, we could give teachers meaningful questions to ask, to help them focus on pausing and nominating.) Having designed a focused practice task, we can plan what to do if teachers struggle with the prerequisites, what to do when they practise successfully, and when to revisit the skill.

Planning around prerequisites: When we choose a target skill, we believe that teachers have mastered the prerequisites (if not, we would target them instead). During practice, however, we may find colleagues struggle. We can offer individual support: if a teacher struggles to call for silence before asking a question, we could offer a reminder, a model, or feedback. Alternatively, if everyone struggles, we could target this skill in a future session.

Planning next steps: After two or three successful rounds of practice, we can make things harder. We may invite teachers to practise the logical next step. For example, having nominated a student to answer a question, they could practise responding to the student answering, "I don't know." Integrating skills gets teachers nearer classroom reality, while ensuring they keep experiencing success.

Planning to revisit skills: Just like students, teachers forget things. They may practise successfully, but a single session is rarely enough for a skill to stick. We should plan to revisit the target skill within a few weeks. This could be a short activity: before a future session targeting choosing activities, Jen plans to ask colleagues to set objectives. Alternatively, we could integrate the skill into practice. For example, in a future session practising giving sanctions, Daniel plans to ask teachers to use a non-verbal reminder, then a sanction. (We look at other ways to make change stick in Chapter 4.)

Planning for prerequisites, next steps, and revisiting skills, prepares us to respond to teachers' needs. During practice, we can step back, if teachers struggle, or forwards, when they succeed. We've approached progression in the context of a single training session, since this is the focus of the chapter. We can plan progression and revision when we develop a programme; we discuss this in Chapters 5 and 6.

Effective training helps teachers progress by planning for prerequisite skills, logical next steps, and revisiting the target skill.

Action 4a) Identify prerequisites of the target skill; plan how to address them if colleagues struggle. Identify logical next steps; plan how to integrate them when colleagues succeed. Decide when to revisit the target skill.

Step 4b) Promote insight

As well as teaching skills, a training session may promote insight: a new way of seeing the world, teaching, or a teacher's own practice.[29] An example: when I began seeking student misconceptions, I was astonished to realise how extensive and fundamental they were. Students asked, for example, why the Spanish Armada ran into storms - could they not have checked the weather forecast on TV? Insights are crucial for teacher development: they show teachers that change is needed, and, often, what kind of change might help.[30] Recognising how much my students were missing, I changed how, and how often, I checked student understanding, how long I spent on topics and how soon I revisited them.

Important as insights are, they are a tricky target for professional development. First, insights alone do not improve teaching. Teachers need the insight - students have misconceptions - and the skills to do something about it.[31] Second, we can't predict when individuals will attain insights. I was told, "Effective teachers plan backwards" many times, before I understood why this mattered. Insights require external stimuli - models, feedback, discussion - and internal preparation: knowledge and dissatisfaction. Teachers may need to encounter an idea (perhaps many times), teach with it in mind, then discuss it. Third, we can't assess whether teachers have attained an insight. If we ask them how to plan, and they say, "Backwards", have they internalised the insight, or told us what we want to hear? We can plan a session to practise planning lessons backwards; we cannot plan a session which ensures teachers grasp why it matters. Effective sessions identify and promote key insights; they don't target insights alone. (Again, we are planning backwards. We may promote insight early in the session - but we plan for it having prepared the practice activity.)

Insights show teachers what change is needed: effective training promotes insights, but doesn't rely on them for improvement.

We can identify target insights by asking, "What must teachers grasp in order to see why this skill matters, and use it effectively?" They may need to recognise a problem: too many students are confused, for example, or marking is taking too long. They may need to see how a solution - a particular skill - can help. Daniel wants his colleagues to appreciate the value of non-verbal reminders. The underlying insight: verbally challenging off-task behaviour is sometimes necessary, but it distracts other students and can create a power struggle. A non-verbal reminder may solve off-task behaviour while avoiding confrontation. Jen wants colleagues to see that the objective is the core of the lesson. She needs them to grasp the difference between assembling a mix of activities and selecting tasks to pursue a specific goal. Having identified a target insight, we can plan how to promote it.

As we have discussed, teachers must make sense of an insight, not just hear about it. One researcher describes this as discovery: teachers, "Reexamine familiar events and come to see them differently", through discussing provocative questions.[32] Others describe helping people, "trip over the truth", by directing their attention and stretching their thinking.[33] An example: Alex Douglas, at Mossbourne Community Academy, wanted colleagues to grasp the importance of students thinking about meaning. First, he asked them which way the monarch's head faces on a pound coin. Then, he asked how many table tennis tables were in the school yard. Despite walking through the yard every day, no one could answer correctly. The penny dropped: teachers realised that exposure alone doesn't cause learning; students need to think hard about what is to be learned. Daniel demonstrates the value of subtle interventions by giving one colleague a thumbs up, and talking to another across the room. We promote insight by choosing a stimulus (new information or past experience), posing questions, and giving teachers time to consider them.

One note of caution. We could show teachers that shouting in the classroom is unpleasant by shouting in the session. This would be an effective demonstration, but an unpleasant experience. Likewise, a multilingual teacher educator could start the session in another language - showing how tough the classroom is if you don't understand it. Teachers could find this patronising and frustrating. I would rarely recommend creating negative experiences to promote insight.

Effective training helps teachers grasp the insights needed to teach differently.

Action 4b) Promote insight: identify what teachers need to grasp to see why the target skill matters. Choose a stimulus and questions; make time for teachers to consider them.

Step 4c) Track impact

Once teachers are practising, we may draw breath and wonder what to do next. Most usefully, we can track their progress with the target skill, choosing success criteria (from those set in Step 1b) to look for while circulating. One approach is to count; for example, the number of colleagues who:

- Write instructions sequentially;
- Use non-verbal reminders while teaching; or,
- Pause for three seconds between asking a question and nominating a student to respond.

This rapidly reveals how well the group is doing. It also allows us to give feedback (and convey social norms) in neutral and objective terms: "Twelve of the eighteen people I saw practising managed a three-second pause." Some things can be counted; others must be assessed qualitatively. For example, we can look at how clear instructions are, how warm non-verbal reminders are, and how the teacher spends the three-second pause. Finally, we can track teachers' increasing willingness to practise, monitoring how much of the time they are in role. (We discuss building this culture of practice in Step 5, below.) Tracking impact allows us to recognise colleagues' successes, suggest improvements, and adapt the session to meet their needs.

Tracking teachers' success during practice allows us to highlight successes, suggest improvements, and adapt the session.

We also need to know how training affects teaching. Our questions mirror those during the session:

- How many colleagues are using the skill?
- What's going well?
- What needs improvement?

At Daniel's school, leaders do weekly lesson visits. After his session, he asks them to record how many teachers they see using non-verbal reminders, and any strengths and weaknesses they notice. Using existing observations tracks impact without creating additional work. (If the school doesn't have regular lesson visits, we'll need to make time for them.) These quick checks show the impact of the session and allow us to plan future training and support for individuals. (We further discuss transferring skills from training to the classroom in Chapter 4, and measuring impact in Chapter 7.)

Effective training changes teaching: we must track the impact of our session

Action 4c) Track impact: check whether the target skill is being used, and how well, during training, and in the classroom.

Step 5 - Build a culture of practice

We've chosen a skill, designed a practice activity, and prepared support to make it work (Steps 1-3). In Step 4, we looked at ensuring impact, by planning progression, promoting insights, and tracking the results. One crucial challenge remains. Practice is hard and, for many teachers, unfamiliar. They may avoid it, saying:

- "This feels artificial."
- "I don't feel comfortable."
- "It's more useful to plan what to say/discuss what to do (than to practise it)."
- "I'll practise later."
- "I'll be fine in the classroom."

These reactions are understandable. But, as we discussed above, teachers are under intense pressure. If they won't try something in training, they almost certainly won't try it while teaching. We need to overcome their objections and get them practising, so they can test and refine the skill, gain confidence, and, hopefully, recognise the value of practice. Again, we're planning backwards. We'll build a culture of practice throughout the session. But, in planning, we set a goal, decide how to achieve it, *then* work out how to ensure participation. We're helping teachers *pursue the objective* in comfort - not pursuing comfort for its own sake. To develop a culture of practice, we'll build conviction, make practice comfortable, and challenge colleagues to participate.

What does Step 5 look like?

Daniel first plans how to build conviction that the session is worthwhile. He'll demonstrate the value of non-verbal reminders by highlighting the problem they address: spirals of disruption, in which reminding one student disturbs others. Daniel will explain how he got this wrong, interrupting teaching to say, "Stop chatting", distracting the whole class. He can't ignore students who are talking, he'll explain, but non-verbal reminders gain their attention without disturbing others. (He'll also explain that using them doesn't preclude using more robust interventions, or sanctions, where needed.) Daniel will remind teachers of the value of practice by emphasising the cognitive load placed on them when they give reminders while continuing to teach complicated ideas. Practice is essential if they are to do both simultaneously.

Daniel builds comfort by giving teachers time to choose the non-verbal reminders they will use. This allows them to prepare themselves for practice, and make the skill fit their teaching style. Initially, teachers will practise in pairs; this gives them a degree of privacy. Later, he'll reinforce the benefits of practice by asking what has gone well and how they have improved.

Teachers may delay starting practice, or pause between rounds of practice. If so, Daniel plans to approach them and ask, "Who's next?"[34] This avoids implying criticism, or getting caught up in what they're doing: it simply reminds and invites them to continue practice. Teachers may say, "We're just discussing what to do if students don't respond." If so, Daniel will reassure them that the session will come on to this.

Jen plans to build conviction that objectives matter by describing three things she once struggled with:

- Planning from objectives. She'll describe her planning process as a new teacher: choosing engaging activities, then thinking about the objective.
- Specifying objectives. She'll give examples of objectives which sound precise but aren't (like "Analyse language structures in Act 2, Scene 3").[35]
- Time pressure. She'll remind colleagues how much is in the curriculum and how quickly students forget things.

She hopes to convince colleagues that precise objectives are essential. She'll also note an immediate benefit of practising setting objectives: teachers will get ahead with their planning.

Practising lesson planning is less discomforting than practising teaching. Jen plans to make starting easy by giving colleagues a clear initial focus (setting objectives for a specific upcoming lesson). Once they have exchanged feedback, she'll emphasise the value of the process by asking what they have taken from the feedback and from seeing each other's objectives.

Jen anticipates colleagues wanting to go beyond setting objectives. It would be easy to begin discussing activities and exit tickets. There's obvious value in doing this, but Jen wants to ensure everyone can set excellent objectives first. She plans to remind colleagues of the importance of getting objectives right and explain that they'll tackle other elements of planning in future sessions.

Step 5a) Build conviction

If they believe in the session's focus and approach, teachers will participate more enthusiastically. We must build conviction in the target skill and in practice.

BUILD CONVICTION IN THE TARGET SKILL

We need to convince teachers of the target skill's value. To do so, we can appeal to their experience, to evidence, or to authorities. For example:

We can appeal to...	*To show the value of...*	*By...*
Teachers' experience (in the classroom)	Retrieval practice	Asking teachers to recall examples of students forgetting things they had previously learned.
(outside the classroom)	Modelling	Asking teachers to consider how models have helped them master skills (for example, in sport, cooking, music).
Evidence	Checking student understanding (rather than using self-report)	Telling teachers: "Among patients who died in intensive care, doctors who were 'completely certain' of their diagnosis were wrong 40% of the time."[36]
Authorities	Students responding to feedback	Telling teachers: "Dylan Wiliam says 'Feedback should be more work for the recipient than the donor.'"[37]

The initial sections of each chapter in this book offer further examples. In this chapter, I appealed to evidence (the systematic review of professional development), the reader's experience (of learning skills) and authorities (such as medical training). I also discussed possible counter-arguments, and why I didn't think they applied. In person, we might elicit and tackle these doubts explicitly, asking "Why might we be sceptical about this?"

Teachers must see the value of the target skill.

BUILD CONVICTION IN PRACTICE ITSELF

We also need teachers to believe that practice works. The best evidence is experiencing effective practice: teachers will believe it works when they see themselves improve. But we need colleagues to take the first step: to begin practising. When I introduce practice, I start with a pitch, presenting the arguments made in the Introduction to this chapter. I ask teachers about their experience learning skills. I expand on the examples: describing the challenges Civil Rights protesters faced at lunch counter sit-ins, for example, and how practice helped. This seems to satisfy most teachers. It also provides a touchstone. We can remind teachers of it in future sessions; we can return to it when talking with sceptics. Initial efforts to convince colleagues are essential - but when they are deeply sceptical, ongoing debate is a dead end (true sceptics can debate indefinitely). We must get them practising so they can *feel* the benefits. We discuss how to do this in Step 5c, below.

Teachers must see the value of practice.

Action 5a) Show teachers the value of the target skill, appealing to evidence, authorities, or their experience. Show teachers why practice matters - then get them practising so they can experience its value.

Step 5b) Make practice comfortable

No matter how good a case we make for practice, many teachers find it uncomfortable initially. We want them practising - and experiencing success - as soon as possible. We can refine the session to make starting easier, success more likely, and progress more noticeable.

MAKE STARTING EASY

We can make practice more comfortable by easing teachers into it. Let's look at doing this for teachers' first experience of practice. We choose a simple initial task, like practising a sentence (such as a question or a reminder). This is easy, unthreatening, and guarantees teachers succeed. We ask them to write their sentence, then stand facing a partner. We ask one teacher (the taller one, say), to sit, while their partner speaks. Nominating the first speaker and having them standing already allows everyone to start straight away (and shows us who's practising). Once they've swapped, we skip feedback, so teachers don't feel they're being judged. We've made practice feel easy and unthreatening. We can do something similar in *any* session: start small, ease teachers in, limit perceived threats. Once they're practising, we can increase challenge and add feedback.

Practice should feel easy and unthreatening.

ENSURE SUCCESS

We want teachers to succeed in most practice attempts.[38] Success fosters new habits and increases teachers' confidence and enjoyment. The steps we've taken in planning the session should ensure this. We can revisit them to address (or pre-empt) teacher discomfort. For example, if teachers struggle, we can offer additional models (Step 3a), more time to prepare (Step 3b), or move to a simpler, prerequisite skill (Step 4a). Planning practice and specifying how teachers playing students should respond is particularly important, so they don't act out and put off the teacher practising (Step 2c). We must ensure teachers succeed: if they struggle, revisiting these steps should help.

Practice succeeds when teachers succeed.

HIGHLIGHT SUCCESS

We want teachers to succeed *and to recognise their success.* We can ask questions which encourage this, for example:

- After teachers' first experience of practice, we could ask "How did that feel?" and "What did you like?" (We might also ask what they're unsure about.)
- After multiple rounds of practice, we could ask "How are you seeing yourself improve?"
- After peer feedback, we can emphasise the positives, asking "What did your partner do well that you might copy?" or "What useful feedback did your partner offer?"

Brief opportunities to consider questions like these, and share answers with the group, can help teachers recognise the benefits of practice.

Teachers need to recognise their success.

Action 5b) Make practice comfortable: make it easy to start, ensure teachers succeed, and help them recognise their success.

Step 5c) Challenge colleagues

Despite all we've done – planning carefully, building conviction, making practice comfortable – some teachers may still avoid practice. Perhaps they still see it as artificial or unnecessary. They may still feel uncomfortable. But as teacher educators, we're responsible for helping everyone to improve. Only practice tests and refines a new skill, prepares teachers to use it in the classroom, and turns good intentions into action. We must challenge colleagues to participate.

Our immediate goal is not to convince colleagues: sceptics can debate indefinitely. Instead, we want to acknowledge their concerns and get them practising. We can do this by *affirming* their objection, *rationalising* it, and *redirecting* it towards practice. For example, imagine a teacher saying, "My Year 9s are far more challenging than this practice task - how is this going to help?" We:

- **Affirm**: "I appreciate they're a particularly tricky class."
- **Rationalise**: "We're starting with a simple scenario. Once everyone is using the skill successfully, we'll make things more difficult."
- **Redirect**: "Can you show me how you'd respond to the scenario? Then we'll adapt it."

We've acknowledged their concern and nudged them to practise. Their participation and success should build confidence and begin to form a habit. (If we face many sceptics, we have other options, like testing changes with pilot groups of volunteers, and using behavioural science techniques to encourage participation. We discuss these in Chapters 4 and 6.)

Teacher educators must challenge teachers to participate.

Action 5c) Challenge colleagues to practise: affirm their concerns, rationalise the situation, and redirect them towards practice.

What does an effective training session look like?

We've looked at the steps in the order we plan them. Now let's see how Daniel's plans come together as a session (the steps are in bold).

The **target skill** for Daniel's session is non-verbal reminders. He begins **building conviction** they are worthwhile by highlighting the problem they address: spirals of disruption, in which reminding one student disturbs others. Daniel explains how he got this wrong, distracting the whole class by interrupting teaching to tell a couple of students to "Stop talking." Non-verbal reminders can gain the attention of distracted students without disturbing everyone else.

Next, Daniel shows two video **models** which demonstrate non-verbal reminders in different contexts. He asks teachers what they notice, highlighting the success criteria the videos illustrate and the scope for teachers to adapt reminders to suit their teaching style.

Before introducing practice, Daniel **builds conviction** in it by emphasising the cognitive load teachers face when giving reminders while teaching. He tells them that practice is essential if they are to do both simultaneously.

Daniel then gives teachers time to **prepare for practice**. He invites them to skim over the text they'll be using and choose gestures to regain students' attention (**making**

practice comfortable). He also uses this preparation time to **promote insight** about the value of non-verbal reminders. While teachers are working individually, he gives a thumbs up to one colleague, then loudly asks another how they're getting on. Afterwards, he asks who noticed each action; several teachers nod in understanding.

Before practice begins, Daniel **clarifies the task and teachers' roles.** One person, the teacher, reads the text; the other loses focus. When the teacher offers a clear non-verbal reminder, they focus again. This simple, paired activity **makes practice comfortable**, and Daniel soon sees most colleagues practising.

Daniel circulates to **track the impact** of the session. He checks whether teachers are using non-verbal reminders and how clear, subtle, and integrated into teaching they are. He finds one pair deep in discussion. They turn to him, saying, "We're discussing what to do if students don't respond." Daniel **challenges** them, affirming the importance of the question, explaining why they need to get non-verbal reminders right before dealing with resistance, and redirecting them by asking "Who's next?" The pair return to practice.

After the first round of practice, teachers give each other **feedback** using the success criteria. To **make practice comfortable**, Daniel asks them to focus solely on positives. Daniel's feedback highlights a common issue: non-verbal reminders which are so exaggerated they seem unnatural. He invites teachers to practise again. They improve further and Daniel decides they're ready to **progress** on to harder practice. First, he invites them to practise in fours, challenging the person teaching to spot who's off-task. Then, he asks the distracted colleague to remain off-task after the first reminder, challenging the teacher to intervene more actively.

After the session, Daniel **tracks its impact** by looking for non-verbal reminders during lesson visits. He sees many more reminders being used, but he believes they could be clearer and more smoothly integrated into teaching. Daniel plans to revisit them in the next session.

Case study

In this case study, Lucy Davies, Assistant Principal at Manchester Communication Academy, describes how using deliberate practice changed her approach to setting session goals and promoting insights.

SETTING OBJECTIVES (AND CREATING SUCCESS CRITERIA)

Previously, I didn't identify one clear skill for practice. It's difficult to believe this now as when I'm teaching students, I always set a clear objective and know exactly what I want students to be able to do by the end of the lesson, but it hadn't occurred to me to be this specific about the professional development sessions that I designed. My process for creating training was to select an area of teaching or a theme, such as "checking for understanding", and to choose a range of strategies to share with the trainees. This approach often involved a number of strategies which meant that they weren't covered in enough depth. Often, I would explain the strategies, model them myself with trainees playing the role of students, and provide resources for trainees to take away to implement into their teaching.

I now begin to plan training sessions by identifying the skill that I want trainees to develop. This has meant that I have had to revisit some past training sessions and refine them. One of the training sessions that I spent time designing and refining was on "effective explanations". When creating success criteria, I realised that this session needed to be separated into two parts; one on scripting an explanation and the other on delivering an explanation. I set the following success criteria for scripting an explanation:

- Define the idea, process, or word simply.
- Elaborate using diagrams, analogies, or examples.
- Make explicit links between the definition and the elaboration.
    - It's similar to... because...
    - It's a bit like... except...

The impact of focusing on a particular skill and employing success criteria has been that trainees are much clearer about exactly what they need to do to develop the skill at hand when they come to practise. The outcome of this is that practice is more purposeful, resulting in trainees becoming more confident and therefore, more likely to implement this in their own classrooms. By narrowing down the focus of the session, more time can also be dedicated to exploring the rationale behind developing this skill and therefore in increasing "buy-in".

FRAMING THE PRACTICE (BY ENCOURAGING INSIGHTS AND SHARING "THE WHY")

Although my past training sessions referenced cognitive science and included questions, analogies, or examples when introducing a topic, I now feel that they weren't effective in promoting "aha" moments or really explaining "the why" behind the ideas that were being shared. The main reason for this was most probably that I was creating this content before deciding the skills that were to be practised and refined. The inclusion of cognitive science had become almost habitual rather than meaningful and would take place at the start of the session, sometimes never to be referred to again and questions posed at the beginning were generic rather than designed to promote insight.

I now start to design activities to promote insight that is intrinsically linked to the practice task. An example of this was a session where I wanted trainees to practise planning for potential misconceptions. At the start of the training, I posed the question, "Why might misconceptions arise?" Although this seems really simple and obvious, by giving the trainees enough time to discuss this in depth, they were able to produce all the answers that I had pre-prepared.

Pre-prepared potential answers to the questions 'Why might misconceptions arise?'

WHY MIGHT MISCONCEPTIONS ARISE?

1. Because something feels logical. — For example, students might think that shredding paper is a chemical reaction because they can't imagine it being reversed.

2. Because teachers try to simplify things for students. — For example, students might believe that we use a comma when we want the reader to take a breath.

3. Students have an incomplete understanding of something. — For example, students might think that we add an apostrophe to any word ending in an 's'.

4. Student pick them up through everyday experience. — For example, students might think that Vikings wore horns on their helmets.

In pairs, discuss the following question: **Have you come across any misconceptions since you started teaching?**

This meant that when they moved onto the practice task of identifying potential misconceptions, not only did they find the task easier to access, but they felt a sense of ownership which seemed to motivate them.

Conclusion

If teachers are to adopt new skills in complex, busy classrooms, they must first practise them. Effective training focuses on this practice. We ensure teachers experience success by focusing on a target skill, and offering models, preparation, and feedback. We build a culture of practice and aim for lasting impact on teachers' thinking and actions. This approach reflects current best evidence around teacher professional development: success depends on promoting insights, motivating change, teaching techniques, and embedding changes. This is a lot to consider – we can build these steps into our sessions gradually. Having looked at effective training, in the next chapter we'll apply these principles to supporting.

Next steps

Reflection questions

1) Review a recent professional development session (one you experienced or led). To what extent did:
   - The session focus on a single target skill?
   - Teachers practise using that skill?
   - Teachers see models, prepare for practice, and receive and use feedback?
   - The session promote insight?
   - Leaders track the impact of the session?
   - The session build a culture of practice?
2) Think about how you might refine this session (or a future session). Which step could you focus on? What could be done differently?

Checklist

1) Choose a target skill
   a. Choose a goal
   b. Select a skill and success criteria
2) Design the practice activity
   a. Focus practice on the target skill
   b. Choose how teachers will practise
   c. Clarify the task and teachers' roles
3) Prepare support to make practice shine
   a. Select models
   b. Plan how teachers will prepare for practice
   c. Choose how teachers will receive feedback; prepare key points
4) Ensure practice has lasting impact
   a. Plan the next step and any steps which they may need to review
   b. Identify the insights teachers need and how to promote them
   c. Track impact during and after the session
5) Build a culture of practice
   a. Build conviction in the target skill and in practice
   b. Make practice comfortable
   c. Challenge colleagues to participate

Getting started

Based on your answers to the reflection questions, pick one sub-step to work on (the first sub-step in the sequence which you think needs work). Focus on improving this in your next session.

Success in different roles

You can apply the ideas in this chapter, whatever your role:

- **As a teacher. . .** you can help yourself improve by choosing a single target skill and practising it before trying it in the classroom. Better still, find colleagues to practise with.
- **As a middle leader. . .** you can apply these steps to planning training for your department or team. You can push for this approach to training to be adopted across the school.
- **As a leader working across schools. . .** you can encourage and support your schools to design training which applies these principles; you can model this approach in the training you lead.

3 How can we coach individual teachers to improve?

Chapter map

Effective coaching tailors training to individual teachers' needs.

↓

Effective coaching:

- Is frequent, focused, developmental, and promotes change
- Promotes insight, motivates goal-directed behaviour, teaches techniques, and embeds change

↓

Step 1: Observe teaching and gather evidence

a) Check progress
b) Identify a priority

↓

Step 2: Offer feedback and support change

a) Highlight success
b) Agree the next step
c) Model the step
d) Plan and practise the step
e) Commit to action

↓

Step 3: Coach responsively

a) Ensure the teacher grasps their step
b) Ensure the teacher succeeds
c) Add challenge incrementally

↓

Step 4: Build a culture of coaching

a) Make coaching feel comfortable
b) Nudge teachers to act
c) Highlight progress
d) Learn from other coaches

↓

Step 5: Adapt to teachers' expertise

↓

We can then support teachers to change (Chapter 4) and improve teaching across the school (Part II).

DOI: 10.4324/9781003439622-5

In Chapter 1, we established principles of teaching and learning: what we want teachers to do. In Chapter 2, we looked at designing training to help groups of teachers apply these principles. Now, we turn to supporting individual teachers. Our purpose is unchanged. We want teachers to understand the principles, wish to pursue them, know how to put them into practice and apply them in the classroom. In this chapter, we'll look at how coaching allows us to tailor our pursuit of these purposes to an individual's needs. We can agree a goal and offer support which directly reflects their current practice. First, we'll examine how effective coaching can make a difference.

Why does effective coaching matter?

Let's look at three ways to support individual teachers: feedback dumps, growth coaching, and instructional coaching. Pratibha's initial approach - feedback dumps - reflects her experience as a teacher. She observes lessons termly. Giving feedback, she first describes everything the teacher did well, then lists possible improvements. Pratibha tries to make the discussion supportive, inviting the teacher to contribute at every stage. But she feels she should mention everything she has noticed, so they receive a feedback dump. Listing suggestions doesn't mean teachers improve - it's overwhelming for them. Pratibha is spending a lot of time but achieving little: she looks for alternative approaches.

Pratibha decides to try growth coaching. She no longer dumps feedback on teachers: they lead the discussion. Her questions elicit their thinking, rather than guiding it. Pratibha hopes that giving less feedback and putting teachers in control will make meetings more positive. Most colleagues enjoy the discussion; more experienced teachers get the most out of it. But few teachers improve as a result. Some focus on issues which bother them, but aren't crucial. Others know what's needed, but not how to achieve it. Pratibha bites her tongue to avoid taking charge, but gradually becomes as frustrated as they are. Teachers want to improve - she isn't helping.

So Pratibha turns to instructional coaching. Feedback is focused: instead of Pratibha making multiple suggestions, she and the teacher agree one aspect of teaching to improve. To address it, they select a single step to work on; Pratibha shares a model and helps the teacher practise the step during the meeting. On her next lesson visit, Pratibha checks whether the teacher has achieved the step. If so, they move on to another step; if not, she offers further support. Teachers make rapid progress, so they increasingly welcome coaching.

Instructional coaching helps teachers improve, for several reasons. First, it feels manageable. Unlike feedback dumps, teachers focus on one thing. Second, it pretty much guarantees teachers' success. Unlike growth coaching, teachers get the models, guidance, and practice needed to master their action step. Third, it offers Goldilocks guidance: the coach invites the teacher to lead at every stage, but supports them if they struggle. Finally, through follow-up visits, the coach reminds the teacher to act and offers further support if needed. Effective coaching allows us to help individual teachers improve - and makes them feel successful.

Effective coaching focuses on a single improvement, guarantees teachers' success, and makes them feel successful.

What makes coaching effective?

There's growing evidence that coaching can substantially improve teaching.[1] Asked whether their school's observation and feedback process helps them improve however, just one third of teachers agree. The rest are split: some say observations only check for compliance; some say the process is meant to help them improve, but doesn't; some say there is no observation process.[2] What needs to change to make coaching effective?

Effective coaching is frequent

For many teachers, observations remain infrequent. Most are observed one to three times a year. Just 4% of teachers are observed fortnightly; 14% aren't seen all year.[3] Changing this seems difficult: for one recent study, schools promised to observe teachers 12 times in a year. They managed just three.[4] Infrequent observations present two issues. First, it's hard to identify a teacher's needs without seeing them teach. (Occasional observations also raise the stakes for the teacher, making a typical lesson less likely.) Second, a follow-up visit encourages the teacher to act and allows us to offer further support. Delaying this makes change less likely. **Effective coaching is frequent: this allows coaches to accurately identify teachers' needs and provide ongoing support.**

Effective coaching is focused

Feedback is often unfocused. Some coaches expect teachers to identify problems and solutions themselves. But most teachers need guidance on where to focus and how to improve. Others offer a laundry list of suggestions, covering behaviour, assessment, planning, and displays. (When observations are infrequent, observers often feel they should mention everything they have noticed.) Teachers can't address everything mentioned. Some give up, others try the changes that appeal most. Unfocused feedback - too many suggestions or too little guidance - makes it hard for teachers to know how best to improve. **Effective coaching is focused on the most immediate, important improvement a teacher can make.**

Effective coaching promotes change

Feedback meetings often provide information, rather than promoting change. Teachers are told to improve behaviour, explain more clearly, or assess more carefully. They know what's needed, but change may prove hard. For example, they may:

- Know what to change, but not how. An observer might tell a teacher to improve "pace" or "challenge". The teacher will struggle without concrete guidance and models showing how to do so.
- Know how to change, but be left to get on with it. Teachers may be clear during the meeting, but get stuck or confused when they try to change. Or they may just forget, as everyday pressures supplant their good intentions.
- Try the change, but struggle to make it work. They may plan a new routine or activity and find it doesn't work first time. Without further support, they may not know what to do next.

- Make the change, then revert to existing habits. If no one checks, there's no reminder and perhaps little incentive to maintain the change. (This is particularly likely if observations are infrequent and if teachers receive many feedback suggestions.)

In Chapter 2, we discussed evidence showing effective training promotes insight, motivates change, teaches techniques, and embeds practice, using behaviour change mechanisms such as modelling, feedback, and practice. When we coach, we apply these principles to individual improvement. Feedback alone rarely causes change. **Effective coaching promotes change, by encouraging insight, motivating action, teaching techniques, and embedding practice.**

Effective coaching is developmental

Observations often feel judgemental. Some explicitly are: the goal is assessing the teacher. Even when they're not, teachers fear judgement. They worry their mistakes will be reported, triggering further scrutiny. So they perform: they schedule observations for good classes; they prepare especially. They approach feedback defensively, justifying their actions and debating suggestions, rather than listening and learning. When teachers feel judged, they resist coaching. **Effective coaching is developmental: teachers feel safe learning, making mistakes, and trying new things.**

Drawing these ideas together, coaching is more likely to succeed if:

- Observations are frequent, capturing typical practice and offering ongoing support;
- Feedback focuses on the biggest improvement the teacher can make;
- Coaches promote change, rather than providing information;
- The process feels developmental, not judgemental.

We'll call this approach instructional coaching: instructional because we focus on teaching (not personal growth), coaching because we offer individual support. The principles apply whoever we're working with. For example, effective coaching is focused. The focus may be selected by the coach (for a new teacher) by the teacher (if they're an expert) or, most likely, mutually agreed. We'll discuss coaching expert teachers in Step 5, below.

> *Effective instructional coaching - frequent, focused, developmental, and promoting change - helps teachers improve.*

How do we coach effectively?

Step 1 - Observe teaching and gather evidence

A coaching cycle begins with an observation. If these are to be frequent, they must be quick - ideally less than 15 minutes. Our goal is to gather evidence around three questions:

1) Has the teacher achieved their previous step? If not;
2) What is the teacher doing particularly well?
3) What aspect of teaching should we prioritise improving?

What does Step 1 look like?

In this chapter, I have described Rachel coaching three teachers, to illustrate how coaching approaches reflect teachers' expertise. I won't describe every sub-step in depth for every teacher - instead, I'll go into more detail when her approach varies between them.

Setting aside a lesson for observations, Rachel begins with Kamil. He has been working on breaking instructions into chunks - one or two actions at a time. Rachel is pleased to see this working well: he breaks a complicated transition into multiple steps; most students begin the next activity immediately. Nonetheless, challenges remain. While he is giving instructions, some students keep working on the previous task. Others start the new task early, thinking they've grasped what to do. Kamil neither checks students' understanding of the instructions, nor monitors what happens next. Rachel finds some students struggling, or on the wrong track.

Next, Rachel visits Ania. She has been working on giving better explanations. Rachel observes three snippets of explanation - but none includes a concrete example. Rachel notes strengths: Ania is carefully checking students' work and offering clear feedback. But students' confusion means there's a lot of feedback to give. Rachel wonders whether Ania's explanations are vague due to gaps in her subject knowledge. She can't be sure from the observation, but Rachel will focus on this during the feedback meeting.

Finally, Rachel sees Josh. He has been working on checking student understanding before independent work using hinge questions. During Rachel's visit, however, there's no logical moment to try this. Rachel saves looking for hinge questions for future observations. She notes how well Josh has designed the task and how focused students are. Students' grasp of the lesson's key idea is mixed however: some are unsure, others are ready to move on. Josh seems aware of this - he's circulating the room and checking understanding. But he deals with everything through individual feedback, and can't reach every student. Rachel thinks this will be a productive focus for their meeting.

Step 1a) Check progress

When observing, we first look for evidence that the teacher has successfully achieved their previous step (we'll look at how these are chosen below). For example, Rachel checked whether Kamil was breaking instructions into chunks. If they have, we record a telling example: Rachel noted Kamil's instructions helping students transition rapidly between activities. We'll begin the feedback meeting by using this to highlight the teacher's progress. If they haven't met their most recent step, we can identify a different strength - possibly a past step. For example, Rachel notes Ania's feedback to students.

Effective coaches check the teacher has achieved their previous step and record specific evidence of their success.

Action 1a) Begin observations by looking for evidence the teacher has successfully achieved their previous step. If so, record a telling example. If not, identify a different strength.

Step 1b) Identify a priority

Imagine observing a lesson for just sixty seconds. We might spot many things which could be improved: a meandering teacher explanation followed by a confusing task, for example, while students whisper at the back. But telling the teacher everything they *could* improve conveys how much change is needed - dispiritingly - but not where to begin. Teaching is too complicated, and habits are too powerful, for a teacher to make several changes at once. We must prioritise. Here, we'll look at how to identify an area of teaching to improve, a goal, and a next step. In Step 2, we'll see how we can use this model to agree the step to pursue with the teacher.

IDENTIFY THE MOST IMPORTANT AREA TO IMPROVE

To prioritise, we work our way upstream. Picture a winding river. At its mouth, birds are getting sick. We have limited resources and can do only one thing. Should we:

a) Set up a treatment programme for sick birds;
b) Build a water purification programme half-way down the river's course; or,
c) Prevent pollution entering the water?

The answer seems self-evident: challenges are best tackled at their source.

Working upstream in coaching, we consider the fundamental challenges all teachers face, in turn. Effective teachers:

1) Secure students' **attention**
2) **Present** key ideas effectively
3) Ensure students **think** hard about key ideas
4) **Assess** student understanding and give feedback
5) **Consolidate** student learning

These challenges must be addressed in sequence, beginning upstream. For example, we imagined seeing a meandering explanation, a confusing task, and distracted students. We want a better task, but students will struggle with it unless key ideas are presented clearly. We want a better explanation, but students won't benefit from it unless they're listening. The initial priority - the challenge furthest upstream - is maintaining all students' attention. (A better explanation will help, but we can't leave students to opt out of listening to it.) We'll tackle everything, eventually. But we must begin somewhere: upstream.

IDENTIFY A GOAL, AND THE NEXT STEP TO TAKE

With a challenge in mind, we can select a goal which addresses it, and the next step towards it. Back to our imagined observation. The challenge is securing students' attention. The goal is more focused: maintaining attention during an explanation. To achieve this, the teacher must use many skills: calling for silence, monitoring attention, issuing reminders, and perhaps sanctions. We work upstream again: the teacher cannot issue a reminder or monitor attention until they have gained it. The first step – the skill we will focus on in this round of coaching – is successfully calling for silence. Future coaching meetings will tackle other steps until the goal is achieved.

Effective coaching prioritises, identifying the furthest upstream challenge the teacher faces, a goal addressing it, and the next step towards it.

Let's apply this approach to the teachers Rachel coaches. For each teacher, what is the fundamental challenge? What is an appropriate goal? What step might they take next?

1) While Kamil is giving instructions, some students keep working on the previous task; others start the new one. He neither checks students' understanding of the instructions, nor monitors what happens next.
2) Ania's explanations lack concrete examples, leaving students confused.
3) Josh's students' understanding of key ideas in the lesson is mixed; Josh deals with this slowly, using individual feedback.

Once you've chosen, turn the page.

We might conclude:

1) The **fundamental challenge** Kamil is struggling with is *securing students' attention*. He has been working on the **goal** of *giving clear instructions* and ensuring students follow them. This goal needs further work: chunking instructions has helped, but some students are still confused about what to do. Checking their understanding and monitoring their actions will help - but ensuring they listen to the instructions in the first place is further upstream. So Kamil's next **step** is *calling for silence*.
2) Ania's **fundamental challenge** is *presenting key ideas effectively*. Her current **goal** is *giving clear explanations*. Her previous **step** was *scripting the explanation of key points*. She needs to keep working on this step, including concrete examples in her script.
3) Josh's students are thinking hard - but their understanding is mixed. The **fundamental challenge** he faces is gathering evidence of student understanding, and *giving feedback*. He's giving individual feedback, which is taking too long. An appropriate **goal** is using *whole-class feedback* to address student misunderstandings; a possible first **step** is *planning feedback for likely misconceptions*.

Some find the observer's role discomforting. But, in a busy classroom, a coach may well spot something the teacher has missed. Bringing this to the feedback meeting, they should work *with* the teacher to understand what happened and agree what to do next. Rachel noticed Ania's explanations lacked concrete examples. There are many possible reasons: maybe Ania deliberately rejected concrete examples. Maybe there's a gap in her subject knowledge. Maybe she rushed her planning. Together, they will identify the issue and agree how to address it. We'll look at how to do this in Step 2 and, in Step 4, at how coaches can make the process feel comfortable. Teaching is hard; we can always learn more - so teachers *and coaches* should approach observations with humility.

Effective coaches bring what they notice to the feedback meeting and work with the teacher to agree what to do about it.

Meanwhile, coaches may worry about choosing the wrong focus. I'd offer three reassurances. First, observing frequently allows us to establish what's typical and what matters. Second, we aren't seeking certainty: we're helping the teacher improve, not judging their competence. Third, if we do choose the wrong focus, this will soon become obvious, either as the teacher practises or during the next lesson. They'll either master the next step immediately, or struggle - we can adjust the focus. Our goal is small, frequent improvements: this leaves room for small, occasional errors.

Effective coaches seek iterative improvement, not certainty.

Action 1b) Work upstream: identify the fundamental challenge the teacher faces, an appropriate goal, and the next step towards it.

Step 2 - Offer feedback and support change

Giving effective feedback is tricky. To make frequent coaching manageable, feedback meetings should last no more than 20 minutes. Moreover, we have discussed many possible traps, such as judgement, lack of focus, and providing information rather than supporting change. To avoid them, keep to time, and help teachers improve, we need a careful plan and a clear structure:

1) Highlight the teacher's success
2) Agree the next step
3) Model the step
4) Plan change and practise the step
5) Commit to action

This is a scaffold, not a straitjacket; we'll discuss possible adaptations in Steps 3 and 4.

What does Step 2 look like?

Rachel begins her feedback meeting with Kamil by highlighting his success in breaking down instructions. She asks, "What impact has this had?" and he enthusiastically describes the quicker starts and better work he's seen. Rachel then raises students' attentiveness to instructions. First, she checks Kamil's awareness of the issue, asking, "What did you notice students doing while you were giving instructions?" Kamil did spot students not listening, but he doesn't immediately link this to their subsequent confusion. Rachel pushes him: "Marcus and Sadie were chatting - what was their work like later in the lesson?" Kamil makes the link and suggests focusing on ensuring silence himself. Rachel models calling for silence - "I need everybody's eyes on me" - scanning to check students are listening, then giving instructions. She asks Kamil, "What did you spot about the model?" and repeats it to ensure he notices her instructions are succinct and are given in an unhurried, confident tone. Rachel then asks Kamil to choose an upcoming lesson and task. Kamil scripts his call for silence and reviews it with Rachel. Then he practises calling for silence and checking students are listening before beginning the instructions. They practise several times, and Kamil gradually gains confidence. After several successful rounds of practice, Rachel acts as a distracted student; Kamil notices and reminds her to listen. Finally, he creates a reminder to pause and scan, drawing a pair of eyes beside the instructions in his lesson plan.

Rachel begins her meeting with Ania by discussing the strengths of her feedback. Then they consider explanations. Ania recognises they aren't working perfectly, but isn't sure why. But when Rachel asks Ania to choose an upcoming lesson, they review the plan and find gaps in her subject knowledge. They briefly review the key ideas, Ania scripts an explanation, then Rachel helps her add concrete examples. They practise the explanation several times. Ania usually plans with colleagues: she suggests using this time to share planned explanations and get feedback.

Josh has noticed the issue Rachel spotted: some students struggled to grasp key ideas. Rachel suggests looking at consolidating student understanding, but Josh argues whole-class feedback is further upstream. They agree to focus on preparing for whole-class feedback. Josh chooses an upcoming lesson, identifies likely misconceptions, plans feedback, and practises giving it. Rachel promises to observe that lesson.

Step 2a) Highlight success

The first step in the feedback meeting is to highlight the teacher's success. In Step 1a, we identified a strength (ideally, the step the teacher was working on). Highlighting it starts the meeting on a positive note, encourages the teacher to keep going, and emphasises that coaching is working. One strength is enough: exploring several would take too long and could lead the meeting astray. The underlying goal isn't to praise the teacher - *it's for them to recognise their progress*. We can achieve this by:

- **Giving a concrete example.** A vague comment - "relationships were good" - may seem like a platitude (and a precursor to criticism). A concrete example - "you spotted and acknowledged Andrea's confusion, keeping the lesson on track" - has two advantages. First, pointing to a real event makes our praise credible. Second, it makes success replicable: the teacher knows what to do again.
- **Inviting the teacher to comment.** When we describe a strength, *we* are claiming the teacher has succeeded. When the teacher describes the strength, *they* are claiming they have succeeded. So we must ask the teacher to expand on their success. We might ask, "What impact has this had on students?" or, "How have you made this work?"

Effective coaches highlight a strength and invite the teacher to comment on it.

Action 2a) Highlight one strength: give a concrete example and invite the teacher to comment on it.

Step 2b) Agree the next step

We want to achieve a shared understanding of the issue we identified (in Step 1b), why it matters and what to do about it. We can do this by:

1) **Checking what the teacher noticed**. Rachel asks Kamil, "What did you notice students doing while you were giving instructions?" This check has several functions. First, it specifies the issue we want to address, and the event which inspired our thinking. Second, it tells us what the teacher is aware of (and may guide their attention in future

lessons). Third, it invites the teacher to explain their observations and thinking. This may change our interpretation: the teacher might explain, for example, that they didn't overlook a struggling student - they judged the student could succeed without help.

2) **Checking the teacher's understanding of why it matters.** Rachel asks Kamil what impact students chatting had. She prompts him to recognise that it caused their subsequent confusion. Grasping the impact of an issue may motivate the teacher to address it. It also clarifies the *purpose* of the step they choose, helping them to apply it appropriately.
3) **Agreeing the next step.** We need to agree the fundamental challenge the teacher faces, and an appropriate goal and next step. Usually, these will match our conclusions in Step 1b: Kamil suggests the step Rachel had in mind, calling for silence. Sometimes, the teacher will make a better suggestion: Josh convinces Rachel that preparing whole-class feedback would address student confusion better than consolidating student learning.

This may be the hardest part of the meeting. We must balance:

- Giving the teacher time to think and gain fresh insight;
- Being open to new information which alters our interpretation of the lesson;
- Ensuring the selection of a meaningful, manageable step;
- Keeping the meeting to time.

An "ask, tell, ask" approach can help. For example, to agree the next step, we can begin by *asking*, "Is there a specific goal and step you would suggest?" This gives the teacher first choice and allows them to suggest a step we haven't thought of. If they choose a promising step (our suggestion, or something better) we can move on. If not, we can *tell* them our suggestion: Rachel tells Ania, "I was thinking about scripting concrete explanations." We can then *ask* what the teacher thinks, checking whether they understand our thinking and whether they agree. Throughout, we are inviting them to guide the process, while ensuring they choose an appropriate step.

Effective coaches achieve a shared understanding of what happened, why it matters, and what to do next.

Action 2b) Agree the next step: check whether the teacher noticed the issue, check their understanding of why it matters, and agree what to do next. At each sub-step, *ask* what the teacher thinks; if they struggle, *tell* them what you think, then *ask* whether they agree.

Step 2c) Model the step

Models show teachers how to perform the next step. We discussed their value in Chapter 2, noting the importance of selecting a model which foregrounds the success criteria and ensuring the teacher spots these elements of the model. We can choose a video (or an artefact, like a worksheet or lesson plan), or we can model during the meeting. Rachel shows Kamil how to call for silence, standing to say, "I need everybody's eyes on me", scanning the room, then giving instructions. Then, she asks what Kamil has noticed, repeating the model to ensure he spots her tone and choice of words. Some coaches feel uncomfortable offering models, fearing they're imposing their way of teaching. But if the teacher knew how to do the step already, we wouldn't be working on it. They deserve to see it done well. They *may* copy elements of the model; hopefully, they will learn from it. For example, we might model a succinct explanation, then ask the teacher to script an explanation for an upcoming lesson. The model conveys the principle; the script is theirs.

Effective coaches show teachers what the next step looks like.

Action 2c) Show the teacher a model of the step; check that they have spotted the crucial elements.

Step 2d) Plan and practise the step

Practice builds teachers' skill and comfort in using the step before they apply it in the classroom, as we discussed in Chapter 2. We also noted the importance of the teacher *preparing* for practice: planning what to say and do. In coaching, this preparation can be personalised. We can ask teachers to choose a lesson in which they will apply the step: Ania selects a concept to explain; Josh a topic he will check student understanding of. This makes practice feel real, makes it immediately valuable (the teacher gets ahead with their planning), and makes it much easier to apply the step in lessons. We then give the teacher time to prepare: Ania scripts her explanation; Kamil plans his call for silence; Josh identifies likely misconceptions and prepares feedback addressing them.

This done, we can practise. We want the teacher to step into role immediately. If we're coaching in a classroom, we can ask them to stand in their usual teaching position, then offer a clear cue to start, like, "Let's go." To master the step, the teacher must practise it several times. Each time, we can highlight one effective element and suggest one change. For example, in the first round, Rachel praises the clarity of Ania's script and encourages her to speak more slowly. In the second, she praises Ania's slower pace and suggests emphasising key words. Once the teacher is meeting all of our success criteria, we can make things slightly harder. When Kamil has called for silence successfully twice, Rachel asks him to practise again but (acting as a student) she keeps writing, challenging Kamil to notice and remind her to focus. Below, we'll look at adding challenge when teachers succeed (Step 3c) and building a culture of coaching (Step 4).

Effective coaches help teachers practise the step several times in the context of an upcoming lesson.

Action 2d) Invite the teacher to plan what to do and script what to say to apply the step in an upcoming lesson. Practise several times, naming a strength and a suggestion each time.

Step 2e) Commit to action

We want the teacher to use the step, not once, but whenever it will help. Even if the feedback meeting goes well - the teacher understands and embraces the step and practises it successfully - making lasting changes to planning habits and teaching routines is hard. Committing to further action after the feedback meeting can help. For example, we might ask the teacher to:

- Plan when to act: for example, choose other lessons in which to use the step;
- Set prompts: for example, add a reminder to their slides or lesson plan;
- Work with colleagues: for example, commit to checking ideas with an experienced colleague.

Kamil draws eyes on his lesson plan to remind him to scan; Ania decides to ask colleagues for feedback on the explanations she has planned. Inviting the teacher to commit to action only takes a minute, but it makes them more likely to remember and pursue their plans.[5] (We'll look at other ways to help teachers change in Chapter 4.)

Effective coaches encourage teachers to commit to further action.

Action 2e) Ask the teacher to commit to a plan, set prompts, and work with colleagues.

Step 3 - Coach responsively

We've outlined what should happen during the feedback meeting. But many other things *could* happen. The teacher may struggle to grasp the step, struggle to master it, or find it easy. In Step 3, we'll look at how to overcome these challenges and ensure the teacher leaves the meeting skilled and confident to use their step.

What does Step 3 look like?

Rachel soon realises that Kamil hasn't fully grasped his action step. He practises the call for silence successfully, so Rachel makes things harder. Acting as a distracted student, she keeps writing, hoping he will offer a quick reminder. Instead, Kamil begins calling for silence again. "Pause briefly", Rachel says. "Remind me what the call for silence is for?" Kamil answers that it was to get students' attention, so she probes: "Whose attention?" Kamil seems unsure, so Rachel explains: "It's an effective way to get everyone's attention, but an inefficient way to get one student's attention." Then she offers two models: first a call for silence followed by a quick reminder, then one call for silence followed by another. Kamil smiles as he grasps the point. Practising again, he successfully offers a call for silence, followed by a reminder.

Ania masters improving explanations easily, but, in her next feedback meeting, she struggles to integrate checks for understanding into the explanation. After asking questions, Ania can't pick up the explanation again, even when Rachel (acting as a student) answers correctly. Rachel breaks the practice activity into its components. First, she asks Ania to give the explanation she has prepared, without asking any questions. Then Ania gives the explanation, pauses to ask questions but doesn't take answers. Finally, she practises the whole step: explanation, questions, and answers. After doing this twice, Ania seems confident, so Rachel challenges her with an incorrect student answer.

Josh quickly masters new steps, so Rachel adds likely challenges to their practice. Once he has prepared a hinge question and practised asking it, for example, she acts as a student who is reluctant to share her answer. As well as asking the question, Josh must now succinctly encourage her to respond. Next, Rachel insists that her (incorrect) answer is right, challenging Josh to explain why it isn't. The added realism and difficulty leave Josh ready to use hinge questions in the classroom.

Step 3a) Ensure the teacher grasps their step

A teacher may grasp some aspects of their step but miss others. Or they may understand the mechanics of the step but not the principles guiding its use. Kamil quickly grasps how to give a call for silence, but not how this fits into a repertoire of actions to gain and maintain student attention. So he overuses it, repeatedly calling for silence when a simple reminder to an individual student would be better. We can do two things to help. First, revisit the purpose of the step, asking the teacher to explain why we use it (and telling them if necessary). Rachel reminds Kamil that calling for silence gains everyone's attention - there are better ways to gain an individual's attention. Second, we can model again, asking the teacher how this differs from what they're doing (or from a non-example). Rachel models a call for silence followed by an individual reminder, and contrasts this with repeated calls for silence. Having revisited the purpose and/or the model and checked the teacher's understanding, we can invite them to practise again (this is another example of the "ask, tell, ask" approach). If they still struggle, we may need to simplify the action step; we discuss this next.

Effective coaches ensure teachers grasp their step by reviewing its purpose and revisiting models.

Action 3a) If the teacher struggles to grasp the step, review its purpose and revisit model examples and non-examples. Then ask them to practise again.

Step 3b) Ensure the teacher succeeds

If the teacher still struggles with the step after we have revisited its purpose and a model, we may need to simplify it. Teaching is incredibly cognitively demanding (as we discussed in Chapter 2). Selecting a single step helps, but a step may require many skills. For example, Ania's step is checking student understanding of her explanations. To do this she must give the explanation, ask questions, and respond to student answers. Initially, this proves too much. To ensure the teacher succeeds, we can break the step down, practise its components, then rebuild it. Rachel first asks Ania to practise the explanation (this is particularly worth revisiting as it was her previous step). Once this is fluent, they practise pausing to ask a question, then restarting the explanation. Finally, Rachel offers student answers, challenging Ania to respond. (If this still seems too much, responding to student answers could be Ania's next step). This is another example of distorting the setting - simplifying reality to permit focused improvement - which we discussed in Chapter 2. Practising each skill in isolation allows Ania to master them separately before combining them.

Effective coaches break the step down further to ensure teachers succeed.

Action 3b) If the teacher struggles, practise each component of the step to mastery - then recombine them.

Step 3c) Add challenge incrementally

Once the teacher has mastered their step, we can make practice more challenging. We shouldn't rush this. We want the teacher to hone their step first - getting every element right - and then to practise it perfectly a couple of times, to begin forming a routine. Kamil practises calling for silence several times before Rachel makes it harder. We can then add challenge. This should come in manageable increments: *practice is only working if the teacher is succeeding.* Rachel challenges Kamil by playing a student still writing when his call for silence ends; when he reminds her, she responds immediately. Playing a student who is implacably opposed to listening would be unhelpful. So, rather than improvising, we need to plan possible increments before the meeting. We can revisit the teacher's recent steps, or identify issues they may face in using their current step. Practising hinge questions, Rachel presents Josh with two common barriers: she plays a student who is unwilling to respond, then another who insists her answer is right. Incrementally adding challenge prepares the teacher to use their step successfully in the classroom.

Effective coaches plan to make practice incrementally harder.

Action 3c) Once the teacher is practising successfully, add challenge incrementally. Plan to include recent steps or likely barriers to using the current step.

Step 4 - Build a culture of coaching

We've looked at observing teaching, offering feedback, and coaching responsively (Steps 1-3). Some teachers initially find this process challenging and discomforting. In Chapter 2, we discussed building a culture of practice. In Step 4, we'll look at developing a culture of coaching, by making it comfortable, nudging teachers to act and highlighting progress. We'll also see how leaders can help.

What does Step 4 look like?

When Rachel starts coaching a teacher, she builds comfort and conviction by sharing a few key ideas. "I had some misgivings when I first experienced coaching", she told Kamil in their initial feedback meeting.

> I worried about being caught out by my coach. It took me a while to believe that coaching is confidential and that my coach really did just want to help me. I also thought frequent feedback might be too much pressure. But focusing on one change makes me feel less pressured. Now, I look forward to feedback meetings: I know I'll get the help I need to improve.

Alongside this initial message, she reviews her plan before each feedback meeting, looking for opportunities to increase comfort. Meeting Kamil to discuss calling for silence, she plans to encourage him by mentioning how much student behaviour has improved in his lessons this year. She will also normalise improvement by explaining that her model non-example reflects her own mistakes. Rachel works towards the teacher leading the feedback meeting. At each step, she asks their opinion first, prompting them to think through their own improvement. Often, this teaches her something new about the challenge and their thinking. Rachel finds teachers' confidence grows as they understand, participate in and, increasingly, lead the meeting.

Rachel has become used to nudging colleagues towards action, gently but firmly, to ensure they benefit from coaching. In Kamil's initial feedback meeting, when she invited him to practise, he started to describe what he would do in the lesson. "Let's practise that now", she suggested. Apparently nonplussed, Kamil asked why. "Doing this without students may seem artificial", Rachel said,

> but it's great preparation for using the step in the classroom. When we're busy, it's much easier to try a step we've practised already. Practice also helps us identify barriers, like obstacles to circulating around the classroom. Would you like to stand where you'd normally teach?

Slowly, Kamil stood up to practise. "All set?" she asked. Kamil nodded. "Great, let's go."

Ania, on the other hand, practises willingly, but finds it hard to stay in role. She begins her explanation, then pauses, saying it would be better to start with a concrete example. Beginning again, she immediately stops to suggest a better example. "You're right, there are pros and cons to each approach", Rachel tells her. "Let's practise the explanation you've scripted first and see whether it works. After a couple of rounds of practice, we can discuss alternatives." Ania starts again. A few words later, she pauses. Rachel offers an encouraging smile. Ania nods and keeps going.

With years of experience, excellent results, and a cynical view of new initiatives, Josh was initially sceptical about coaching. Rachel soon felt stuck: Josh neither suggested improvements nor accepted her ideas. When she first mentioned hinge questions, he stonewalled: results were good; he marked students' books frequently; some student confusion was inevitable. "I know your classes do well", Rachel said. "I also know we can always improve. I want to make this work for you. Can you tell me how you're feeling about coaching?" Josh said he was unsure about it: he had faith in the teaching routines he had spent years refining. "I can see they work and I'm in awe of how often you mark your books", Rachel replied.

> I do think identifying student misconceptions early can save time and confusion later. I'd like to take fifteen minutes to look at how hinge questions might work. If, at the end of the meeting, you don't want to try them in the classroom, we'll say no more about them. Is that fair?

Josh nodded. Having practised using a hinge question, he saw their value and decided he would use them in the classroom.

Since Ania struggled to integrate questions and explanations, Rachel makes a point of highlighting the progress she has made. She asks how Ania found the meeting. "Tricky", she replies, "but I'm glad we did it". Rachel waits, inviting Ania to continue. "At one point, I thought, 'This is too difficult, I'm just going to let students read the textbook.' But now we've worked through it, I'm much more confident. I know I'll be able to explain it properly." Rachel asks about practice itself. "I felt more comfortable staying in role", Ania smiles, "Thank you!" Rachel is relieved, but wonders whether she should have made practice easier initially. She decides to ask another coach to join her for Ania's next observation.

Step 4a) Make coaching feel comfortable

Coaching is invaluable, but teachers may initially find it discomforting. There's nowhere to hide from individual feedback. To increase comfort, we can:

1) **Build conviction in coaching.** We can use a teacher's first feedback meeting to introduce key messages about how and why coaching works. Rachel tells Kamil why she likes being coached and how she overcame her initial misgivings. We can also elicit and address the teacher's concerns. As with practice, we need only convince them to give coaching a chance. When they see themselves improving, teachers will feel comfortable being coached.
2) **Plan ongoing encouragement.** We can review our plan for the feedback meeting, adding encouraging phrases to offer as the teacher thinks, scripts, and practises. Coaching Kamil, Rachel mentions how much behaviour has improved before she suggests working on calls for silence. She normalises improvement by explaining that her non-example reflects her mistakes. As Ania finishes scripting her explanation, Rachel says, "This looks great, let's try it", to introduce practice. Ongoing encouragement maintains teachers' confidence.
3) **Hand over control.** Coaching works because it supports the teacher to make a single, powerful change. Once they grasp the coaching process - selecting a step, preparation, practise - teachers may lead it themselves, jumping to the next step unprompted. We can encourage this. We've discussed the "ask, tell, ask" approach (in Step 2b): with time, we hope to tell less, as the teacher thinks through each step unaided. More broadly, changes should reflect the teacher's preferences. This means attending to and building on their ideas. Josh persuades Rachel that a different step would be best; Ania scripts her own explanation, reflecting her understanding of the topic. We want to give the teacher as much control as possible - while ensuring they improve.

Effective coaches build teachers' confidence and hand control to them.

Action 4a) Make coaching feel comfortable, by convincing the teacher to try it, planning ongoing encouragement and handing over control of the process.

Step 4b) Nudge teachers to act

The feedback process described in Step 2 is not innate: it's more natural to discuss many strengths than to focus on one, for example. We may need to nudge teachers to follow it. Consider practice. We want the teacher to test and master their step; they may instead describe what they would do (as Kamil did) or struggle to stay in role (as Ania did). To challenge this, we can:

1) **Pause and clarify.** We can ask the teacher to pause as soon as they go off-track (rather than letting them continue unproductively) and clarify what should be happening. When Kamil describes what he would do in the classroom, Rachel stops him, explains that she wants him to practise, and reminds him why this matters. We can also check the teacher's understanding of the step, offering another model if necessary.

2) **Reset.** We can then help the teacher prepare and begin. Rachel asks Kamil to stand, checks he's ready, then prompts him to start: "Let's go." Getting into position prepares him for practice physically and psychologically; a signal to start separates practice from discussion.
3) **Highlight the difference.** Highlighting the effect of doing things right encourages the teacher to recognise their success and the value of the process. We might ask, "How did that feel?" or, "What did you notice?" and emphasise that we'll do the step this way next time. (We will say more about highlighting progress in Step 4c, below.)

We've focused on practice as teachers often struggle with it initially. But we can use the same approach - pause and clarify, reset, highlight the difference - to support a willing but uncertain teacher with any step.

Effective coaches pause teachers who are off course, reset the step, and highlight the difference this makes.

We may also find some teachers are unwilling to be coached, having previously experienced unhelpful feedback (and perhaps been free to ignore it). We can acknowledge their concerns; we can't let them derail feedback entirely. Experiencing coaching working may convince them; discussion and reassurance alone will not. To nudge them towards action, we can:

1) **Elicit the issue.** First, we need to identify the underlying issue. A teacher may tell us they don't believe the step or process will work for them. More often, however, they express discomfort obliquely: "This sounds great, can I practise it in my own time?" We can ask something like, "It feels like you're unsure about this. Can you tell me what's bothering you?" They may have immediate concerns about the feedback, broader worries about coaching, or unrelated issues.
2) **Acknowledge the concern.** Teachers' concerns are usually justified on some level. Practice is great, but it is uncomfortable initially. Change is invaluable, but it does upset routines. We can express understanding and agreement. Rachel acknowledges to Kamil that practising without students is artificial; she agrees with Josh that his routines are effective. (We *can* discuss this at length, but we must keep moving towards action.)
3) **Rationalise the step.** We can explain why the action we want them to take matters. Rachel reminds Kamil that practice makes change easier. She suggests to Josh that identifying student misconceptions will save time and pre-empt confusion. Again, this should be brief. When a teacher's response is driven by emotion - they feel scared or uncomfortable - a lorryload of evidence won't convince them. A reminder of the rationale allows us to invite them to act.
4) **Redirect towards action.** We then reset the step (as we discussed above), inviting the teacher to prepare - standing to practise, for example - and then begin. We can frame this tentatively: "Can we try this once?" or, "Let's see how it might work." Rachel asks Josh to work on the step for 15 minutes; if he remains unconvinced, she promises to drop it.

Hopefully, the teacher will succeed; if so, we can highlight this. If not, we can offer feedback or discuss alternatives, based on what they have tried.

Effective coaches elicit and acknowledge concerns - then nudge teachers to act.

Action 4b) Nudge teachers to act. If they are uncertain, pause to clarify, reset, and highlight the difference it makes. If they are unwilling, elicit, acknowledge, and rationalise their concerns, then redirect the meeting towards action.

Step 4c) Highlight progress

We want to establish a virtuous cycle in which teachers make progress, gain confidence, and look forward to coaching. By the end of the feedback meeting, they should be confident to use their step in the classroom. But they may focus on what has proved hard and miss the improvements they have made. Explicitly highlighting their progress can help. We can encourage the teacher to attribute improvement to their efforts by asking *them* to explain what has changed (as in Step 2a). We could highlight a strength and ask them to comment: Rachel mentions Kamil combining a call for silence with a reminder and asks, "How did that feel?" Or we could ask them to identify what's improved: Rachel asks Ania, "How did you find the feedback meeting?" and Ania describes persevering to success. Doing this routinely should help teachers recognise their progress and the value of coaching.

Effective coaches help teachers recognise the progress they are making.

Action 4c) Invite the teacher to comment on their progress.

Step 4d) Learn from other coaches

We're most likely to encounter the challenges discussed in Step 4 when we're new to coaching, or the teacher is new to being coached. Anticipating them, we can script and practise possible responses. If we keep encountering a particular challenge, we may want to reconsider our approach. We're better at spotting others' missteps than our own,[6] so a second opinion - from a leader or another coach - can be invaluable. We can:

- Invite another coach to observe a feedback meeting;
- Film a feedback meeting and review it, individually or with others; or,
- Observe another coach (perhaps working with our teacher).

This reinforces a culture of coaching and builds a culture of improving coaching. There's more that leaders can do to support coaches - we will look at leading improvement more generally in Part II.

Effective coaches learn from other coaches.

Action 4d) Learn from other coaches: observe them coaching; ask them to observe you.

Step 5 - Adapt to teachers' expertise

We've touched on how coaches can support experienced teachers throughout the chapter. Here, we'll draw these points together. First, the principle: coaching can benefit everyone, including experts. Teaching is hard, classrooms are complex: every lesson can be improved. Moreover, teachers can plateau (as we discussed in the Introduction). Experienced teachers form stronger habits and receive less feedback (they are more likely to be among the 14% of teachers who go unobserved all year). Coaches offer them a fresh perspective and prompt new thinking. To do so, we use the process described in Steps 1 and 2: gathering evidence, agreeing a step, planning and practising change, applying it in the classroom.

Coaching experts is slightly different, however. First, we'll often work on more subtle improvements - such as small but significant changes to wording or supporting specific students - rather than the bigger changes newer teachers need to make. More importantly, once they've grasped the coaching process, we'll increasingly hand each step to them (as we discussed in Step 4a). We've looked at the ask, tell, ask approach (Step 2b): we should find ourselves telling the expert much less, as they decide what matters, what to change, and how to practise. We may also add challenge faster during practice (Step 3c). Experts benefit from coaching - but, increasingly, they should lead the feedback meeting, and their own improvement.

Expert teachers benefit from coaching - they should increasingly lead the improvement process.

Step 5) Coach expert teachers, but encourage them to lead the improvement process.

Case study

Steve Allen, Assistant Principal at Farnborough Spencer Academy, shares its experience working with Steplab to develop a whole-school coaching model.

A school on a rapid improvement journey

Farnborough Spencer Academy, part of Spencer Academies Trust, is located in Clifton, Nottingham. The school has been on a clear improvement trajectory since joining the trust in 2018. Following the appointment of the current executive principal and the development of the senior leadership team, a renewed focus on teaching was established, with professional development viewed through the prism of instructional coaching.

This shift led to transformed classroom experiences for students and steady improvements in outcomes. The school was judged "Good" by Ofsted in 2022, following almost a decade of being rated "Inadequate". By 2025, Farnborough Spencer Academy had seen a dramatic rise in student results, placing it:

- Fourteenth most improved nationally for Grade 5+ in English and maths.
- Top 100 nationally for most key attainment measures.

These outcomes position the school among the highest-attaining "similar" schools nationwide.

Establishing a whole-school approach to professional development

As part of Farnborough Spencer's continued journey of improvement, it became clear that a structured and sustainable whole-school approach to professional development was required if the school was to positively impact teaching and learning. As a leadership team, we knew the strong evidence about the power of instructional coaching and so we decided that this was the direction we wanted to invest our energies in, with the powerful lever of Steplab to support. We knew from experience that it was important to get implementation right, so the introduction of the coaching programme was carefully phased to ensure buy-in from staff before gradually scaling the programme.

Early foundations and piloting

Lesson visits were already established through high presence in lessons from middle and senior leaders, which led to a request from staff to receive more ongoing feedback. Beginning in the summer term, a small group of teachers were trained and began piloting instructional coaching using Steplab, focusing on a cycle of lesson observation and structured feedback. The leadership team also worked on creating and establishing a shared language, mirroring this in the bespoke professional development curriculum we built on Steplab.

Scaling drop-ins and building a coaching culture

At the start of the academic year, we launched drop-ins on Steplab. Initially, this was led by senior leaders and then widened to include faculty heads and early career teachers. Alongside this, early career teachers received fortnightly coaching from their mentor and, by the second term, all teachers were engaged in peer drop-ins, solidifying a culture of collaboration and feedback. This laid the foundations to introduce a whole-school coaching model the next academic year, following some intensive training in a summer training day.

Introducing the 20:20:20 model

When we moved to peer coaching across the school, we decided to use a 20:20:20 model. This means that teachers give coaching feedback all in one room, with an hour of directed time protected at the end of each cycle.

- First 20 minutes: we train teachers on one aspect of the coaching model, such as giving precise praise. To help us do this effectively, we use Steplab's Coaching Quality Check to dig into coaching planning and see which areas we can further develop.
- Second 20 minutes: the first of our reciprocal coaches feeds back.
- Final 20 minutes: the second coach feeds back.

Coaching all in one central space allows us to do some additional monitoring of quality and also helps build our culture of modelling and rehearsal.

Transformative impact on professional development and teaching

Our coaching programme, powered by Steplab, has had a transformative effect on both professional development and teaching quality across the school. Observations and feedback have become valued everyday practice, with teachers reporting:

- Increased confidence in their teaching.
- Enjoyment of the opportunity to observe and learn from other colleagues.
- More frequent coaching conversations and corridor discussions about teaching.

The structured approach to lesson observations and coaching has helped create a more consistent and expert standard of teaching across the school.

A sustainable model for continuous improvement

By embedding structured coaching cycles, prioritising staff engagement, and aligning coaching with whole-school priorities, the school has created a sustainable model for continuous improvement. With thoughtful planning, clear communication, and a phased approach, instructional coaching has - and can - drive meaningful change in schools.

Conclusion

Instructional coaching tailors the effective training approaches we discussed in Chapter 2 to individual teachers' needs. The feedback process allows us to agree, plan, and practise a step, and to respond to the teacher's needs and expertise. By observing again, we can check progress and offer further help. In this chapter, we've looked at what the coach does. Leaders play a crucial role too: training and supporting coaches, making time for coaching and monitoring progress. We'll look at leading professional development within a school in Part II. First, however, we'll examine the behavioural science of teacher change, in the next chapter.

Next steps

Reflection questions

1) Review your most recent feedback meeting (whether you were coaching or being coached). To what extent did:
    - The teacher feel successful?
    - The teacher and coach agree a single step to work on?
    - The coach share a model?
    - The teacher plan and practise the step?
    - The teacher commit to action?
    - The coach respond to the teacher's needs?
    - The meeting build a culture of coaching?
2) How might you improve the feedback meeting? Which step would you focus on? What would you do differently?

Checklist

1) Observe teaching and gather evidence
    a. Check progress
    b. Identify a priority
2) Offer feedback and support change
    a. Highlight success
    b. Agree the next step
    c. Model the step
    d. Plan and practise the step
    e. Commit to action
3) Coach responsively
    a. Ensure the teacher grasps their step
    b. Ensure the teacher succeeds
    c. Add challenge incrementally
4) Build a culture of coaching
    a. Make coaching feel comfortable
    b. Nudge teachers to act
    c. Highlight progress
    d. Learn from other coaches
5) Adapt your approach to reflect the teacher's expertise

Getting started

If your school isn't yet using coaching, find a colleague who is willing to be coached and try coaching them. Then consider growing the coaching team. If your school is already using coaching, audit coaching practice, using the reflection questions. Pick an element to refine with your coaching team.

Success in different roles

You can apply the ideas in this chapter, whatever your role:

- **As a teacher. . .** you can ask observers to help you to choose a single step and to practise it with you. You can coach colleagues using this approach.
- **As a middle leader. . .** you can apply this approach when observing your team. You can push for it to be adopted across the school.
- **As a leader working across schools. . .** you can support your schools to adopt instructional coaching; you can model this approach when giving feedback.

4 How can we help teachers change?

Chapter map

Improving teaching means helping teachers make lasting change.

↓

Helping teachers change means:

- Focusing on habits
- Influencing their environment
- Applying behavioural science

↓

Step 1: Design a habit

a) Decide what teachers should do
b) Identify when they should act

↓

Step 2: Build conviction in the change

a) Give a reason for the change
b) Show the change is immediately worthwhile
c) Show that others are already trying the change

↓

Step 3: Encourage teachers to commit to action

a) Choose when to act
b) Plan what to do, and with whom
c) Set prompts and reminders
d) Make a Plan B

↓

Step 4: Make starting easy

a) Break the change into steps
b) Simplify the change
c) Set defaults
d) Practise the change

↓

Step 5: Make change stick

a) Track what's changing
b) Offer feedback
c) Relaunch the change

↓

We can then improve teaching across the school (Part II).

DOI: 10.4324/9781003439622-6

We've mentioned how busy teachers and classrooms are and how hard this makes teaching and improving teaching. The approaches discussed in Chapters 1-3 - pursuing coherence, leading effective training, and coaching - help. But we can do more to support teachers to change. Behavioural science offers ways to encourage teachers to believe in, commit to, initiate, and maintain change. These strategies can be applied to training and coaching; some have been mentioned already. This chapter adds two things. First, it explains the underlying principles of behaviour change. Second, it shows how they can be applied, not just to training and coaching, but to the many other ways we can influence teachers, such as emails, briefings, bulletins, meetings, and line management. First, we'll see what difference they can make.

Why does helping teachers change matter?

Let's contrast two ways of introducing a change. This term, the school's focus is students discussing thought-provoking questions. Christopher tells staff this is a priority during briefing, and sends an email explaining the technique. Later, he models writing questions and leading discussion during professional development. He asks middle leaders to offer support during team meetings. But when he observes 20 lessons a few weeks later, Christopher sees only three teachers attempt to use the technique. One appears to have misunderstood, encouraging students to debate a simple question at length. Another leads an effective discussion, but reveals he's been doing so for years. The third worries he's not doing enough.

Christopher tries another approach. The tools are the same: briefings, emails, training, observations. But he uses them differently. Recognising how many demands teachers face, he makes change as easy and attractive as possible. First, he simplifies the desired change - students discussing thought-provoking questions - into a habit: discuss one thought-provoking question each lesson. Next, he tries to show this is worthwhile. Teachers often complain that students articulate sophisticated ideas poorly; Christopher introduces discussion questions as a partial solution. In the initial professional development session, he invites teachers who are already using them to describe what works for them. In subsequent sessions, he makes time for teachers to plan questions for upcoming lessons. Each week, he asks middle leaders to share good examples and mentions these in briefing. Christopher also asks coaches to look for effective approaches and to ask teachers about barriers. Observing again, he finds most teachers are using discussion questions - but some students are still struggling to articulate their ideas. He plans a follow-up session to share successes and address this issue.

Teachers are busy and teaching is hard; change is effortful and often unappealing. Behavioural science offers strategies to address these barriers. Choosing a habit gives teachers a clear focus and encourages lasting change. Showing the habit is worthwhile and popular motivates action. Ongoing support keeps the change in teachers' minds. Applying behavioural science doesn't create more work: we still send emails, lead training, and offer support. Instead, it makes change easier and more appealing - and so, more likely.

Helping teachers change means applying behavioural science to make action seem easier and more appealing.

What helps teachers to change?

Helping teachers change means changing habits

Much of our everyday behaviour is habitual.[1] Teachers develop habits early in their career.[2] They are invaluable, allowing teachers to respond rapidly under pressure: sanctioning a student without losing the lesson's thread, for example. But, once formed, habits are hard to change,[3] even when the stakes are high. After a heart bypass, patients must eat differently and exercise more. Two years later, most have reverted to their former habits.[4] It's far harder for teachers to deliberate and experiment. They may intend to give gentle reminders, but, busy and under pressure, revert to habit and give a sanction instead. Effective teacher development promotes insights, motivates goal-setting, teaches skills, *and helps teachers embed changes in practice*.[5] **To help teachers change, we focus on habits.**

Helping teachers change means influencing what influences them

Training is rarely sufficient to change teachers' habits. Many years ago, I saw this in my own work. Having led an intensive and apparently effective training programme, I visited trainees' classrooms a few months later. I could see no evidence it had helped. Training matters, but, if we're lucky, we spend an hour a week with teachers. Their context - their day-to-day experience and the actions of colleagues and students - is a far greater influence.[6] Helping teachers change is as much about influencing these wider influences as it is about planning training. We can tweak almost everything the school does, to model, encourage, and support improvement: briefings and bulletins, meetings and performance management, marking policies and lesson plan proformas. **To help teachers change, we influence their environment.**

Helping teachers change means applying behavioural science

Behavioural scientists study what influences people's actions and why they change. In our systematic review, we found that techniques they advocate, such as setting goals and planning action, help teachers improve.[7] Behavioural science shows us how to influence teachers: how to make a reminder motivating and actionable, for example. The effect of any single technique is small: a reminder alone will not change a teacher's habits. But, taken together, many motivating, actionable influences (reminders, action plans, and feedback, for example) encourage habit change, while costing us nothing (we are doing briefings and bulletins anyway). There is little behavioural science research in schools.[8] We will draw on what there is, and on the broader evidence base and general principles behavioural science offers. I examined the evidence and its limits in detail in a previous book, *Habits of Success*; here, we will focus on applying it. **To help teachers change, we apply behavioural science.**

Drawing these ideas together, lasting change is elusive. Training and coaching are important, but we can do more to help. First, we can focus on changing habits: a new habit is the epitome of a lasting change. Second, we can apply the principles and techniques of behavioural science to help teachers build and maintain those habits. This chapter provides a framework for this approach.

To help teachers change, we apply behavioural science to support them to form new habits.

How do we help teachers change?

Step 1 - Design a habit

We have discussed narrowing the focus of training or coaching from a big goal, like improving assessment, to a specific skill, like asking better hinge questions (in Chapters 2 and 3). If change is to last, using this skill must become a habit; we begin by designing this habit.

What does Step 1 look like?

Claire's current focus is models. She wants teachers to create better models, use them more often, and ensure students see their merits and apply them to their work. There will be training on each skill, but Claire wants to ensure it leads to lasting change. Initially, she decides to focus on ensuring teachers are planning models: they are unlikely to use models if they don't first plan them. She designs a habit. She will ask teachers to review each lesson when they finish planning it, checking:

1) What is the crucial task? This is the most important or newest thing students will be doing.
2) Is there a model for the task, and three questions to help students see the model's strengths?

There is much to do to make this stick, but by specifying what to do when, Claire has turned the general idea - using models more - into a habit.

To design a habit, we must decide what is to be done *and when it is to be done*. Habits come in many sizes: starting each lesson with a quiz, pausing after a question to let students think, scanning the room while speaking. Each is an automated response to a situation - this is what makes them habits.[9] So designing a habit means distilling a broad goal into a precise action - a what - and choosing a specific situation in which to act: a when. Let's say we want teachers to give clear, memorable explanations. First, we choose a specific skill, like giving concrete examples. Then, we choose the situation in which teachers will use it. We could create a planning habit by asking them to review each lesson once it is planned, checking it includes concrete examples. Or we could create a teaching habit by asking teachers to respond to student confusion with a concrete example.

We can design a habit by asking two questions:

- **What should teachers do?** Our answer should be simple, precise, and meaningful. A simple action becomes a habit more easily than a complicated process. A single change to lesson planning is simple, a new planning approach is not. (Complicated changes may be necessary, but the more we break them up and simplify them, the more likely they are to stick.) A precise action is easier to grasp, recall, and take. Asking teachers to encourage risk-taking could mean anything; asking them to thank students for sharing answers, even if they're wrong, conveys exactly what to do. Finally, the action must be meaningful - must improve learning - as well as simple. Starting every lesson with a retrieval quiz is simple; ensuring students think hard about the questions is meaningful.
- **When should teachers act?** Since a habit is an automated response to a situation, to design a habit, we must define the situation - when to act - as precisely as the action. Sometimes, the action we choose dictates the situation: if a teacher is working to discourage shouting out, they will act when students shout out (or just before they usually do). If the action doesn't dictate when to act, we can identify an appropriate moment within their existing routines (for lesson preparation or giving feedback, for example).

This may seem unsurprising, but teachers often receive vague, complicated, and unmanageable requests; they rarely receive guidance on when to act. Planning habits may seem directive, but just as teachers can lead the coaching process (as we discussed in Chapter 3), they can share in or lead the process of habit design. We're helping them change, not binding their actions: Claire supports colleagues to use models more; they decide where models are needed and what they should be.

Helping teachers change means designing a habit: what should be done when.

Action 1) Design a habit: choose a simple, precise, and meaningful action, and exactly when to act.

Step 2 - Build conviction in the change

If teachers believe a change is worthwhile, they're more likely to pursue it. We can try to convince them that the habit we have designed matters in three ways: giving a rationale for it, showing its immediate value, and highlighting social influences in its favour.

What does Step 2 look like?

Claire thinks some colleagues will resist using models, worried about discouraging independent thought, or the time they will require. Introducing them, she first asks staff about times students have tried hard, but struggled to create high-quality work. She suggests that students don't always grasp what a good piece of work looks like. Models may help. Next, she mentions some of the research in their favour. Then, she shares success stories, asking colleagues who are already using models to describe what they do and the impact it has. Her eventual aim is for staff to use models in every lesson. She starts with something far less demanding, however, framed as an experiment: she invites teachers to try using a model one lesson a week for the next six weeks, to see whether it helps.

We can build conviction by showing that the change is popular and worthwhile. Let's say we want teachers to approach feedback differently, ensuring students act on it. First, we might explain the change and offer evidence for it: "The Education Endowment Foundation review shows students benefit from engaging with feedback."[10] This is worth mentioning, but it may leave colleagues unmoved. More powerfully, we can show that the benefits of the change will outweigh the costs. We might begin by eliciting teachers' experience of the problem we hope to solve, asking "How often do students ignore your feedback?" We can also reduce the effort change requires: Claire could have asked teachers to use models in every lesson; instead, she suggested using them in one lesson a week, for a few weeks. Finally, we can show the change is popular by highlighting individual role models and group norms. We could ask colleagues to share ways they've helped students engage with feedback; we can mention how often we observe this happening. Together, this should make the change seem attractive and immediately worthwhile.

To build conviction, we can offer teachers answers to these questions:

- **What is the reason for the change?** We can give a succinct explanation and supporting evidence for the change. For example, to explain the importance of breaking new ideas down for students, we might mention the limits of working memory.
- **Why is the change worthwhile?**
    - **What problem does it solve?** Eliciting teachers' experience of a problem can clarify the need for change. For example, we might ask, "Can you think of a recent time when students struggled to grasp a new idea?"
    - **What are the immediate benefits? How can we reduce immediate costs?** To show a change is worthwhile, we can highlight immediate benefits. For example, if breaking new ideas down reduces student confusion, lessons should run more smoothly. We can also limit the change to make it seem easier. Instead of asking teachers to transform their approach, we can suggest smaller changes: tweaking their practice, using an existing skill more often, or trying the change once.

- **Who has already tried the change?**
  - **Who can act as a role model?** Sharing what other teachers are already doing can make a change seem manageable and attractive. We could show videos, or ask teachers to describe how they break ideas down and the impact this has had.
  - **How common is this?** A change is more attractive if it is already (or increasingly) a social norm. We can draw on observations and surveys to show this is the case.

We hope to convince colleagues that the change is worthwhile. If we succeed, they are more likely to act - and, by acting repeatedly, to build a habit. But many other factors encourage action: picking a viable habit (Step 1), making commitments (Step 3), and making change easy (Step 4). Conviction helps, but we need not persuade every colleague before moving on to the remaining steps.

Helping teachers change means building conviction in the change.

Action 2) Build conviction in the change: explain it, emphasise its immediate benefits and limited costs, show that others are already doing it.

Step 3 - Encourage teachers to commit to action

During training, a teacher may be convinced a specific habit will help, and feel ready to act. But each school day sees an array of events and distractions. Good intentions are easily subsumed by competing concerns. By encouraging teachers to plan what they will do when, we can help them create time, support, and commitment for action.

What does Step 3 look like?

Claire wonders how best to remind teachers to review models in their lesson plans. She considers asking them to set a phone reminder, but suspects this will prove distracting and unsustainable. Instead, she suggests adding the word "model" to whatever they use to plan lessons: a slide in a PowerPoint template; a note on a lesson plan form. She asks teachers who support others' planning - through mentoring or co-planning - to check and discuss models when they meet. Finally, she asks teachers to make a Plan B: to think of a quick way to select a model if they forget to plan one, such as sharing student work using a visualiser.

There's a big difference between a loose intention and a specific commitment. We sometimes hear vague promises: "I'll think about it", or, "I'll try to do it next week." These reflect weak intentions, rapidly discarded in favour of marking books and dealing with behaviour. The more concrete a commitment, the more likely people are to act.[11] Choosing a specific time helps: "morning break tomorrow" is far better than "next week"; it helps teachers safeguard time in advance, and recall their plan in the moment. We can strengthen these commitments further by thinking through the details. This might mean planning where to act: do teachers need a quiet space in which to rehearse, for example? It might mean setting reminders or involving others in the plan to prompt action or check its impact. Encouraging teachers to make specific commitments makes action more likely.

To help teachers commit to action, we can invite them to choose:

1) **When to act.** Teachers may pick a specific class or lesson; a time, like after school on Wednesdays; or an event, like a student expressing confusion (informed by the habit design we did for Step 1). A precise when turns an intention into a plan.
2) **What to do, and with whom.** Alongside a time, we can prompt teachers to think through the details of their action. Will they need to prepare a script, or print resources? When will this happen? Involving others can encourage action: who might be able to offer help or check progress? These details make the plan viable.
3) **Prompts and reminders.** Plans are easily forgotten. We can invite teachers to put reminders on their phones, annotations on their lesson resources, or sticky notes on their laptops. We could develop a checklist to show key steps succinctly.
4) **Plan B.** Well-laid plans are often derailed by *predictable* challenges. A free period can easily become a cover lesson; students often reveal unexpected knowledge gaps. We can invite the teacher to make a Plan B which addresses possible obstacles: if you're put on cover, what alternatives do you have?

Helping teachers change means planning what to do when, and setting reminders.

Action 3) Encourage teachers to commit to action: ask them when they will act, what they will do and with whom. Then ask them to set a reminder and make Plan B.

Step 4 - Make starting easy

Teachers are convinced the habit is worthwhile and have committed to a plan: we should see action. But there are many barriers to taking the first step for the first time; it's often tempting to defer. The easier we make starting, the more likely we are to see change.

What does Step 4 look like?

Claire identifies several ways to make using models easier. She breaks creating and discussing them into smaller steps. For example, to discuss models, teachers need to introduce them, direct students' attention to specific features, then check their understanding. Breaking this down makes what to do seem clearer and more manageable. Claire knows that newer teachers sometimes find developing models tough. She asks departments to share a pool of models for one unit of work: teachers can use these if they struggle to make their own. Finally, Claire helps teachers practise planning and discussing models during training. Her approach makes using models seem simple, familiar, and manageable.

The simplest and most powerful insight behavioural science offers is this: making change easy encourages action. Think about the most frustrating computer program you've had to use. Was it unintuitive, tedious, and frustrating? Did you avoid or defer using it? Now think about the most successful online retailers. They've relentlessly removed barriers to ordering: your details are saved, postage is free, you can "buy it now". It works. This isn't surprising, but we can overlook it when we're busy, or asking teachers to complete tasks we find simple. So it's worth reviewing the change to overcome possible barriers: breaking it down, simplifying it, setting defaults, and practising it. Making the first step easier makes change more likely.

To make starting easy, we can:

- **Break the change into steps.** Experience and expertise allow us to act fluently. We simultaneously give out worksheets, answer questions, and catch a distracted student's eye. A teacher learning a new skill will struggle to achieve this fluency, just as a new driver struggles to integrate clutch, gears, and accelerator. This can make change feel overwhelming: breaking it down helps. To change an entry routine, for example, we might suggest choosing a starter activity, standing at the door, greeting students, and so on. Showing that change is a series of manageable steps makes it seem much easier.
- **Simplify the change.** Teaching, managing behaviour, and checking student understanding is already demanding. Making complex changes to teaching routines is hard. The more we cut steps and simplify change, the easier it is. A complete entry routine has many steps. But just standing at the door and monitoring students' actions is a good start. Once teachers are doing this, we can build on it.
- **Set defaults.** The demands of teaching absorb much of a teacher's decision-making capacity. If change requires new decisions, they may struggle. Imagine a teacher thinking hard about an explanation. They can't simultaneously think hard about phrasing a reminder for chatting students. We can help teachers plan default responses, which should work most of the time. For example, teachers could script a default phrase to

ask a student to calm down when entering the classroom. Under pressure, they don't need to think through what to say: they can use the default. If they have more time, they can adapt it.

- **Practise the change.** Practice makes starting easy by building teachers' fluency and confidence in the change before they launch it in the classroom (as we discussed in Chapter 2). Practice allows teachers to refine their entry routine before using it.

Helping teachers change means making starting easy, by breaking down, simplifying, and practising change.

Action 4) Make starting easy: break down and simplify the change; set defaults and practise.

Step 5 - Make change stick

Maintenance matters. Steps 1-4 have helped teachers begin to change. But too often, an initial burst of energy is followed by increasing neglect, as interest wanes and priorities shift. How we maintain momentum determines whether change sticks - or teachers revert to old habits.

What does Step 5 look like?

Claire tracks how teachers' approaches to models are changing. She asks everyone observing lessons to record whether teachers use models, their strengths, and any issues. In briefing, she mentions how many lessons included models the previous week, showing they are becoming more common. Claire revisits key ideas and invites colleagues to share their successes during professional development sessions. They also practise checking students' understanding of models, since observations suggest this is a weakness. Some teachers struggle to create models: Claire asks middle leaders to share examples for upcoming lessons during department time. By the end of term, observations show teachers are using models more and better. Claire plans a relaunch for next term, focusing on using models to support independent work, with additional help for teachers who have struggled.

Launching change demands detailed and diligent planning; sustaining change is no different. First, we must track what's happening. What are teachers doing differently? How well is change working? This informs everything else we do. We have discussed the power of role models and social norms (in Step 2). We can now offer new examples, showing what's possible and how the school is changing. The change must remain a priority for teachers. We can use feedback and refresher training to keep it at the forefront of their thinking, revisiting key ideas and addressing weaknesses. Finally, change often falters: we may need to adapt and relaunch.

To make a change stick, we can:

- **Track what's changing**. We must first establish whether change is happening, and whether it's helping. We want a handful of light-touch measures: a handful because no single measure is perfect; light-touch to avoid making work for teachers, or us. Let's say teachers are working on using probing questions to encourage deeper thinking. We could track change through three existing tasks: lesson observations, staff surveys, and reviews of student work. This would tell us what teachers are doing, their perceptions, and the effect the change is having. (We will discuss how to assess the impact of professional development in Chapter 7.)
- **Offer group feedback:**
  - **Share quantitative feedback.** Having tracked what's changing, sharing our findings highlights progress and encourages further effort. For example, we could tell teachers, "We saw probing questions in three quarters of lesson visits last week – twice as many as last term." In a few positive words, this reminds teachers of the goal, shows leaders are focused on it, recognises progress, and challenges teachers to keep going.
  - **Highlight success.** As colleagues try to change, highlighting their success creates new social norms and role models (influences we discussed in Step 2). Telling teachers we are seeing more probing questions emphasises a developing norm. Inviting individuals to share their efforts and reflections offers new role models. We can encourage teachers to keep going by showing that their colleagues are using the change more and finding it worthwhile.
  - **Revisit key points.** Tracking what's changing may also reveal gaps in teachers' knowledge or skill. We can tackle them by revisiting key points and leading further practice. Reminders are intrinsically valuable; moreover, they show the change remains a priority and promote insight as teachers reflect on their efforts (we discussed promoting insight in Chapter 2). We could model probing questions and revisit why they matter in as little as two minutes. With more time, we could also invite teachers to plan and practise questions for their next lesson.

  We could also offer individual feedback, drawing on the ideas discussed in Chapter 3.
- **Relaunch the change.** Change often falters: our focus and approach may not be quite right; initial success may be interrupted by exams, holidays, or competing pressures. A relaunch may be needed to make change stick. The rhythm of the school year helps: a new term allows a new start. We can modify our approach based on what we've learned: adapting the habit, improving support, refining feedback. Working on probing questions, we may learn more about how discussing them encourages deeper thinking: we can redesign the habit accordingly. Or we may find teachers struggle to formulate effective questions: we can break the process down further. Relaunching begins the change process again: building conviction, encouraging commitment, making starting easy – and so making change stick.

> *Helping teachers change means making change stick: tracking it, giving feedback, and relaunching it*

Action 5) Make change stick: track what's changing; share feedback, highlighting success and revisiting key points; refine and relaunch the change if needed.

Case study

Lucy Newman, at Oasis Academy South Bank, was working to build a staff habit of reading more about teaching. This is the text of an email she sent to colleagues. She has used many of the strategies discussed above: she seeks to build conviction that the reading will be worthwhile, explains that it will be quick and makes it easy to access, and highlights the work of colleagues who are reading regularly.

This week's reading is a very short blog by the one and only Doug Lemov. It is on "tracking not watching" which Doug calls one of the "most important skills for any teacher".

The blog is only 400 words!

There are five more working days to read this blog as a new blog will be out next week.

The blog aims to help solve this problem at the heart of teaching: how do we know our pupils are achieving?

I have really enjoyed the extreme honesty of teachers' reflections so far this week and I personally can really identify with the challenges other teachers are facing. There is a huge gap between the teacher I am and the teacher I want to be and I find it really helps me to read where other teachers at Oasis are struggling to change habits and get tips from them.

The blog is here, you can comment on it here.

Shout outs for comments on last week's reading to Mark, Josh, and Rob:

Mark had some geeky maths reflections: "I think this links well to the effective modelling we were previously looking. With a great model [in maths especially] it 'can guide an individual through with potentially less understanding but a successful' outcome..."

Conclusion

The key to lasting change is building habits: developing effective, automated responses to classroom challenges. We can help teachers form habits by showing change is easy, worthwhile, and popular, inviting them to commit to it and supporting them to make it stick. The behavioural science underpinning these steps informs the approach to training and coaching discussed in Chapters 2 and 3. We can apply it to offer wider support for teachers to improve, beyond training and coaching (or to encourage any change within school). No single step will transform a school overnight. But the more we draw on them in our training, coaching, and day-to-day tasks - emails, meetings, briefings - the more likely teachers are to change. We have discussed four steps to designing effective teacher development: building a coherent programme, designing training, coaching teachers, and supporting change. In Part II, we turn to improving teaching across the school.

Next steps

Reflection questions

1) Think about the most recent change you have asked teachers to make (or been asked to make). To what extent did it lead to lasting, meaningful change? Why?
2) To what extent:
   - Did change focus on a specific habit?
   - Were teachers convinced that change mattered?
   - Were teachers encouraged to make commitments?
   - Was the change made easy to start?
   - Were teachers supported to make the change stick?
3) How might you have made the change work better? Which step would you focus on? What could you do differently?

Checklist

1) Design a habit
   a. Decide what teachers should do
   b. Identify when they should act
2) Build conviction in the change
   a. Give a reason for the change
   b. Show the change is immediately worthwhile
   c. Show that others are already trying the change
3) Encourage teachers to commit to action; invite them to choose:
   a. When to act
   b. What to do, and with whom
   c. Prompts and reminders
   d. Plan B
4) Make starting easy
   a. Break the change into steps
   b. Simplify the change
   c. Set defaults
   d. Practise the change
5) Make change stick
   a. Track what's changing
   b. Offer feedback: share numbers, highlight successes, revisit key points
   c. Relaunch the change

Getting started

Pick something you want colleagues to do, such as practising in a session, responding to a request, or observing one another. Pick one big barrier - like struggling to get started - and try one technique from this chapter to try to overcome it.

Success in different roles

You can apply the ideas in this chapter, whatever your role:

- **As a teacher. . .** you can use this process to make changes to your own teaching, or to support your colleagues to change.
- **As a middle leader. . .** you can use this process to support individual teachers, or your team, to make changes.
- **As a leader working across schools. . .** you can follow these steps in designing organisation-wide change; you can work with school leaders to help them plan change.

Part II

How can we improve teaching across the school?

Part I looked at building blocks to improve teaching: a coherent programme (Chapter 1), effective training (Chapter 2), coaching (Chapter 3), and support for change (Chapter 4). We can begin using these strategies immediately – to refine our next training or coaching session, for example. We may take time to master them. At some point, however, we must go beyond them. Effective training sessions, and the efforts of a single teacher educator, can help teachers improve. But they aren't sufficient to improve teaching across the school. We need a systematic approach which coordinates our work, and that of our colleagues, around a shared focus.

Part II shows how we can plan, coordinate, and evaluate professional development across the school. It allows us to use the building blocks discussed in Part I to the greatest effect, by identifying a focus for improvement, applying an effective model of change, and assessing our impact accurately. We will consider three challenges:

- In Chapter 5, we examine picking a focus for professional development. We have built a coherent model of effective teaching (in Chapter 1), but we cannot work on every aspect of it at once. How can we choose what to prioritise?
- In Chapter 6, we look at planning, coordinating, and refining improvement efforts. Schools are graveyards of failed initiatives. Having chosen a priority, how can we pursue it effectively?
- In Chapter 7, we discuss the evaluation of professional development. We need to know what's working and adapt our efforts accordingly. How can we assess progress accurately and easily?

Part II offers simple, effective approaches which help us deploy training, coaching, and support to achieve focused improvement across the school.

DOI: 10.4324/9781003439622-7

5 How can we choose a focus for improvement?

Chapter map

Effective improvement focuses on the school's most pressing need

↓

To choose a focus we:

- Carefully analyse existing practice
- Gain a complete picture of the school
- Establish the changes needed

↓

Step 1: Identify issues to investigate

Choose a few broad issues as a jumping-off point

↓

Step 2: Examine effective and existing practice

a) Examine effective practice, in theory and reality
b) Examine existing practice

↓

Step 3: Review and decide

Distil the findings and agree a priority with leaders

↓

We can then lead change (Chapter 6) and assess our impact (Chapter 7)

DOI: 10.4324/9781003439622-8

We've established a model of teaching and learning to guide our professional development programme (in Chapter 1). But we cannot pursue every aspect of it at once. Effective training, coaching, and habit formation are focused. A focus is crucial for teachers, who have little time to spend on improvement, and leaders, who may otherwise work at cross purposes. Yet we have said little about how to choose one. This is deliberate. We first built the skills needed to help teachers change. We can now set goals, confident in achieving them. This chapter looks at how to assess teachers' needs, and possible changes, to choose a focus for improvement.

Why does choosing a focus matter?

Benjamin has just taken responsibility for teacher development. He knows the school's approach must change. The previous incumbent, Humza, came from a turnaround school, and rapidly produced an ambitious professional development plan. But he worked alone, replicating his former school's approach; the link to teachers' needs was unclear. The programme itself seemed unfocused, switching from topic to topic. Humza announced a priority early in the year: challenging students to think hard. Minutes later, however, he was talking about growth mindset, asking teachers to promote it every lesson. Across the term, training jumped around: modelling, then psychological safety; feedback, then behavioural expectations; praise, then setting lesson objectives. Some teachers focused on getting students to think hard. Others panicked, trying to act on each new idea, or switched off, as conflicting messages drowned one another out. The programme was neither coherent nor built around teachers' needs: it did little good.

Benjamin wants to focus professional development where it will make the greatest difference. Recent leadership team discussions have raised two concerns: behaviour obstructing learning and teachers struggling to adapt teaching. Wary of jumping to conclusions however, Benjamin sets out to assess teachers' needs carefully, and to work collectively, gaining colleagues' support for change. First, he examines existing practice. He looks for patterns in staff surveys and lesson observation notes. With these in mind, he conducts joint observations with middle leaders, using feedback meetings to probe teachers' thinking. In parallel, he studies effective practice, observing excellent teaching and discussing key texts on classroom management and responsive teaching with the new teaching and learning group. His report to the leadership team shows that behavioural issues are isolated and can be tackled with individual support. His findings about responsive teaching are more nuanced. Teachers know the techniques - but they struggle to respond to students' needs due to gaps in their planning and subject knowledge. Leaders agree that professional development should focus on addressing this next term. Benjamin develops a sequence of sessions and resources: with a clear focus and plenty of support, teaching improves rapidly.

Carefully identifying priorities has a number of benefits. It allows teacher educators to go beyond superficial concerns and identify underlying issues. We are more likely to find lasting solutions which meet teachers' needs as a result. The work required to choose a focus is valuable preparation for leading training: it helps us understand the ideas and skills involved, and identify good examples to share with teachers. Finally, this approach demonstrates procedural justice: we are choosing an appropriate focus *and being seen to do so*. Colleagues are more likely to support it as a result. Combined, this increases the chances our programme will succeed.

Effective improvement focuses on the school's most pressing need.

What makes a choice robust?

The stakes are high: our choice determines how considerable time and effort will be spent. We must choose carefully: avoiding hasty conclusions; building and sharing a convincing rationale for change. What makes a choice robust?

A robust choice rests on careful analysis

A robust choice of professional development focus rests on careful analysis. It's tempting to skip this, especially when we're busy, and the problem seems urgent. But we don't know what we don't know. It's easy to jump to conclusions based on what we do know. Once we have an initial hunch, we may seek evidence for it - not alternative explanations.[1] Imagine Benjamin choosing a focus in this way. Concerned about responsive teaching, he could have focused on techniques like exit tickets. He would have seen apparent success: teachers using exit tickets more. But, having overlooked the underlying planning and subject knowledge issues, this would increase teacher workload, without improving learning. An incomplete analysis leads to partial solutions - and new problems.[2] We can choose a professional development focus in a heartbeat. But **a robust choice rests on careful analysis and resists rushed judgement.**

A robust choice requires a complete picture

On eighteenth-century ships, changing course meant rousing the whole crew to adjust every sail. Schools are just as complex. To make a change work - to improve feedback for students, for example - we may need to change the tasks teachers set, their marking and teaching routines, how students respond, what parents expect, *and* the support leaders offer.[3] So, as we choose a focus, we must consider the many adjustments it may require. They may not be obvious. Like the blind men in an ancient tale - one held the elephant's trunk and believed it was a snake, another touched its leg and insisted it was a tree - we sense the school's complexity in part. We noted that senior leaders are twice as likely as teachers to think professional development is working,[4] but this gap between perspectives is more general. For example, leaders are also twice as likely as teachers to believe they are listening well, recognising success, and enforcing the behaviour policy consistently.[5] Overcoming this is hard: colleagues may not express their views out of politeness or nervousness. But **a robust choice requires a complete picture of the school - and of teachers' perceptions of it.**

A robust choice establishes the changes needed

Analysing existing practice reveals issues, but we must also choose how to address them. Organisations learn by identifying, codifying, and spreading effective practice. For example, struggling to make a better breadmaker, a designer apprenticed herself to an exceptional baker. Grasping exactly how he kneaded dough - his tacit knowledge - helped her redesign the breadmaker successfully.[6] Like her, we must identify teachers who are succeeding already (in school and beyond), understand their approach, and establish what others can take from it. If we're looking at modelling, for example, analysing existing practice will reveal gaps: teachers using models poorly, or not at all. We must then find teachers who are using models effectively, identify what they're doing, and understand why it works. **A robust choice establishes the changes needed to improve existing practice.**

Drawing these ideas together, to choose a focus for improvement, we must do three things. First, pursue a careful analysis and avoid jumping to conclusions. Second, gain a complete picture, seeing the school through others' eyes. Third, identify effective alternatives to existing practice. The implications may seem unsurprising: think hard, listen, choose something good. I often feel tempted to skip this step. But it deserves time and effort, for two reasons. First, this chapter's steps - practical strategies to help choose a focus - invariably generate fresh insight about the school's needs. Second, our exploratory work helps generate consensus among leaders and colleagues: they inform the choice of focus; in doing so, they begin to accept the coming change.

> *To choose a focus we carefully analyse existing practice and identify effective alternatives.*

How can we choose a focus for improvement?

Step 1 - Identify issues to investigate

We begin by choosing a few broad issues to investigate. This is a jumping-off point: in Steps 2 and 3, we will deepen our understanding of them, unearth underlying challenges, and select a priority. For now, we simply need to identify issues we might wish to address.

> *What does Step 1 look like?*
>
> Choosing what to investigate takes Narayani an hour. First, she creates a longlist of ideas, using staff surveys, the school improvement plan, and the most recent inspection report. Senior leaders make further suggestions, then help her whittle the list to three big issues: planning, challenge, and behaviour around the school.

To identify issues we could investigate, we can briefly review existing documents and collate our hunches. We might consider:

- Existing priorities set out in school and trust improvement plans;
- The perceptions of colleagues, students, and parents, expressed in survey reports or discussion;
- The views of outside observers, in reports by inspectors, consultants, or peers;
- Promising ideas we've encountered recently in training or reading.

The long list of possibilities this offers can then be reduced to two or three broad issues. We can merge related ideas: disruption in lessons and students struggling to focus can be tackled together, for example. We want to maintain a broad focus at this stage: "improving planning in maths" is fine; "developing better unit plans for Year 8 maths" is too narrow - we can't yet know if this is the biggest issue or the best solution. Inviting leaders to help us prioritise makes this step easier, and involves them in choosing a focus from the start.

Choosing a focus starts with the identification of two or three broad issues to investigate.

Action 1) Briefly review existing documents and agree two or three issues to investigate with senior leaders.

Step 2 - Examine effective and existing practice

We now want to understand what's currently happening around the issues chosen in Step 1, and what's possible. In Step 2, we examine effective and existing practice in parallel. As we learn more about effective practice, we can better spot the strengths and weaknesses of existing practice. As we learn more about existing practice, we can identify the potential for, and barriers to, more effective practice.

What does Step 2 look like?

Narayani begins examining the three issues agreed by leaders. For each, she first clarifies for herself what effective practice looks like, watching lesson footage and reading blogs and research reports. She identifies teachers who manage each issue well, observing and learning about their approach. This helps her understand, for example, what kind of behaviour students are capable of, and what teachers (and schools) do to achieve it. With these criteria in mind, she examines existing practice. For example, with principles of effective planning in mind, she observes lessons and discusses how teachers actually plan. Narayani establishes whether they understand the principles, whether they apply them and, if not, what's stopping them. By the end of Step 2, for each issue, she knows what's currently happening, what could or should be happening, and the barriers improvement faces.

Step 2a) Examine effective practice

We can begin by looking at the ideas underpinning effective practice. This means reading around each issue, reviewing the evidence available and considering how robust it is. We'll read critically, separating assertions from ideas which have been tested rigorously. But we're not academics, and this isn't an academic literature review. We can begin with blog posts, the books recommended in Chapter 1, and evidence reviews from the Education Endowment Foundation. Given time, we might dig into the sources they reference. There's often less evidence than we might wish for. There's almost never a careful trial with a clear result in a context like ours - sometimes, there's no trial at all. But our goal isn't finding evidence telling us what to do. It's gaining new insights: a sense of what might and might not work, and why. Drawing on our reading, we can establish principles of effective practice for each issue.

We then need to find out how teachers make these principles work. Having established what effective planning looks like in theory, for example, we need to know how successful teachers actually plan - around teaching all day and stacks of marking. This means spending time with effective teachers, in our school and beyond, observing their actions and asking about their approach. (Videos of effective teaching help too.) Looking at support for early career teachers, for example, we might first establish what great mentoring and training look like in principle. We would then want to observe the training, coaching, and support offered by schools with a good record of retaining early career teachers; to hear from teachers, their mentors, and leaders; and to understand what's really working, and why. At the end of our examination of effective practice, we should have a set of principles for each issue *and* an understanding of the practical strategies teachers actually use.

Choosing a focus requires an understanding of effective practice - in theory and in reality.

Action 2a) For each issue, establish what effective practice looks like in principle, and find out what successful teachers and schools actually do.

Step 2b) Examine existing practice

We must understand existing practice if we are to change it. Imagine examining questioning. We have clarified how to question effectively, in Step 2a. To choose a focus, however, we must establish how teachers' current approaches differ from this ideal. We may wonder:

- How many questions are teachers asking?
- What kind of questions are teachers asking?
- How are teachers phrasing questions?
- When are teachers asking questions?
- Who is being asked questions?
- Who is actually answering questions?
- To what extent are students attending to questions/answers?
- How long are teachers waiting for an answer?
- To what extent are questions promoting thinking/discussion/retrieval?
- How do teachers respond to student answers?

Knowing what teachers are doing well and where they're struggling helps us choose a worthwhile focus for improvement. Identifying colleagues who are using questions effectively will also help us show the desired change can be achieved with "our kids".

To examine teachers' current approach, we can:

- **Review existing data.** Schools have extensive data on existing practice, such as planning documents, observation records, survey reports, and student results. Studying questioning, we may learn about the questions teachers plan (from curriculum documents), how they are used in lessons (from observation records), and how students perceive them (from survey reports). Comparing this with test results hints at their impact.
- **Seek new evidence.** Having exhausted existing data, we can seek new evidence. We might visit lessons, speak to colleagues, and examine student work. This shouldn't be onerous, for us or them: a handful of conversations and lesson visits can tell us a lot. Our goal is to test and refine our initial impressions. For example, we might think teachers aren't asking many probing questions. We can check: are they asking questions, and if so, how good are they? More broadly, we might think questioning has a big impact on learning. It's worth seeking counter-examples: do some teachers achieve impressive results without much questioning? If so, are explanations and practice more important? This clarifies what teachers are and aren't doing, how this affects student learning, and so, what's worth focusing on.

This process also prepares colleagues for change. We can emphasise how their views shape the choice of focus, as we listen and when we come to launch the change.

Choosing a focus requires an understanding of existing practice.

Action 2b) Establish what existing practice is like: review current data and seek new evidence as to what teachers are doing and the impact it is having.

Step 3 – Review and decide

Having examined effective and existing practice for the issues we identified in Step 1, we now review our findings and choose a focus for improvement.

What does Step 3 look like?

Narayani presents her findings to the leadership team. She explains what she's done, what she's learned about current practice and teachers' needs, and how each issue could be addressed. She doesn't suggest a focus however. Instead, she invites leaders to agree the most important, urgent, and tractable issue. Some argue planning is crucial. But the disruption to lessons Narayani has reported makes behaviour more urgent. It's also tractable: she has outlined small changes which could improve learning significantly. Leaders agree to focus on routines for gaining and maintaining students' attention. With their support, Narayani begins planning professional development to achieve this.

In Step 3, we distil what we've learned, present this to leaders, and agree a focus for improvement. Step 2 will have suggested conclusions. But summarising our learning in a presentation or report helps us weigh the evidence, gain new insight, and convey our findings. It also shows colleagues that careful thought has gone into choosing a focus. Working with those involved in previous steps, we can explain what we've done, what we've learned, and what could be done next. Then, we invite leaders to agree a focus. We might ask them which issue seems most:

- Important: what will cause the biggest improvement to student learning?
- Urgent: what needs immediate attention?
- Tractable: where are teachers likely to succeed?

Working upstream may help us prioritise: we must secure students' attention before refining explanations, for example (we discussed working upstream in Chapter 3). With a focus for improvement agreed, we can move on to helping teachers pursue it, the subject of Chapter 6.

Choosing a focus means distilling findings and agreeing a priority for change.

Action 3) Distil what you've learned, present it to leaders, agree a focus - prioritising change which is important, urgent, and tractable.

Case study

Alex Douglas, Head of Teaching and Learning at Mossbourne Community Academy, wanted to understand how the school could better support early career teachers. Here, he describes what he learned through Step 2, looking at effective practice - in theory and reality - and existing practice.

My first reading around what other teacher educators look to focus on was from The New Teacher Project and their focus on new teacher training and accelerated classroom expertise.[7] They have distilled the key skills teachers need in early training down to four things that they practise until mastery (those four techniques were: 100%, Positive framing, Strong voice & What to do). This is supported with deliberate practice and coaching. The thinking around refining to essentials is useful for me and it is good to get oversight of initial teacher training, but it is a step before early career teaching (ECT), which is my focus. It made me think about the difficulty of designing effective ECT programmes. Each one of my ECTs has been trained by a different provider, which means they arrive with different skills and preferences, as well as priorities. I need to think deeply about what the gaps the ECT programme should fill without it being a re-training process.

Key insight: narrow initial teacher training skills to highest leverage techniques.

After these readings, I had conversations with Belinda Goodship (Bedford Free School) and Susie Fraser (Manchester Community Academy) about their initial training and ECT provision. I asked about the sequence and component parts of the planning and design of these courses. A key difference between the two was the amount of reading/assignments that were required differed greatly. I found the Bedford programme compelling and felt that there was a clear rationale and alignment with the principles of the school, outlined in the first page of the training materials. After analysing these documents I read the Early Career Framework. A question I have still concerns the sequencing of this material. There is no suggested order. I would like to read something that thinks about the order of developing/practising these elements. I also wonder about priority. There are so many elements and I believe that an ECT programme should prioritise. These three pieces of evidence all failed to articulate a vision for the sequencing of a programme. However, two sources had considered and planned around the sequencing of teacher training. First, Josh Goodrich's Steplab sequence starts with behaviours and routines. This was apparently influenced by Bamrick-Santoyo's *Get Better Faster*. In his first 30 days of teacher training, he focuses on behaviours and routines of the classroom. My reading around sequencing and experience in the field has compelled me to believe that starting with behaviour is the best bet.

Key Insight: Sequence the training by starting with behaviours and routines.

At the beginning of the year, I completed an audit of early career provision. I revisited this to explore if any of the entire programme had aligned with everything I read and heard about elsewhere. It didn't. The previous programme was not aligned to any particular philosophy, had no apparent sequence, lacked priorities, and was not evidence-informed. In addition to this audit, I interviewed my counterpart at our sister school about the early career programme there. The findings were similar. Essentially, they are continuing with the ad hoc (little thought given to sequence, cog-sci, etc.) approach taken at my school before I took over. They freely admitted that it was sub-par and that they are looking to change it. This was a very fruitful call as we discussed how we could work together to align the school programmes and create a high-quality off the shelf model for their school. I shared both *The Learning Curriculum* [discussed in Chapter 1] and *Learning: What is it and how can we catalyse it?*[8] We agreed to meet early in the next academic year to discuss further and to share my findings. To support my interrogation of the programme, I conducted a survey of early career provision this year. In order to learn, iterate, and adapt I needed insights from those that completed the programme. These findings have already challenged my thinking and helped to clarify my ideas around sequence and priority.
Key Insights: There is no academy leadership on an aligned initial/early career programme + regular feedback provides real-time insight to help iterate based on student need.

Conclusion

This chapter supports us in choosing an appropriate professional development focus with confidence. Step 2 helps us understand the issues and teachers' needs. We can use it to collate ideas and examples which will make training successful – and to prepare colleagues for change. Involving leaders in the decision should elicit the support we need from them to pursue improvement. We end the chapter with a focus; in Chapter 6, we will look at how to address it.

Next steps

Reflection questions

1) Think about previous professional development programmes you have led (or experienced).
    - To what extent was there a clear focus for improvement?
    - What was the process for choosing this focus?
    - How deeply did leaders examine existing and effective practice?
    - To what extent was the choice a collective, considered decision by leaders?
    - How successful was the professional development?
2) How might you have improved the process of choosing a focus? Which step would you prioritise? What could you do differently?

Checklist

1) Identify issues to investigate
2) Examine existing and effective practice
    a. Examine effective practice
    b. Examine existing practice
3) Review and decide a focus

Getting started

Do one thing - an observation, an interview, some reading - to learn more about effective and existing practice. Discuss what you learn with your immediate colleagues - other leaders, or the teaching and learning team - to share insights and get their feedback.

Success in different roles

You can apply the ideas in this chapter, whatever your role:

- **As a teacher. . .** you can simplify this process, examining your current practice and effective alternatives to choose a focus for improving your own teaching.
- **As a middle leader. . .** you can use this process to select a focus for your team.
- **As a leader working across schools. . .** you can follow these steps to identify an organisation-wide focus; you can support leaders to choose a focus for their school.

6 How can we lead change?

Chapter map

Effective change leadership applies Problem-Driven Iterative Adaptation

↓

Problem-Driven Iterative Adaptation:

- Focuses on a problem
- Finds solutions which work for our school
- Tests ideas iteratively

↓

Step 1: Get to the heart of the problem

a) Identify a tractable problem
b) Establish the causes

↓

Step 2: Choose actions

a) Identify possible actions
b) Assess the options

↓

Step 3: Plan first steps

Select promising steps which can be taken immediately

↓

Step 4: Act

↓

Step 5: Review progress and identify next steps

Review what's been done and learned and agree what to do next

↓

Step 6: Keep going; keep building

Maintain the cycle; scale solutions; choose the next problem

↓

We can then assess the impact of our efforts (Chapter 7)

DOI: 10.4324/9781003439622-9

Part I provided tools for teacher development: coaching, training, habit building. Chapter 5 gave us a focus for improvement. We now turn to making change happen. Pursuing our focus means initiating action, coordinating training, and guiding colleagues. We must navigate conflicting priorities and unexpected barriers. This is notoriously difficult: schools are littered with the remnants of failed initiatives. I suspect every reader has seen projects introduced prematurely, expanded carelessly, and abandoned unlamented. This chapter looks at how we can avoid this fate - and lead change successfully.

Why does leading change matter?

Dave's school has chosen a professional development focus for next year: improving lesson planning. Visiting other schools convinced Dave that co-planning would help. His goal is to get all teachers co-planning lessons by the end of next year. He spends the end of the current year preparing training sessions and, across several meetings, persuading leaders to make time for departments to plan together. He launches co-planning at the start of the year, training teachers and leaders to use it. After a term, Dave checks progress, observing planning, surveying staff, and talking to heads of department. He addresses the gaps this reveals by preparing further training and asking leaders to offer more support. As the year ends, results are mixed. Enthusiastic teachers are co-planning well. Sceptics have given up. Some teachers are planning better - others aren't.

Sam's school has chosen the same focus, but his approach is very different. Dave spends the last few weeks of the year preparing training and timetables to launch co-planning. Sam uses this time to test how best to improve planning. His examination of effective practice has revealed many options, including co-planning, improving unit plans, and working on curriculum documents. Sam approaches two middle leaders with an appetite for innovation, Jeevan and Marie. They each ask two teachers to try co-planning during the next department meeting. Afterwards, Sam, Jeevan, and Marie review their lesson plans. There are strengths, but key ideas are missing or buried. Marie and Jeevan draft knowledge organisers for the relevant units, then ask teachers to try another round of co-planning. The key ideas are clearer, but they aren't linked to the themes of the unit. So Marie and Jeevan amend the unit plans, emphasising these links.

Sam, Marie, and Jeevan review what they have learned. Two other middle leaders hear about the pilot and also ask to join. Knowledge organisers and unit plans are helping, but co-planning in pairs isn't working. They agree to test "team planning": drawing on the whole department's expertise to develop a single model lesson (one newer colleagues will teach the following week). By the end of the year, all four departments are doing this successfully. Teachers' plans - and their understanding and use of those plans - are improving. Like Dave, Sam launches the change to the whole school at the start of the following year. Unlike Dave, Sam has tested his ideas and evolved an approach that works. Four departments are already using team planning; they offer models, advice, and enthusiasm. The launch goes well. After a term, all departments are team planning, most teachers are planning better, and Sam is ready to make further refinements.

Initiatives fail when leaders adopt solutions which don't fully address the problem, or don't work in their school. Sam's approach - Problem-Driven Iterative Adaptation (PDIA) - overcomes these barriers. Dave sees co-planning in another school, predicts it will work, and focuses on implementing it. Sam focuses on making planning better, experimenting until he finds a solution which works for his colleagues. This also limits opposition to change. Sam takes tentative steps with enthusiastic volunteers. He doesn't mandate change school-wide until he has a viable solution. While iterating, he builds momentum, demonstrating progress, attracting more volunteers, and creating advocates. PDIA helps him lead change successfully.

Effective leaders iteratively develop solutions to their school's problems.

What makes change leadership successful?

Change often ends in failure, and not just in teaching. Foreign donors funded a project to build a case management system for Mozambique's judiciary. After five years, the money had been spent, no system had been created, and case management remained a problem.[1] To lead change better, international development researchers have evolved an approach called Problem-Driven Iterative Adaptation, or - the only acronym I have included in the book - PDIA.[2] What can we learn from it?

Successful change focuses on a problem

PDIA encourages leaders to focus on addressing a problem. In our case, this will usually be some element of classroom practice. This matters because, while schools are changing all the time - adopting new structures or curricula or wellbeing programmes - this rarely affects what's crucial: how teachers and students interact in the classroom.[3] Change is elusive when we work with individual teachers (as we discussed in Chapter 4). It's even more elusive when we work with the whole school. Tackling a problem - the focus chosen in Chapter 5 - guides our team's efforts towards a meaningful goal. **Leading change means focusing on a specific problem.**

Successful change finds solutions which work for our school

School leaders often copy other successful schools. Doing so meets teachers', parents', and inspectors' expectations.[4] It's rational, given that schools, "face ambiguous goals, are risk averse, uncertain about the means to achieve them and are dependent to varying degrees on external bodies."[5] But, as a result, "Many school reform initiatives fail to achieve sustained improvements in performance because schools pretend to reform by changing what policies and organisational structures *look like* rather than what they *actually do*."[6] These failed initiatives eventually make "failing and flailing schools both internally resistant to reform and immune to external pressures for any real change".[7] These quotations come from researchers studying international development: I've replaced the word "states" with "schools". Yet the description - of ambiguous goals and external pressure, superficial change, and resulting incapacity - rings true. We can learn from others: processes of memory, practice, and habit formation are universal. But imitating them rarely works: **leading change means finding solutions which work for our school and build our capacity to improve.**

Successful change test ideas iteratively

When we plan, we assume the best. We are often disappointed. This is most obvious in big infrastructure projects like the HS2 railway: delayed, under-delivering, and over-budget. This is not new: Concorde and the Sydney Opera House arrived years late and cost *ten times* original estimates.[8] It reflects human frailty, not engineering difficulty: under pressure to promise success, people plan optimistically and overconfidently.[9] Our school improvement and professional development plans are no different. Once made, they are immediately and unforeseeably undermined, as colleagues move role, new priorities emerge, and external pressures shift. Ambitious, inflexible, multistep plans are soon upset by unexpected events and diverted by new insights. PDIA encourages us to make small plans, test ideas, and adapt our approach, iterating towards success. **Leading change means testing ideas, adapting, and iterating.**

Drawing these ideas together, we see initiatives falter when leaders try to imitate successful schools, when optimistic plans meet harsh reality, and when teachers experience disruption which doesn't improve classroom practice. PDIA increases our chance of success. It focuses on a core problem: some element of classroom practice. It discourages unrealistic or imitative plans - guiding us instead to iterate towards a solution which works for our teachers. Some of the steps below may seem obvious. But I encourage you to complete them all - preferably with colleagues. Invariably, they help teacher educators gain fresh insight and make meaningful changes. Through PDIA, we can overcome the barriers to change and improve teaching across the school.

> *We can lead change successfully by using Problem-Driven Iterative Adaptation.*

How can we lead change in schools?

Step 1 - Get to the heart of the problem

In Chapter 5, we examined existing practice and chose an area of focus. The first step in applying Problem-Driven Iterative Adaptation is to turn that focus into a specific problem and to establish its causes. This clarifies our goal - solving the problem - and the changes that will be needed to achieve it.

What does Step 1 look like?

School leaders have agreed to focus on challenge in lessons. Now, Emma meets the teaching and learning team to decide how to make improvements. First, they take the broad concern - challenge - and specify the problem they will address: most students already know much of what they are being taught. Then, they dig into possible causes. They identify many, including gaps in teachers' subject knowledge, weak assessment of students' existing understanding, poor planning processes, and lack of time and support to plan better.

Step 1a - Identify a tractable problem

Write your answers to the following questions.

1) What problem do you wish to solve?

____

2) What is a solution to the problem?

____

Sometimes, our framing of the problem dictates the solution. Imagine a teacher educator saying the problem is, "teachers not using retrieval practice enough". There can be only one solution: help teachers use retrieval practice more. Let's check whether your problem fits this pattern.

3) Write three other solutions to the problem.

____

____

____

If we haven't yet captured the underlying problem, formulating three further solutions is hard.[10] In this example, what matters is not teachers' use of retrieval practice, but students forgetting key ideas. Retrieval practice may help. But there are other solutions: rethinking how ideas are introduced, revisiting them across the curriculum, and better assessing students' initial understanding.

The next set of questions should help turn our focus into a problem which is tractable and worth solving. We want to get to the heart of the issue, not just address symptoms. For example, all teachers are short of time. There is no simple solution. Rather than seeking one, or becoming discouraged, we need to establish why this matters.[11] Perhaps lack of time means teachers can't plan effectively, or offer actionable feedback. These are tractable problems, worth addressing. Finding more efficient, effective ways to give feedback should improve student learning.

> *Effective leaders choose a tractable problem worth solving.*

Action 1a) Beginning with your chosen focus, use these questions to identify an underlying problem which can be solved, and is worth solving.

Question	*Emma's answers*	*Your answers*
1) What is the problem?	Lack of challenge in lessons.	
2) Why does this matter?	Students are bored; they are making less progress than they could be.	

(Continued)

Question	*Emma's answers*	*Your answers*
3) Why does this matter?	It creates disaffection; leads to worse results.	
4) Why does this matter?	We want students to learn a lot, succeed, enjoy learning.	
5) To whom does it matter?	Students, parents, teachers, leaders, society.	
6) Who needs to care more?	Teachers, heads of department, senior leaders.	
7) How do we get them to give it more attention?	Highlight easy alternatives? Share student survey results?	
8) How will things look when the problem is solved?	More challenging teaching; greater student progress; increased student engagement.	

Step 1b – Establish the causes

One problem may encompass or conceal many others.[12] We can identify the causes of our problem by asking five whys. Japanese manufacturers used this approach to create the most efficient factories in the world.[13] On finding a problem, they asked what caused it, what caused that cause, what caused that cause, and so on. This gives us profound insight into what's happening, and allows us to identify lasting solutions. Consider a student who has been sent out of a lesson. We ask, "Why?"

"I answered back."

"Why?"

"I was frustrated."

"Why?"

"I was confused about the task." (Note that we're asking them to explain each answer they give, not asking, "Why were you sent out?" five times.) Identifying every cause – frustration, confusion, answering back – allows us to address them all, making change more likely. Applying this to establish the causes of our problem guides our choice of actions, in Step 2.

Effective leaders establish the causes of the problem, and the causes of those causes.

Action 1b) Write the three most obvious causes of the problem. Then ask, "Why?" five times, to identify the causes of the problem.

	Emma's answers *Cause: Teachers underestimate students*	*Cause 1*	*Cause 2*	*Cause 3*
Why?	They haven't seen what students can achieve			
Why?	They have limited exposure to models of excellence			
Why?	Most professional development is internal; we rarely visit other schools			
Why?	The school has been quite insular in its approach			
Why?	We see our challenges and students as unique			

Step 2 - Choose actions

We've seen the many causes of our problem. We can now decide what to do about them. Poor student retention could be addressed through retrieval practice, for example. But we might also want to improve student focus, teach key ideas more memorably, and check understanding of them more frequently. In Step 2, we'll consider how the causes could be addressed, then assess how feasible each action is.

What does Step 2 look like?

Emma's teaching and learning group identifies ways to address each cause of lack of challenge in lessons. First, they look for *possible* actions, drawing on their work examining effective practice. Some are fairly simple: sharing excellent work would show teachers what students are capable of. Others are more complicated: creating external partnerships could make the school less insular. Once the list is complete, they review each action, asking three questions. Do we have the authority to act? Would colleagues accept the action? Could the school make it work? This helps them identify what they could do immediately, such as sharing model work, and what would take more preparation.

Step 2a - Identify possible actions

We can organise the causes of our problem and identify possible actions using a fishbone diagram. First, we add the causes named in Step 1b to the diagram. We can then work with colleagues to suggest actions which *could* address each cause. Our work examining effective practice (in Chapter 5) should help. We need not get bogged down in how feasible each action is at this stage: we'll assess this in Step 2b. For example, partnering with another school will take longer than sharing model work, and may be complicated by relationships and rivalries between schools. But it's an action which could make the school less insular, so Emma adds it to the list. This step should leave us with at least one possible action to address each cause.

Effective leaders identify actions which could address each cause.

Action 2a) Complete the fishbone diagram. Add the causes you identified in Step 1b to the left-hand columns. Write possible actions to address each cause in the right-hand columns.

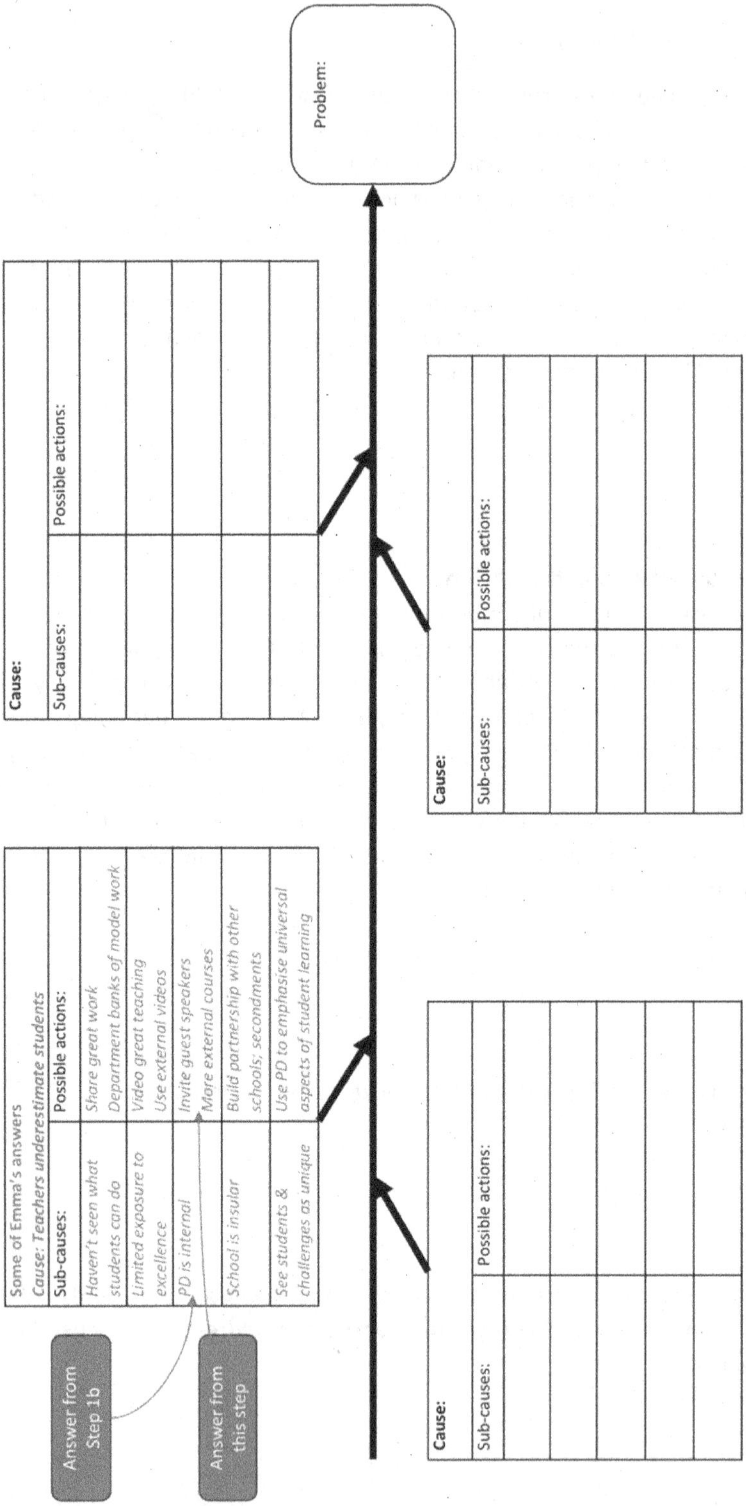
Problem:
Cause:
Sub-causes:
Possible actions:
Cause:
Sub-causes:
Possible actions:
Some of Emma's answers
Cause: Teachers underestimate students
Sub-causes:
Possible actions:
Haven't seen what students can do
Share great work
Department banks of model work
Limited exposure to excellence
Video great teaching
Use external videos
PD is internal
Invite guest speakers
More external courses
School is insular
Build partnership with other schools; secondments
See students & challenges as unique
Use PD to emphasise universal aspects of student learning
Answer from Step 1b
Answer from this step
Cause:
Sub-causes:
Possible actions:

Step 2b – Assess the options

We now assess how feasible each action is. An action should succeed if we have three things:

- Authority: responsibility or permission to act;
- Acceptance: staff enthusiasm for, or at least acceptance of, the action;
- Ability: the knowledge and skill required (individually and collectively) to make the action work.

Reviewing possible actions against these criteria shows us where to begin. For example, imagine wanting to introduce deliberate practice in professional development sessions. The sessions are our responsibility, so we have authority to act. Deliberate practice is novel, so we'll need to work to gain staff acceptance. We may feel able to use it already – if not, we can seek training or support. Another example: teachers might welcome changes to the performance management system, but we would need to design a better system and gain leaders' permission to use it. Our assessment reveals where we can act now and where we need further preparation; it sets us up to plan action, in Step 3.

Effective leaders assess how feasible each action is.

Action 2b) Complete the Venn diagram, placing each action identified in Step 2a to reflect whether you have the authority, ability, and acceptance to act.

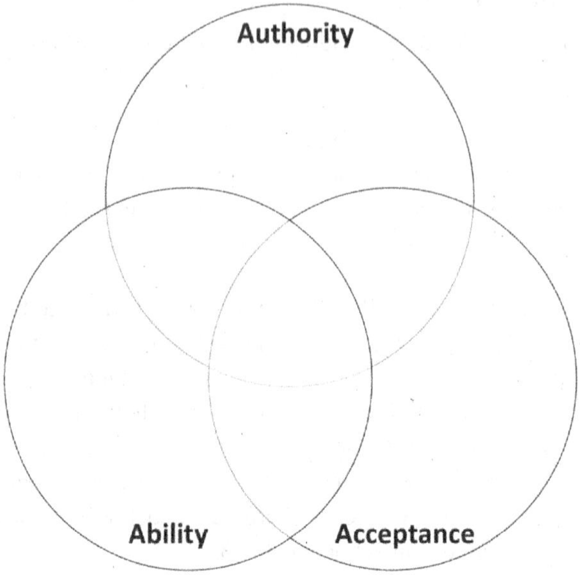

Step 3 - Plan first steps

Problem-Driven Iterative Adaptation encourages us to gain momentum: to act fast and keep going. A swift start - as opposed to lengthy planning - has several benefits. First, if we try several actions, some of them should work. Second, our actions activate others, highlighting problems, eliciting interest, and encouraging colleagues to take part. Third, each small success is a platform for further action. Solving problems increases our team's capacity and coherence. Change promotes acceptance: enthusiasts expect further progress; sceptics recognise the direction of travel. Showing managers evidence of our impact helps us gain authority for further action. Starting fast matters: in Step 3, we will plan where to begin.

What does Step 3 look like?

Emma's teaching and learning team reviews their Venn diagram, planning how to begin to address lack of challenge in lessons. First, they look at the middle: actions which they have the ability, authority, and acceptance to take now. Three seem worth trying immediately: sharing model work, training teachers to assess prior knowledge, and drop-in sessions to support new teachers' planning. Next, they look at actions which seem important, but for which they lack ability, authority, or acceptance. Subject departments seem crucial for improving planning. Emma promises to speak to middle leaders, seeking authority to get departments working on this. The team has discussed co-planning, but no one has tried it: they lack the ability to make it work. They agree to test different approaches. Finally, they're unsure teachers will accept that the gaps in their subject knowledge matter. They decide to ask teachers what makes planning hard. This seems an ambitious but achievable set of first steps.

We want momentum, not perfection.[14] This means planning, not the perfect path to success, but the quickest way to get started. As we review our Venn diagram, we're looking for two things. First, actions we can take now. These are the actions - in the middle of the diagram - for which we already have ability, authority, and acceptance. We can replan the next professional development session today, for example, using Chapter 2. Second, steps which will build the ability, authority, or acceptance needed for future action.[15] For example, if we want to change the performance management system, but lack the authority, we could raise the issue with the head. If we want to change the marking policy, but lack the ability and acceptance required, we could seek examples of better policies and survey staff on problems with the existing one. We plan, not perfect first steps, but immediate action.

Effective leaders select promising steps which can be taken now.

Action 3) Review your Venn diagram. Circle actions which you can take immediately. Then note steps you can take now to build the authority, acceptance, or ability to change.

Step 4 - Act

The next step is simple: act. Set a deadline no more than two weeks away, and take as many actions as you can in that time (preferably as a team). Be bold, make time, act.

What does Step 4 look like?

Emma and her team take most of their planned actions. They lead training on assessing prior knowledge and receive positive feedback. Two new teachers attend the first drop-in planning support session; both say it's helpful and promise to return. They collate examples of model work, but can't find a good time to share it. The team's attempts to build ability, authority, and acceptance for further action prove harder. They identify ways to improve planning, but don't have time to test them. Their survey receives only a handful of responses; the middle leaders' meeting Emma hoped to speak at is postponed.

Effective leaders act.

Action 4) Set a deadline, within two weeks; take as many actions as you can in that time.

Step 5 - Review progress and identify next steps

Problem-Driven Iterative Adaptation intentionally moves in short cycles. This has many merits. Reviewing progress early helps us learn and iterate fast. Planned pauses prevent us from getting stuck: we can rethink failing approaches and relaunch our efforts. A review is also a chance to identify, celebrate, and build on success. Reviews work best when they are collective: the group holds us to account for our actions and offers fresh perspectives. As we take stock of what we've achieved, we can plan our next steps.

What does Step 5 look like?

After two weeks, Emma's team meets again. First, they review what they've done: team members briefly describe the training, drop-in sessions, and emails. Next, they discuss what they've learned. Some findings are unsurprising: middle leaders are busy; they couldn't immediately create a better planning process. But the discussion also fosters new insights. One colleague asks how they'll track whether teachers are applying the training on assessing prior knowledge. This crystallises a concern of Emma's: the weak link between training, observations, and department meetings. Another colleague suggests brief, superficial opportunities to share model work will have little impact. Teachers need time to examine the work, grasp its strengths, and understand how it was created - this can only be done by subject teams. "Departments are the key", Emma realises. Finally, the team plans next steps. They'll run further support sessions for new teachers, and use them to test alternative ways to support planning. Emma is determined to meet heads of department. She decides she must also convince the leadership team of the need to link training sessions with day-to-day activity. Each teacher in the team commits to starting a bank of model work for their subject. They promise to reconvene in two weeks.

Within two weeks of starting, we pause to take stock. Our review asks three questions:

- **What did we do?** Each team member reports their actions. (If we're working alone, it's also worth recording them briefly.) This clarifies what has been done for the whole group, and holds us accountable, to ourselves and one another.
- **What have we learned?** As our efforts succeed and fail, we should gain fresh insight about what works, what changes are needed, and how we can ensure they succeed.
- **What will we do next?** The preceding questions often suggest next steps. We now canvas ideas and select the most promising. We may revisit our fishbone and Venn diagrams to check how we are working towards our underlying goals.

PDIA's power lies in this process of review and iteration. By learning and adapting, we overcome barriers and achieve lasting and meaningful improvements.

Effective leaders review progress and agree next steps.

Action 5) Review progress. What did you do? What did you learn? What will you do next?

Step 6 – Keep going; keep building

We now have all the ingredients of success: clear goals, targeted actions, and a process of review and iteration. We continue this cycle until we find a solution for our current problem. At that point, we scale the solution to reach all our teachers. Then, we choose a new challenge to which we can apply the PDIA process, and the team we've built.

What does Step 6 look like?

Emma's teaching and learning team settles into a routine of action and review. They make gradual progress increasing challenge in lessons. Starting banks of model work convinces middle leaders of their value; they are soon adopted and refined. This has two effects. First, teachers are clearer about what's possible. Second, unexpectedly, teachers begin using these models to show students what they should be aiming for, reinforcing these higher expectations. Through drop-in sessions with new teachers, the team develops a planning process which helps teachers set and achieve ambitious goals. Departments volunteer to test the process and find students produce far better work. Emma presents these findings to leaders, who agree to adopt the approach across the school – this also creates more planning time for teachers. Implementation monitoring will be needed, but the process of iterative experimentation has come to an end. Reviewing their work, several team members raise gaps in teachers' assessment practice. They agree to address this next.

Our first priority is maintaining the cycle of action, review, and iteration, to keep making progress. As this becomes routine, we can increase its impact by:

- **Trying bigger actions.** Our Venn diagram (Step 2b) recognised limits to our authority, acceptance, and ability to act. Over time, we can build each, to tackle increasingly challenging elements of the problem. We can rarely rebuild the school day and the professional development programme immediately. But, over a couple of terms, we can make the case, build support, explore alternatives, and make bigger changes.
- **Adding participants.** Our activity and successes will attract some colleagues' interest. We can leave an open door for them to help test new ideas or join the teaching and learning team. Adding participants creates more advocates, role models, and supporters of change.
- **Maintaining support.** We need to keep whoever we report to onside, by showing the impact of our work. We should be open about challenges too: an honest relationship and frank feedback is invaluable. But sharing our successes – however small – shows that we are making progress and makes them more likely to sanction further action.

Continuing the cycle and adding these steps should help us maintain and increase our impact.

At some point, the process of experimentation and adaptation nears an end. With enough iteration, we should find a solution which works for our teachers. Spreading that solution may require more testing: does what's worked so far still work with maths teachers, younger students, or less enthusiastic colleagues? But, as we get nearer a solution, we should see less adaptation with each cycle of iteration. When we reach a solution, our goal shifts from experimentation to scaling: getting the solution working across the school. This no longer requires PDIA. Instead, we can draw on ideas from other chapters: designing effective training and coaching (Chapters 2 and 3), building new habits (Chapter 4) and monitoring progress (Chapter 7). The PDIA process will have built a motivated and effective team. Our work will have revealed other challenges, or we may assess need again (using Chapter 5). We can refocus the team on a new challenge.

Effective leaders maintain the PDIA cycle, increase its impact, and scale the solution across the school.

Action 6) Maintain the PDIA cycle. Try bigger actions, add participants, and maintain support. When you reach a solution, scale it across the school. Then, apply PDIA to the next challenge.

Case study

Claire Couves led teaching and learning at Reach Academy Feltham. Here, she describes her application of PDIA. Her goals are to improve teaching and learning, increase its profile, and encourage senior leaders to complete more observations. This account comes partway through the year: she describes what she has achieved so far - increasing senior leaders' observations, and their focus on teaching and learning - and exemplifies the process of iteration, as she moves on to working with middle leaders.

My goal in the last term was to raise the profile of high-quality teaching and learning in the school and encourage leaders to see this as a key lever for school improvement. Initially I started by encouraging senior leaders to do three weekly drop-ins which I tracked on a central spreadsheet. I asked them to write "What went well" and "Even better if" into the spreadsheet, which they could then use as a proforma for feedback. At the beginning of the cycle the uptake was low, with a team of 5 SLT (Senior Leadership Team) averaging around 7-8 drop-ins a week, the majority of which were me. So I decided to introduce some strategies to increase these drop-ins.

Increasing SLT drop-ins

In order to build this new habit in senior staff, I wanted to make it as easy as possible for them, so I removed the need to make certain decisions, such as who to see, while maintaining the flexibility of when. I started directing staff to specific teachers, I chose these primarily based on teachers who had not yet been seen by SLT and our new staff, I emailed these out and put them in the SLT briefing to remind teachers. Although initially resistant to being directed in this way, a week later it was clear from the increase in drop-ins that this was useful. To further increase the motivation to complete drop-ins I asked for feedback from drop-ins to be a part of the standing agenda of our weekly meetings. SLT had to provide feedback on the drop-ins that they had seen and the action they had taken as a result. This raised accountability and made senior staff feel like they had greater clarity on the quality of teaching in the school. Discussing the drop-ins also helped us to reflect on the core habits and norm on what we were looking for in terms of implementation. This made senior staff feel more confident in the decisions they were making and the feedback they were giving. Finally, I decided to add a table summarising the number of drop-ins per week in the SLT briefing. This gave rise to healthy competition and significantly raised the number of drop-ins in future weeks.

Supporting and celebrating staff

Having increased the number of drop-ins, we had a much better understanding as to the quality of teaching, this meant that we could have productive conversations in SLT meetings about staff members who we might need to support. We gave drop-ins a RAG(E) (Red, Amber, Green, Exemplary) rating. This was not shared with staff nor is it in any way related to our performance management system, but helped to facilitate a productive conversation between senior staff. From these discussions we identified three members of staff who needed additional support. For two of these we increased the number of coaching sessions and we introduced co-planning for the third. Having had regular drop-ins allowed us to identify and support these members of staff early and in a way that did not feel punitive. RAG(E)ing the drop-ins also allowed us to identify and celebrate some of our exemplary teachers. As often happens to great teachers they had not been observed by anyone except their coach for some time and the fresh perspective and additional praise was motivating in a very difficult term. Raising the number of SLT drop-ins increased the amount of feedback teachers received on a weekly basis, showing that this was a priority for SLT this year. As drop-ins primarily focused on our Continuing Professional Development (CPD) focus it also drew greater attention to the fortnightly action step.

Next steps – empowering MLT (middle leadership team)

Next, I would like to focus on empowering MLT to raise standards of teaching. We recently conducted a CPD review, and while the feedback was generally positive, I identified two main areas for improvement:

- Increasing the impact of culture CPD.
- Increased time devoted to subject knowledge/translating CPD into subjects.

Culture CPD

During this cycle, we ran culture CPD in morning briefings. Due to time constraints this proved very difficult to manage and thus did not get the buy-in we had hoped for from staff. There was also not sufficient time for staff to practise in a meaningful way. Going forward I would like to empower the culture team to run CPD at the beginning of their phase (age group team) meetings, I think that this will give these techniques the time and status that they deserve. To facilitate this, I am going to work with the phase 3 and 4 (11-16 year-olds) culture leads to develop their "curriculum" and run some MLT training for heads of year/phase before implementation.

Developing pedagogical content knowledge

In the survey, staff also identified that they would like more time to focus on their subject in CPD. In the last year we have made the transition to including a CPD review in department time. In different departments this has taken too long or has just not been included, the main push back being the time required. This term I would like to bring department leads together to think about the best use of this time and how they can develop subject knowledge within their department. Empowering middle leaders to drive teaching and learning will increase the impact that we are able to have across the school.

Barriers

I think the main barriers that I will face are curriculum directors and heads of phase prioritising time in their meetings for CPD and practice as this is a culture shift and requires staff to engage with admin tasks outside of meeting time. It is also difficult for me to quality assure these meetings as I currently run my own department. To support this, I will ask other members of the SLT to drop-in/be present at meetings so that I can get a better understanding of what is going on and how to further develop curriculum leaders.

Conclusion

Problem-Driven Iterative Adaptation helps us make change work in busy, complicated environments. It balances precise aims with a flexible approach to achieving them. Beginning with a focus, we break down the problem, identify and test multiple ideas, and iterate towards a solution which works for our school. As we make bigger changes, assessing their impact becomes increasingly important. We turn to this in Chapter 7

Next steps

Reflection questions

1) Think about a previous change effort you led (or experienced):
   - To what extent did leaders break down the problem?
   - How were possible actions identified and selected?
   - How achievable were the initial steps?
   - How soon were actions reviewed?
   - How did leaders iterate to ensure success?
2) How might you have improved the process?

Checklist

1) Get to the heart of the problem
   a. Identify a tractable problem
   b. Establish the causes
2) Choose actions
   a. Identify possible actions
   b. Assess the options
3) Plan first steps
4) Act
5) Review progress and identify next steps
6) Keep going; keep building

Getting started

Identify a tractable problem, with a group of colleagues or volunteers.

Success in different roles

You can apply the ideas in this chapter, whatever your role:

- **As a teacher. . .** you can adopt this approach to solve classroom problems: breaking them down, testing small steps, and iterating towards success.
- **As a middle leader. . .** you can use this process to lead change within your team.
- **As a leader working across schools. . .** you can follow these steps to pursue change across the organisation; you can support leaders to use this process within their schools.

7 How can we assess improvement?

Chapter map

Effective assessment identifies what has improved and what is needed next

↓

Meaningful assessment:

- Cuts windows to reveal the improvement process
- Seeks the first broken step
- Chooses simple, rapid checks

↓

Step 1: Create a logic model

↓

Step 2: Cut windows to view the logic model

a) Check training
b) Check teacher change
c) Check impact on learning

↓

Step 3: Draw conclusions and plan next steps

↓

We can then begin another cycle of improvement.

DOI: 10.4324/9781003439622-10

We've looked at a range of teacher development activities, from training and coaching (in Part I) to leading change (in Chapter 6). Now, we turn to a final, crucial question: what impact are our efforts having? Assessing this accurately is vital. First, it allows us to course-correct, refining our sessions and programme to better meet teachers' needs. Second, we can judge whether money and time are being spent well (as can our managers). Finally, knowing the impact of our actions helps us become better leaders of professional development. Effective evaluation is hard. We must pinpoint what should be changing, choose suitable measures, and collect data - without over-burdening our colleagues. In this chapter, we look at how to assess impact accurately and efficiently.

Why does assessing improvements matter?

A few months after Magda takes responsibility for professional development, the head asks her to write a report he can share with governors about the programme's impact. Magda knows that time and money are tight. She wants to prove that professional development is working - to herself, and to the head. She examines student assessment data. She also asks staff to share lesson plans and student work showing how they've applied their learning. After two follow-up emails, she has very few examples, so she sets aside a training session for teachers to collate evidence. This goes down badly: some teachers don't normally write lesson plans; others complain about, "making evidence for evidence's sake". Magda ends up with a wide range of resources, which she tries to understand and annotate. Student assessment data shows no obvious pattern - certainly nothing which demonstrates the impact of her efforts from other changes in the school. She writes this up carefully, but the report is lengthy and vague; she's asked to rewrite it. Magda is frustrated: she believes things have improved, but demonstrating this is hard.

Determined not to repeat this experience, Magda starts the next term with a fresh approach. The professional development focus is better classroom discussions. Magda maps the sequence of events she hopes to see, then identifies simple checks that each has happened. The first session, for example, should show that discussions matter, share strategies, and inspire teachers to try them. Magda plans an exit ticket checking teachers' understanding and enthusiasm for the strategies. Next, she hopes to see teachers using them in lessons and discussions improving. She organises drop-in observations to check. Her new approach helps in two ways. First, Magda has early evidence of successes and barriers. The initial exit ticket shows teachers believe discussions matter, but are unsure how to improve them. She revisits this next session. Second, when the head asks for a report, Magda can quickly assemble one, using existing data to show what has improved.

Obtaining an accurate grasp of the impact of professional development is invaluable. We're more likely to achieve this if we plan our assessment from the outset. This allows us to identify the evidence we need - and easy ways to obtain it - assess what has improved, and plan how to refine our programme.

What makes an assessment of professional development meaningful?

Professional development should improve student learning. But proving it has caused better results is extremely difficult. To distinguish the effect of professional development from other influences on students we would need a randomised trial.[1] (We would have to randomly choose some teachers to get professional development - while an equivalent group of teachers teaching an equivalent group of students gets nothing.) Instead, we assess professional development by checking each step in the process towards better student learning. How can we make this meaningful?

Cut windows to reveal the improvement process

Imagine managing a café. Picture the kitchen as a black box: trays of eggs go in, cooked breakfasts come out. We could inspect meals as they are served. But checking this late in the process reveals problems, not their causes. Better to map out the intended process - unpacking, preparing, and cooking the eggs - then cut windows in the box to reveal each step.[2] We can apply the same approach to professional development. First, we map out the intended process.[3] For example: teachers encounter effective questioning techniques → understand the techniques → practise the techniques → use them in lessons → students think harder → they write better answers.[4] Knowing what should happen at each step, we can cut windows to reveal what *is* happening. Do teachers understand the techniques? Are they practising them? Are they using them? If so, this suggests that professional development is succeeding. If not, we know where the issue is. **A meaningful assessment maps out the intended process and cuts windows to reveal each step.**

Seek the first broken step

We want to find the first broken step in the process. First, because each step depends on the preceding steps. To understand better questioning techniques, teachers must first encounter them. To use the techniques, they must first practise them. So we check and address the steps sequentially (just as we begin upstream when coaching, as we discussed in Chapter 3). Second, because we can check and fix earlier steps more easily. For example, we can check teachers understand questioning techniques with a quick exit ticket. We can address their misconceptions in the next session. Imagine instead checking first whether teachers are using the techniques. We must observe lessons, so checking takes longer. If teachers aren't using the techniques, we may need to address several preceding steps - and we won't know which. Making professional development work better is more valuable than trying to prove it works. **Meaningful assessment shows us how to improve, by finding the first broken step in the process.**

Choose simple, rapid checks

We want enough data to assess progress confidently - but we must collect it pragmatically, treading lightly on our colleagues' time. Certainty would require multiple trained observers visiting many lessons. That's fine for full-time researchers - not for us. Similarly, pursuing certainty by asking teachers to record their thoughts and actions is onerous. We risk intruding disproportionately on their work as we create evidence for its own sake. Instead, we need simple, rapid assessments. We can easily check teachers' understanding, practice, and intentions during training - this is integral to an effective session. We can include the professional development focus in existing measures, targeting questioning in observations and surveys, for example. If a new assessment is unavoidable, it must be quick, easy, and worthwhile for teachers. For example, we could ask departments to share a good question used the previous week. This is quick, revealing their collective understanding in five minutes' discussion and a one-line email. It's also worthwhile: we're encouraging them to discuss pedagogy and collect model work. Finally, choosing simple checks also makes assessing progress easier for us. **Meaningful assessment is simple and rapid for all involved.**

Drawing these ideas together, we can't directly link professional development to improved student results. Instead, we map the sequence of steps that leads to better learning. Then we cut windows - design simple, rapid checks - to reveal each step. For efficiency, we focus on finding the first broken step. Meaningful assessment helps us both check our impact and refine our work.

To assess meaningfully, we map the steps to better learning, then use simple checks to seek broken steps.

How can we assess improvements in teaching?

Step 1 - Create a logic model

We begin by creating a logic model. This shows how the actions we have planned are linked to the changes we hope to see. Once we establish the intended sequence of events, we can decide how to assess them.

What does Step 1 look like?

Munira's focus is helping teachers use exit tickets to check student understanding. She creates a logic model showing the intended process of change. She begins simply: training in exit tickets should encourage teachers to adopt them, which should improve student learning. Next, she breaks this into steps. Through training, teachers should see the value of exit tickets and practise using them. Munira hopes they will then use exit tickets in the classroom, and do so effectively. She records her assumptions too - that teachers will attend training, for example. Munira seeks feedback on the logic model, then begins to choose checks for each step.

A logic model, or theory of change, shows the steps we plan to take and how they are connected to one another, and to our goal. The fundamental logic model of professional development is:

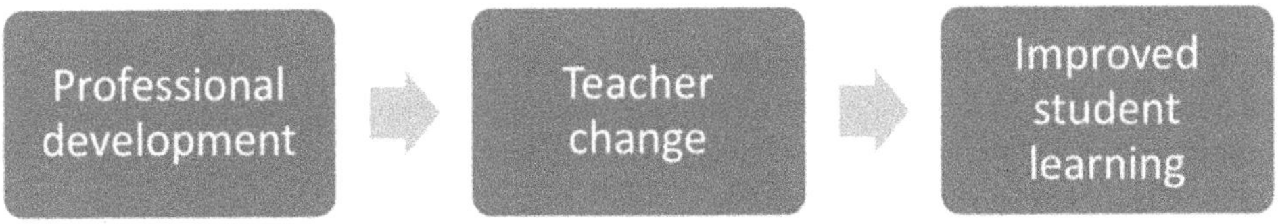

We can replace these generic statements with our goals. For example, Munira writes:

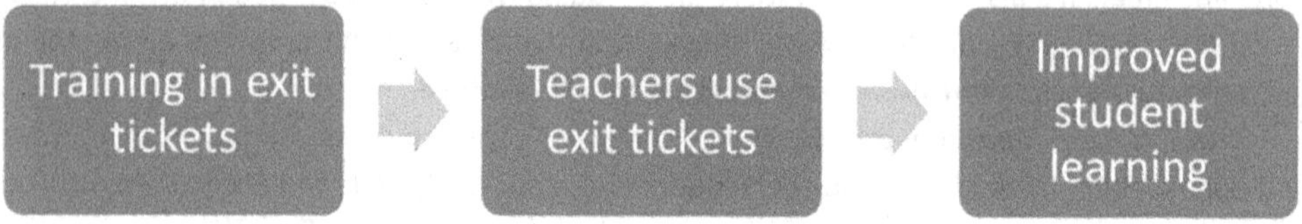

We can now identify the steps under these headings. Specificity is key: the more detailed our model, the less likely we are to miss something crucial. For example, training should encourage teachers to use exit tickets. Specifying how - by changing knowledge, skill, and intention - lets us check each step. This helps us catch issues: perhaps teachers know and can use exit tickets, but don't intend to do so, for example. Munira adds the following steps:

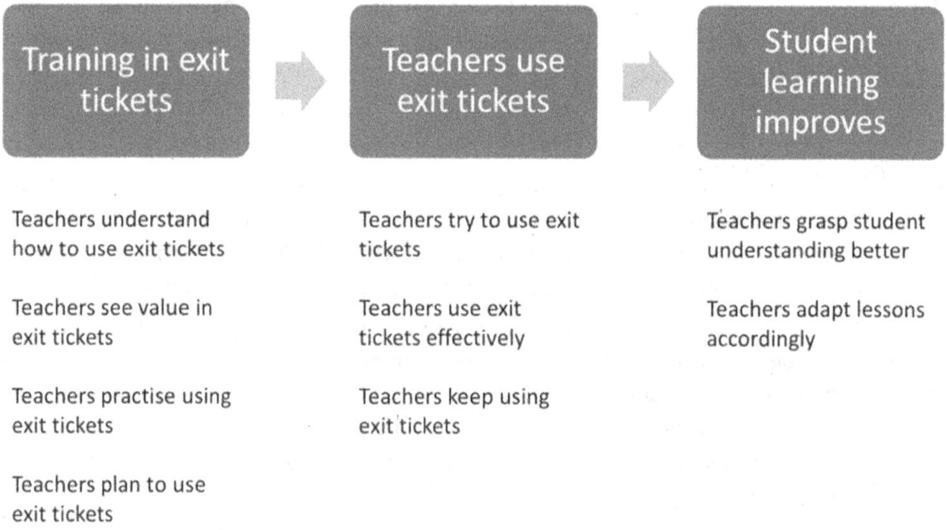

Munira is using training to encourage change. If she were also using coaching, she might include other steps, such as coaches giving feedback on exit tickets.

Finally, we can add our assumptions. These are often left unsaid. But they're crucial, particularly when we're designing or evaluating professional development for the first time. Will training sessions take place as planned, or be derailed by events? Will teachers attend, or cite other pressures? Munira adds several:

Assumptions	Training happens Teachers attend training	Teachers have time to plan exit tickets Leaders support teachers to change	Exit tickets capture student learning Teachers respond to exit tickets

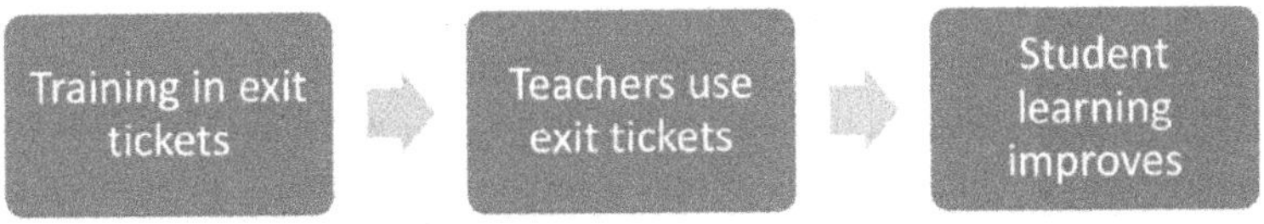

Teachers understand how to use exit tickets	Teachers try to use exit tickets	Teachers grasp student understanding better
Teachers see value in exit tickets	Teachers use exit tickets effectively	Teachers adapt lessons accordingly
Teachers practise using exit tickets	Teachers keep using exit tickets	
Teachers plan to use exit tickets		

Having designed a logic model, we can seek feedback on it. We could also review our professional development plan to ensure there is support in place for each step. In Step 2, we will look at ways to check the logic model is working.

Effective evaluation begins with a logic model which clarifies the intended sequence of events.

Action 1) Create a logic model. Specify every step required for professional development to improve student learning. Add your assumptions.

Assumptions	• • •	• • •	• • •

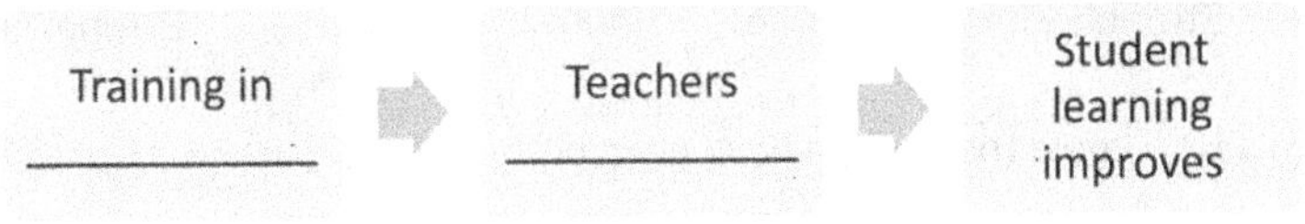

•	•	•
•	•	•
•	•	•

Step 2 - Cut windows to view the logic model

We have a logic model: the series of actions we hope will happen. Those actions are hidden in a black box. In Step 2, we cut the windows which will reveal them. Issues can emerge at any stage: teachers may miss key points, struggle to practise new skills, or find classroom application difficult. The more windows we create - the more checks we have on teachers' thinking, actions, and impact - the easier it is to identify and address barriers. The three sub-steps below correspond to the three stages of the logic model. In Step 2a, we'll check whether training is working as intended. In Step 2b, we'll look at how teachers are changing. In Step 2c, we'll examine the impact on students. Throughout, we'll choose checks which are simple, rapid, and revealing.

What does Step 2 look like?

Munira reviews her logic model for teachers adopting exit tickets. First, she looks at training. She hopes teachers will value, understand, and plan to use exit tickets. Munira designs an end-of-session check (itself an exit ticket) to test this and gain teachers' feedback. She also plans to monitor practice during the session.

Munira's exit ticket.

1) I believe exit tickets are valuable
Strongly agree   Agree   Neutral   Disagree   Strongly disagree

2) It's crucial that exit tickets:
   a) Come at the end of the lesson
   b) Are marked
   c) Are on a separate slip of paper
   d) Capture students' understanding of the lesson's key point

3) For an upcoming lesson, please write the objective and the exit ticket question you will use.

4) The session was useful.
Strongly agree   Agree   Neutral   Disagree   Strongly disagree

5) How could the session have been better?

Next, Munira looks at how teachers are changing. Asking them to submit exit tickets from their lessons would reveal who's doing what, but she dismisses this as onerous. Instead, she asks senior leaders to focus regular observations on the end of lessons. Do they see exit tickets? Can they share good examples and issues? Munira also asks each department to submit an exemplar "exit ticket of the week" and say what teachers learned from it. Once teachers are using exit tickets, leaders will switch to observing the start of lessons. They'll look at how teachers respond to exit tickets and check student understanding of recent lessons. Munira reviews her logic model. Through exit tickets, observing practice, visiting lessons, and asking departments to share examples, she has created simple checks to assess whether the model is working.

Step 2a - Check training

Effective training promotes insight, motivates change, teaches techniques, and embeds practice (as we discussed in Chapter 2). Our checks, during and after the session, should reveal whether we're achieving these four purposes.

ASSESSING INSIGHT

Have teachers grasped the learning principles on which our training builds? The tools we use to check students' understanding in lessons can help us find out. Teachers' responses during discussion offer clues: "This could help with Year 9", or, "I'm not sure how this fits my subject", for example. More powerfully, we can prepare ways to check all colleagues' understanding. One option is an exit ticket at the end of the session. In a session on forgetting and retrieval, we might ask, "Why do students forget what they learn?" or, "How can we help students remember new ideas?" During the session, we can assess understanding with a hinge question, in which answer choices are designed to elicit likely misconceptions.[5] We might check whether teachers understand the process of forgetting by asking:

If students have been introduced to a new idea today, retrieval quizzing will be most useful...

a) Every lesson for the next fortnight.
b) In one week, one month, and six months.
c) In one month and six months.[6]

The Learning Curriculum (discussed in Chapter 1) offers more questions like this - they can be used during a session, as an exit ticket, or after a sequence of sessions. Has the session helped teachers to see the world in a new way? Assessing this is far harder, but we can ask - "How did this session change how you see memory?" Together, these checks reveal whether teachers understand the ideas behind our professional development focus.

ASSESSING MOTIVATION

Motivation is harder to assess. Teachers' questions, body language, and attentiveness give us a sense of their enthusiasm. We may learn something by asking what value they see in an idea or technique. During the session, we could invite a show of hands to represent degrees of enthusiasm, for example; the doubts teachers express can prompt useful discussion. This only works, however, once we have built enough trust to elicit colleagues' true beliefs. Anonymous exit tickets asking similar questions - "How valuable do you think this technique is?" or, "How motivated are you to use this approach?" - may give us more honest answers. Our understanding of teachers' motivation will always be imperfect. But it's always worth asking: the more we know about colleagues' concerns, the better we can address them.

ASSESSING SKILLS

We can assess how well teachers apply the session's target skill through planned checks, observing practice, and exit tickets. A quick check for application is a good start. Looking at retrieval questions, for example, we could name a topic and ask teachers to suggest questions - or suggest questions and ask teachers to choose the most promising. (Focusing the check - instead of letting teachers pick any topic - makes assessment easier: we know what kind of responses to look for.) Asking for a non-example offers further evidence teachers have grasped the skill: "How might a teacher's questions differ if they were *less* worried about promoting retrieval?"

Next, we can observe teachers' preparation for practice, and practice, seeking qualitative and quantitative evidence (as we discussed in Chapter 2). For example, how many teachers have successfully planned retrieval questions? What are their questions' strengths? (Observing practice also reveals teachers' insights and motivation.) Finally, we can check all colleagues' application of the skill with an exit ticket. For example, we might ask teachers to respond to a prompt - "What retrieval questions would you ask in this scenario?" - or invite them to share the questions they have planned. Planned checks, observing practice, and exit tickets allow us to assess teachers' mastery of the target skill.

CHECKING READINESS TO ACT

The final aspect of effective training is embedding change into teaching. We can't assess this during the session - but we can check whether teachers are ready to act. Action is more likely if they have clear intentions, a detailed plan, and have prepared the necessary lesson resources. In our exit ticket, we could ask teachers to describe their next steps, say when they plan to use the target skill, or share their resources. We will assess their changing practice in Step 2b.

Teachers may worry initially about being caught out by these checks. We can mitigate their concerns by:

- Analogising to the classroom: like teachers, we must check what has been learned.
- Framing checks as ways to improve training: "The exit ticket will help me plan our next session."
- Using training activities to check teachers' understanding. For example, if we are developing subject knowledge, we can give teachers exam questions and ask them to predict student misconceptions. This is a useful activity - and it may reveal gaps in their knowledge.
- Offering anonymity - for example, on exit tickets and feedback forms.

Effective evaluation assesses whether training is promoting insight, motivating action, teaching techniques, and preparing teachers to act.

Our focus is assessing how training has helped teachers improve, but it's also worth checking their perceptions. Not to, "make it look as if your improvement project has worked",[7] but to identify how we can improve, by establishing whether the session seemed helpful, the focus made sense, and the logistics worked.[8] On the exit ticket, we can invite teachers to rate the session, say what went well, and suggest improvements.

Action 2a) Plan to check - during and after the session - teachers' understanding of the underlying principles, motivation to change, mastery of techniques, and readiness to act. Ask how the session could be improved.

Step 2b - Check teacher change

Next, we need a window revealing whether teachers' classroom practice is changing. Our task seems obvious: observe teaching, or collect evidence of it. But there are two caveats. First, we need simple, light-touch checks. Teachers and observers - peers, coaches, leaders - are busy. They will not welcome time-consuming requests or complicated observation forms. Second, we should plan how to collate and analyse the data in advance. We don't want to find ourselves reviewing pages of irrelevant observation notes, for example.

We can check teacher change using focused observations. (We may first need to encourage colleagues to do more observations - Claire Couves's case study in Chapter 6 offers valuable guidance.) Just as an exit ticket targets the lesson's key idea, observations should target the professional development goal. Imagine leaders are spending an hour a week visiting lessons and emailing teachers feedback. We could review all that feedback. But we may learn nothing about the target skill - we are not using the observations well. Instead, we want to focus our efforts. This means ensuring observers know the target skill, know what it looks like, seek it in lessons, and report what they find. For example, Munira asks leaders to observe the end of lessons, look for exit tickets, and share strong examples and concerns. This approach has three advantages. First, we channel existing activity towards our goal, rather than creating more work. Second, we reinforce the focus for *observers*, ensuring they understand, look for, and encourage it. Finally, we can check far more teaching than we could manage alone.

Effective evaluation focuses observations on the professional development goal.

We can also seek artefacts showing how teachers are changing. We could ask them to submit lesson plans or resources. But, as we discussed earlier in the chapter, we want to avoid creating this kind of task. Instead, we can use planned collaboration time (meetings and training sessions) to review practice: this should be intrinsically useful, and should produce artefacts which illustrate what's changing. For example, Munira asks middle leaders to let teachers share and refine the exit tickets they have planned for the coming week. This approach has a few advantages. First, these windows reveal the teacher's thinking, planning, and decision-making - things which are hard to discern through observation. Second, it's less labour-intensive: no additional observations; no timetable implications. Third, it reinforces training, by reminding teachers of the goal and encouraging learning from the colleagues who can best help them improve (since they teach the same lessons). We can then ask middle leaders for a summary of what's working, and where support is needed - Munira asks for an "exit ticket of the week".

Effective evaluation uses meetings to elicit evidence.

Action 2b) Check how teachers' practice is changing, using focused observations and/or planned time for collaboration.

Step 2c - Check impact on learning

Better teaching should lead to better learning. But proving professional development has improved exam results is almost impossible. So many factors influence students' performance: how could we isolate the role of professional development? We have the same challenge with internal tests - and they're less reliable, since we rarely standardise their administration and marking.[9] Moreover, learning enough to improve an entire grade takes time. Even if we knew improvements were attributable to professional development, we might wait two or three years to discern an unambiguous impact on grades. We want better results, but results are of little help in assessing the impact of professional development.

We can, however, seek evidence that changing teaching has had an immediate impact on learning.[10] We aimed to improve something specific in the classroom. Has it changed? If we focused on classroom management, are students more attentive? If we worked on explanations, is student understanding better? We can find out by observing lessons, speaking to students, and reviewing their work. Once teachers are using exit tickets regularly, Munira asks leaders to visit lessons as they begin, checking how well students understand *previous* lessons. Had training focused on behavioural reminders, observers would have looked at student focus. We could also use surveys to check students' perceptions of the classroom environment or the clarity of explanations, for example. (We can look at broader impact too: do teachers value training more? Do students seem happier?) If we can keep achieving these smaller changes - greater attention, more effort, better understanding - improved results will follow. If the previous steps of the logic model are working, and we see an impact on learning, professional development is succeeding.

Effective evaluation focuses most on the immediate impact of the specific changes teachers have made.

Action 2c) Check whether your immediate goals for student learning are being achieved.

Step 3 - Draw conclusions and plan next steps

Having created a logic model and checked progress against it, we can now draw conclusions, report what has changed, and plan next steps. This will lead us back to previous chapters, as we look to refine training, improve coaching, and replan professional development.

What does Step 3 look like?

Munira regularly examines the evidence she is collecting, seeking to discern what is changing. Reviewing it with colleagues challenges her thinking, so each month, she presents her findings to the leadership team. Initially, this helps her identify gaps in training. For example, some teachers form misconceptions about when to use exit tickets. Munira redesigns the next session to revisit this, and rechecks teachers' understanding. Observations show teachers are increasingly using exit tickets, and suggest student understanding may be improving. Leaders challenge her to identify who is struggling to use exit tickets, and find out why. Munira revisits the data, and asks fresh questions. She finds that teachers in the Humanities department are particularly sceptical. Moreover, she had assumed they would have time to plan exit tickets. This proves false. With the head of department, she plans a session for their team meeting; together, they allay teachers' concerns, adapt the strategy to suit their needs, and set aside time to plan future exit tickets. As term ends, Munira produces her final report. She concludes the school is ready for a new focus; she will reinforce the habit of using exit tickets by revisiting them next term.

First, we stick the data together, trying to understand what is happening, and why. Sometimes this is obvious: we may find many teachers express the same misconception during a session, for example. But, having painstakingly designed the professional development programme, we may struggle to spot its flaws. Collectively reviewing the evidence is a powerful antidote. It's worth organising a regular slot in which we share our findings. Creating a report - even just a few slides - spells out our thinking and helps others identify gaps. (It can also be used to share progress with our superiors.) We can then invite critique, from leaders, the teaching and learning team, or colleagues in other schools. This may pose new questions. If classroom practice isn't changing, for example, why not? We can return to our logic model and seek new evidence to establish what's really happening.

This allows us to refine the professional development programme. Initially, we might revisit ideas, replan sessions, and offer further support. For example, Munira planned training to tackle misconceptions about when to use exit tickets, and created a bespoke session for the department which was struggling with them. Longer-term, we may reconsider every aspect of the programme. Did we choose the right focus? Were the training sessions sufficient? Are we doing too much too fast? What further support do teachers need to change classroom practice? With our new experience in mind, we can return to previous chapters and rethink our approach. (Often, we realise we have tried to do too much - we'll discuss this in Chapter 8.) Being transparent about what we're learning with teachers should increase their trust in the process - and their understanding of the own learning. Evaluation makes possible a continually improving professional development programme.

Effective evaluation reviews progress to refine the programme.

Action 3) Create a report and invite colleagues to critique it. Make short-term tweaks to address immediate issues, and longer-term refinements to the professional development programme.

Case study

Claire Couves led teaching and learning at Reach Academy Feltham. In the case study in Chapter 6, she described her improvement efforts. Here, we revisit part of that account, and add to it, seeing how she collected and evaluated data.

Initially I started by encouraging senior leaders to do three weekly drop-ins, which I tracked on a central spreadsheet. I asked them to write "What went well" and "Even better ifs" into the spreadsheet which they could then use as a proforma for feedback. At the beginning of the cycle the uptake was low, with a team of five senior leaders averaging around 7-8 drop-ins a week, the majority of which were me.

In order to build this new habit in senior staff I wanted to make it as easy as possible for them so I removed the need to make certain decisions, such as who to see while maintaining the flexibility of when. I started directing staff to specific teachers. I chose these primarily based on teachers who had not yet been seen by leaders and our new staff. I emailed these out and put them in the leadership briefing to remind teachers. Although initially resistant to being directed in this way, a week later, it was clear from the increase in drop-ins that this was useful. To further increase the motivation to complete drop-ins I asked for feedback from drop-ins to be a part of the standing agenda of our weekly meetings. Senior leaders had to feedback on the drop-ins that they had seen and the action they had taken as a result. This raised accountability and made senior staff feel like they had greater clarity on the quality of teaching in the school. Discussing the drop-ins also helped us to reflect on the core habits and norm on what we were looking for in terms of implementation.

Once senior staff felt confident in their decisions and the habit of drop-ins was ingrained I decided to make them more strategic. We are now able, as a senior team, to see and feedback to every teacher every fortnight. This means that teachers are getting much more regular feedback on their teaching. Teachers have really responded well to this and have praised leaders for their presence in classrooms. To increase our ability to think strategically about these drop-ins we also invested in software called 'SISRA observe'. On SISRA we are able to track the drop-ins and intervene swiftly when members of staff need additional support. Having started using SISRA we are now consistently having productive conversations about improving the quality of teaching on a weekly basis at senior leadership team meetings.

Conclusion

We began, in Chapter 1, by setting learning principles; we have pursued them through training, coaching, and supporting change; we have built a professional development programme. Assessing what has improved completes this cycle of action. Evaluating professional development sounds complicated, but it's no different to what we do with every class we teach: check what has been learned, and adapt accordingly. In the final chapter, we address how we can improve as teacher educators.

Next steps

Reflection questions

1) Think about a previous professional development effort.
   - What was the logic model of improvement?
   - How did leaders:
     - o Check training?
     - o Check teachers were changing?
     - o Check the impact on learning?
   - What conclusions and adaptations did leaders make?
2) How might the process have been improved?

Checklist

1) Create a logic model
2) Cut windows to view the logic model
   a. Check training
   b. Check teacher change
   c. Check impact on learning
3) Draw conclusions and plan next steps

Getting started

Design a logic model. Then identify one element of it which you want to understand better. Assess it and discuss your findings with leaders or colleagues.

Success in different roles

You can apply the ideas in this chapter, whatever your role:

- **As a teacher. . .** you can assess your own improvement - preferably with the help of a colleague - and identify what further training or support you might want.
- **As a middle leader. . .** you can assess the impact of training you lead. You can also assess how schoolwide training is affecting your team, and what support or training they need.
- **As a leader working across schools. . .** you can follow these steps to assess professional development in and across your schools; you can support leaders to use this approach in their schools.

8 How can we improve as teacher educators?

We've examined a cycle of steps to plan, deliver, and evaluate teacher professional development. This chapter addresses important questions which don't easily fit within this structure. Some are relevant to every chapter, such as how to make time, build alignment, and work with heads of department. Others are broader questions we'll consider often, like how we can improve and how our perspectives might change. They are:

a) What are the components of an effective professional development programme?
b) How do professional development programmes evolve?
c) How can we make time for professional development?
d) How can we build alignment?
e) How can we help heads of department to improve teaching?
f) What are the components of an effective professional development programme across a group of schools?
g) How might our perspective change?
h) How can we keep improving?
i) How can we gauge our programme?

DOI: 10.4324/9781003439622-11

a) What are the components of an effective professional development programme?

- **Effective professional development programmes have multiple components, including core sessions, coaching, support for leaders and new teachers, subject-specific elements, and a pilot group**
- **We want a programme which is coherent and tailors support to teachers' needs**

We've discussed how to run professional development: how to choose a focus, lead training, and assess progress. We've said less about who to work with when. This is intentional: the principles of training are the same whether we're working with new teachers, departments, or the whole school. We'll now look at the components of an effective programme. What might we expect to see in a school with a mature programme? What might we establish, given a blank slate?

Core sessions

Core sessions are the training - standalone days and across the year - attended by most or all teachers. Using deliberate practice, they reinforce the school's teaching and learning principles (developed in Chapter 1) and target the current focus for improvement (chosen in Chapter 5). Since they include teachers of diverse experience and specialisms, they are fairly generic. This may be leavened by offering a range of models, and by inviting teachers to practise in subject or experience groups.

Coaching and observations

To make training stick, teachers need individual feedback, support, and encouragement. Ideally, everyone would receive coaching. If time and capacity prevent this, we might focus on new and struggling teachers. (The more teachers we can coach, the better, and the more accepted coaching becomes.) Where coaching is limited, regular drop-in observations are an invaluable alternative: they tell leaders what's happening in classrooms, and give teachers feedback on their progress.

Support for new teachers

Most schools offer additional support to teachers who are new to the school or profession (alongside the training to which early career teachers are entitled). This often means interspersing additional training between core sessions. We can use this to introduce the school's teaching and learning principles, share expectations and habits, and check new teachers' progress.

Subject-specific elements

Necessarily, much schoolwide professional development is generic. But opportunities for subject- and phase-specific learning and collaboration are vital. We can begin by inviting colleagues to plan and practise in departments (or year teams) during training. Similarly, we can arrange for coaches to observe their immediate colleagues. We might also establish subject-specific sessions (usually focused on the school's professional development priority), helping middle leaders run them effectively (we discuss this in Section 8e).

A pilot group

A small group of volunteers, meeting to read research and try new things, is invaluable. All new ideas have teething problems; experimentation and iteration make them more likely to work (as we discussed in Chapter 6). With a pilot group, we can test and refine the changes we hope to introduce in a few months' time. This means we have teachers ready to model and advocate change when we launch it schoolwide. There are two other benefits. First, we are offering challenging professional development to our most promising teachers. Second, the pilot group is a recruitment pipeline, helping us find the enthusiasts who will form the teaching and learning team.

A teaching and learning team

A new teacher educator usually leads most of the training. Longer-term, however, we want to share this responsibility with colleagues. Hearing from other presenters offers staff fresh insights. More importantly, we're building a team of experts who can lead sessions, coach teachers, and - one day - replace us. Some of this can be done by the pilot group. But we may also recruit colleagues into more formal roles offering additional time or pay. Jen Calvert, deputy head at Ashcroft Academy, recruited a team of "TLR3s".[1] They applied and interviewed for the role, led training, and received additional pay. Creating a team helps us - and builds lasting expertise and support to keep improving teaching.

Developing leaders

Middle and senior leaders play a crucial role in shaping and advancing the professional development programme. They need to understand and model effective practice, and support teacher improvement. But many leaders are experts in management or pastoral care - not pedagogy. We need to achieve a shared understanding of effective teaching (the principles developed in Chapter 1) and their role in promoting it (for example, through coaching). This means making time to develop leaders' expertise and skills. Some teacher educators build knowledge by discussing key readings in leadership team meetings. We can seek leaders' understanding and support by introducing, modelling, and practising changes with them first. We can then enlist their help: planning what to look for in observations, for example, and how to reinforce key ideas through line management. (We discuss pursuing alignment in more detail in Section 8d.)

Achieving coherence

These components should form a symphony, not a cacophony of clashing ideas. We achieve coherence by grounding each component in our learning principles and focusing it on our professional development priority. An idea mentioned once in training, then contradicted in another session, is soon forgotten. It will stick if teachers encounter it, revisit it, adapt it with their team, and get feedback on its application. Establishing all these components takes time. But while there are many sessions, they draw on one body of knowledge and preparation. A reading we find for our pilot group can also be used with leaders. A core session can be simplified for new teachers and tweaked for middle leaders. A range of coherent components ensures teachers improve, by reiterating key ideas while offering tailored support.

b) How do professional development programmes evolve?

As professional development programmes evolve, we often see that:

- **They cover less, in more detail**
- **The teacher educator spends less time leading training, more time helping others to do so**
- **More professional development takes place in teams and departments**

Programmes cover less, in more detail

Most teacher educators' first professional development plans are ambitious. Focusing on responsive teaching, we might cover lesson planning in week one, modelling in week two, and exit tickets in week three. Teachers cannot master strategies that fast. Modelling alone includes many sub-skills: choosing models, introducing them, helping students spot and apply their features. Turning these skills into successful habits takes time. We could spend a term on what we planned to cover in a session. As our programme evolves, we often spend more time doing fewer things in greater depth.

We lead less training, and spend more time helping others to lead training

We often inherit a limited professional development programme. This means there are few colleagues on whose expertise we can draw. Initially, we must plan the programme, lead sessions, and follow up. Short term, this is unavoidable; long term, it's undesirable and unsustainable. As colleagues' expertise grows and we gain support (by developing a pilot group, team, and leaders, as we discussed in Section 8a), we can increasingly hand control to them. We'll spend less time training teachers - and more time helping others plan, lead, and review their own training.

More professional development takes place in teams and departments

Through the same dynamic, we can move towards more professional development in teams. Initially - with a limited programme and few colleagues who can help - we will lead most training; necessarily, it will be whole school. But eventually, more training should take place in subject or year teams. (What makes a technique effective depends on what we are teaching; to ask better questions about fractions, I'd want help from a maths teacher.) This is only possible once middle leaders are ready to guide improvement: to focus time on teaching, manage practice, and support colleagues to change. As we help leaders become better teacher educators, they can increasingly lead professional development for their teams. (We discuss how to support them in Section 8e.)

c) How can we make time for professional development?

- **Find and create time**
- **Ensure professional development time is used for improvement**

Find and create time

We want as much time as possible for professional development. (It's easier to get time if leaders share our goals; we'll discuss this in Section 8d.) This time is more valuable if it's broken up. A single training day is soon forgotten. Converting an eight-hour day into hour-long sessions over eight weeks lets teachers test, revisit, and refine new ideas - making improvement more likely.

Our initial options (the examples are English, the principles universal) include:[2]

- Training days: we can spread these across the year, and ensure they focus on improving teaching, not administration and announcements.
- Breaking up training days, allowing us to offer sessions most weeks.
- Voluntary sessions at lunchtime or after school: we can meet the pilot group and teaching and learning team outside working hours.

We can make more time by:

- Using briefings to remind teachers of our current focus, share models, and highlight success.
- Using department, team, and leadership meetings for tailored training.
- Redesigning the school day. During some morning assemblies at Dixon's Trinity Academy, for example, students do retrieval practice in the hall, supervised by leaders - freeing half an hour for teachers to practise.

To make time for coaching, we can:

- Ask coaches to schedule a regular feedback meeting with each coachee. This encourages the coach to observe regularly, and avoids delayed feedback after the observation.
- Alternatively, schedule a single meeting for all coaches to feed back to their coachees (as in the case study in Chapter 3). This ensures the meeting happens, reinforces a culture of practice, and makes monitoring easier.

Ensure professional development time is used for improvement

Professional development time is always at risk. Teachers are distracted by incidents, calls, and marking. Leaders like to make announcements and address other priorities. We must keep it sacrosanct. Refusing colleagues time to make announcements feels hard. But improving teaching is hard if sessions always start late. (Scheduling realistically helps: many schools skip sessions when teachers are marking exams, for example.) When colleagues are leading sessions, it's worth checking they're using time well too. We must ensure professional development time is used for improvement.

d) How can we build alignment?

1) **Alignment won't build itself**
2) **Pursue collective understanding**
3) **Surface and address conflicting ideas**
4) **Agree next steps, and follow up**

Imagine a teacher in a school where leaders aren't aligned. Training might focus on assessment, while department meetings discuss planning. One observer suggests giving clearer instructions; the next says this diminishes student responsibility. The teacher's limited attention is pulled in conflicting directions. They plan lessons around what observers look for - not what students need. Professional development becomes noise, to be ignored where possible, paid lip-service where necessary.

We can avoid this by building alignment. This means having shared goals, a shared understanding of how to pursue them - and acting accordingly. We have touched on this when agreeing principles of learning (Chapter 1) and a focus (Chapter 5). Here, we examine how to ensure colleagues subscribe to the professional development programme. We can use these steps to enlist the support of senior leaders - they also apply when working with a coaching team, heads of department, or colleagues across a group of schools.

1) Alignment won't build itself

Broaching alignment means asking colleagues to reconsider what they believe about teaching. This may feel awkward. But we cannot pursue alignment without raising questions like, "What is effective teaching? What do our students most need? How should we make that happen?" It's up to us to initiate this. This means securing time, launching discussions, and planning how they may develop. An experienced deputy head once realised that, in a decade on the leadership team, they had never discussed what kind of teaching they wanted. The first step towards alignment is beginning that conversation.

2) Pursue shared understanding

We want to achieve shared understanding of three issues: what is, what could be, and the path there.

- What is: we can establish what's happening in classrooms, and what our students and teachers need, by discussing existing data, or inviting colleagues to visit lessons and review books.
- What could be: we can examine principles and practices of effective teaching, through reading, watching lessons, and visiting other schools.
- The path there: we can make plans, agree colleagues' roles, and prepare them to act - as observers, presenters, and line managers, for example.

(Chapter 5 discusses ways to examine the first two bullet points more fully.)

3) Surface and address conflicting ideas

Achieving shared understanding is difficult. Some colleagues will disagree about elements of what is, what could be, or the path there. It's tempting to let these disagreements lie. But we cannot achieve alignment if we do. Colleagues who don't believe in the programme will undermine it, through inaction or contradiction. We must surface and address conflicting ideas, by:

- Finding out what colleagues believe, through questions and surveys. We can emphasise that we welcome challenge: we want to know what they doubt and to refine our approach.
- Pinpointing areas of confusion or conflict. Moving from abstract to concrete helps enormously here. The abstract is necessarily vague, which poses two risks. One is superficial agreement. We commit to pursuing "responsive teaching": some colleagues anticipate a revolution; others think they're doing it already. The other is unnecessary conflict: we suggest tweaking planning; colleagues believe they must throw out every existing plan. So, when a colleague raises doubts, being more concrete about what they think, and what we mean, can help clarify or overcome disagreement. What, word for word and step by step, do we envisage?
- Addressing conflict. If there is disagreement about:
  - What education should be - we can discuss key texts and visit lessons together to agree what we want for our students.
  - What the focus should be - we can collectively review the evidence informing our choice.
  - What works for their subject (or year group, or teaching style) - we can agree precise changes, which faithfully pursue the focus, and reflect their preferences.

Conflict often derives from an emotional response: understandably, colleagues may be unsure about change. Our goal isn't to win arguments, but to reduce that discomfort, and find enough common ground to allow us to initiate change.

4) Agree next steps, and follow up

We often achieve nodding agreement, but see little change. This may reflect how busy colleagues are. Sometimes, however, we fail to elicit their concerns; we think they will act, they plan to let things slide. We can pursue alignment of action, not just ideas, by:

- Agreeing what colleagues will do: key messages to share, observations to conduct, feedback to offer. (We could practise these to ensure colleagues are prepared.)
- Modelling the actions we expect and reiterating key messages, publicly and privately.
- Tracking actions and offering feedback (the case study in Chapter 6 is a good example).
- Emphasising their role when celebrating success.

e) How can we help heads of department to improve teaching?

Heads of department are key to improving teaching. We must ensure they:

- **Prioritise improving teaching**
- **Lead improvement**
- **Have the time and support they need**

A training session can initiate improvement - can convince a teacher that hinge questions help, for example. They then need support to create, test, and refine these questions in the classroom. In secondary schools, this is usually subject-specific: an effective hinge question in maths differs from one in music. So, at some point, we must devolve the work of putting good ideas into practice - the work of improving teaching - to heads of department. They have two advantages. One is proximity: teaching in the next classroom and working in the department office, they can visit lessons, gauge progress, and offer support. The second is subject-specificity: they can offer the precise feedback teachers need. But a head of department may find the transition to teacher educator tricky. Their promotion often reflects experience and expertise in the subject - not training or coaching. We must give them time and support, and help them to prioritise and plan ways to improve teaching.

1) Prioritise improving teaching

What do heads of department do? Mostly, they teach their own classes - sometimes up to 20 lessons a week. Then they face administrative tasks like exam entries, data analysis, and setting cover. Finally, they manage their former (and often more experienced) peers. Trying to change their teaching may seem presumptuous; it's rarely a priority. Indeed, some heads of department:

- See themselves as peers, ill-placed to assess or improve others' teaching.
- Are passionate and erudite about their subject, but rarely share their expertise.
- Are so busy teaching their own classes that they struggle to observe colleagues.

There's merit in humility, passion for the subject, and teaching well. But a crucial insight helps to reset these priorities. Andy Grove asks, "What is your output as a manager?" - in other words, "What do you achieve as head of department?" He contends that what matters is not meetings and decisions, but the "output" of those under your influence.[3] Translated from business-speak, what heads of department achieve is the teaching students experience *across the department*. We must help them see that, while collegiality and their own classes matter, ensuring all students are succeeding matters more.

When heads of department prioritise improving teaching:

- Their plans and objectives name "improving teaching" as the top priority.
- Their meetings focus on teaching; they challenge colleagues' thinking where necessary.
- They ask for cover to see their team teach regularly.

2) *Lead improvement*

To lead improvement, heads of department must know what teachers' existing practice is like, choose what to improve, and plan how to help:

- To establish what existing practice is like, we want heads of department to observe teaching regularly, and to talk to teachers about their plans, lessons, and students' work. We can encourage lesson visits by organising joint observations (this also builds a shared understanding of effective and existing practice). We can then invite heads of department to share their findings with us.
- We want heads of department to pursue a professional development focus. If we have chosen a schoolwide focus (as we discussed in Chapter 5), we might ask them to tailor it to their subject. If we chose modelling, they might choose lessons to develop models for, or an aspect of modelling to work on: analogy in history; example/non-example in maths. Alternatively, we might ask them to choose a focus for their department, based on existing practice, the school's principles of learning (discussed in Chapter 1) and current priorities.
- Finally, we want heads of department to plan the support they will offer. This will include schoolwide approaches, like coaching. But we particularly want them to plan how they will use their time - department meetings and line management - to pursue the focus. For example, they might lead joint planning (of lessons or resources), collective review (of student work or past lessons), or problem-solving (for teachers to share barriers to using the focus skill).

When heads of department are leading improvement:

- They see their team teach regularly and know how every teacher is doing.
- They have an improvement focus, which connects the school's priorities to the department's needs.
- Every departmental meeting includes work on the focus.

3) *Have time and support*

If heads of department are to do all of this, we must offer them:

- Time: Heads of department are busy. If we also want them to coach, or prepare training, we should allocate time for this - they are more likely to do it, and do it well.
- Knowhow: Most heads of department learn on the job. Having identified what we want them to do - coach, mentor, lead training - we can offer training, guidance, and mentoring in how to do it.
- Support: Alongside the support we offer, we can bring heads of department together to share experiences, ideas, and hacks. Subject networks across schools help too, particularly for heads of small departments.

When heads of department have time and support:

- They are allocated time to work on improving teaching.
- They are trained in how to improve teaching.
- They feel supported to improve teaching.

f) What are the components of an effective professional development programme across a group of schools?

When we work across many schools, our goals are similar, but the challenges are bigger. We can address them by:

- **Building consensus around a core repertoire**
- **Developing a team of teacher educators**
- **Assessing current practice accurately**
- **Prioritising lasting improvement**

Whether we support one school or many, we want:

- Teachers to understand and apply a set of principles;
- Effective training, coaching, and support; and,
- Priorities to be carefully chosen, pursued, and monitored.

But working with many schools poses two additional challenges. The first is scale and distance. Instead of understanding one school and convincing one leadership team, we must understand and convince many. Instead of seeing them every day - building knowledge and trust - we might see them every term. Instead of leading improvement, we rely on others to run training and monitor progress. The second is diversity. We must design a programme which helps schools with established programmes - and schools with almost nothing. How can we overcome these challenges?

1) Build consensus around a core repertoire

A successful programme is founded on a core repertoire of ideas and practices. When we work with many schools, this repertoire may be limited, given how long establishing it can take. Five teaching principles and a couple of training methods (like practice and feedback) might be enough. Principles are a good place to begin. We might invite leaders to make suggestions, give feedback, and debate the final draft - then introduce them to their schools. Reaching agreement around naming and exemplifying the principles will take time. But the process encourages leaders to support their introduction and creates a mechanism for further improvement. Building consensus should mean teachers encounter more coherent principles and professional development practices.

2) Develop teacher educators within schools

We have discussed the value of building a team of teacher educators within the school (in Section 8a). This is even more important when working across schools we can visit only rarely. In each school, we need to work with the current lead teacher educator, and identify promising teachers who will form a teaching and learning team. We can then:

- Secure time for their work, supporting their negotiations with senior leaders;
- Develop their understanding, skill, and sense of mission, by training them as a group, and,
- Support and mentor their work.

Developing a team of teacher educators dramatically increases our ability to lead change at scale. We rely on them to share teaching principles, lead training, and monitor change.

3) Assess current practice accurately

Assessing current practice across schools is crucial, and challenging. Visits and lesson observations give us a sense of what's happening. But our capacity is limited - we need much more data on classroom practice and staff perceptions. To get it, we must do two things. First, establish shared platforms for observations and staff surveys, allowing us to aggregate data easily. Second, train observers (starting with our team of teacher educators) in what to look for in lessons, so that the data is valid and reliable. With accurate knowledge of current practice, we can judge what schools need, and what impact our programme is having.

4) Prioritise lasting improvement

It's tempting to lead improvement in our weakest schools. Running a training session no one else can lead is a great short-term solution. This may even be sustainable, if we work with three or four schools. But longer-term, and at larger scale, this limits our capacity to make lasting improvements. (It also reduces the pressure to develop leaders in that school.) Building a core repertoire and a team of teacher educators strengthens all our schools - and gives us many colleagues ready to support those which are struggling. Firefighting may be necessary. But to improve all our schools we must prioritise building consensus, developing teacher educators, and assessing current practice.

g) How might our perspective change?

We may gain new insights about teacher education, such as:

- **Asking people nicely isn't enough**
- **Teaching teachers is like teaching students**
- **We seek to influence everything which might encourage change**
- **It takes (more) time**

Insights - that working memory is limited, for example - change how teachers see the world (as we discussed in Chapter 2). Teacher educators experience them too. This section shares four important examples. Since explanations rarely convey insights effectively, they are presented as stories.

1) Asking colleagues nicely isn't enough

Clara, the new assistant head, is reporting on her work improving mentoring to the leadership team. It seems successful, but she has struggled to get staff feedback. "I sent review sheets out, and a reminder this week. I've still only had two back. These are adults and professionals - I'm not sure what more I can do."

Richard has been studying a knot in the table. Now he looks up and clears his throat. As the most experienced (and most cynical) person present, all eyes turn to him. "When you give your students homework, do you expect them all to do it?" Clara shakes her head. "Which is why you give reminders, share the homework with parents, and make them catch it up. When you ask people nicely, some of them will do it, and lots won't. Not because they're lazy, although some of them are", Richard chuckles; the head sighs. "But because asking nicely isn't enough. There's too much going on. If I get a request and hear nothing more about it, I'll ignore it". Richard ignores a tut. "If you *really* need those review sheets back, you could send individual reminders, or catch mentors at the end of briefing, or draw a response out of a hat for a prize. If you want something done, you have to make it happen".

Few people, in any walk of life, respond immediately when asked to do something. Teachers are particularly busy. They'll act - if we support, encourage, and remind them. This takes time, so we must carefully choose what we ask them to do.

2) Teaching teachers is like teaching students

After training, Chris asks the teaching and learning team for feedback. "I wondered whether everyone had grasped the key point", Sakshi begins tentatively.

"They said they did, and I saw lots of nods and smiles", Chris offers.

"Absolutely, it felt great. But students nod, even when they don't get it. Or some of them nod, and we miss the confused ones. If it had been a lesson, I'd have wanted an exit ticket".

Chris is unsure. "Do you not think teachers would find it patronising?"

"I can see how they might. I think we can present it in a non-patronising way: it's to see what we need to do next, not to catch them out. We can also emphasise that it's just good practice - when you teach something, you have to check learners have understood".

"Let's try it", Chris agrees.

Whether we're teaching students or teachers, the learning process is identical. We must, for example, link new ideas to prior knowledge, explain them clearly, and check understanding. We can and should apply approaches which work in lessons to our training.

3) We seek to influence everything which might encourage change

Ali is new to leading professional development. He is describing his plan to Jemima, the trust's education lead. "I've got a great training day lined up for October: a keynote on the principles, and several teachers sharing models. Then, in January, we'll revisit the key ideas".

"What will happen between October and January?" Jemima asks.

"I've just focused on the training days". Ali pauses, "But I guess that won't be enough to ensure teachers change, will it?" They discuss options, and Ali promises to come back to her in a few days.

When they meet again, he seems enthused by the possibilities.

There's so much more I can do!" Jemima smiles. "I've planned reminders for every staff briefing. I'm also going to share everything with heads of department, then catch up regularly to discuss progress. I've tweaked our observation proforma to highlight our current focus. That will nudge observers to look for it - and tell me what they're seeing. And I'm launching weekly surgeries so teachers can get help planning."

New to leading professional development, we focus on our most obvious task: planning the training calendar. With time, we seek to influence everything which might encourage change.

4) It takes (more) time

The teaching and learning team are reviewing the term. In the survey, some staff complained training felt rushed. Session exit tickets showed misconceptions about key points; observations found patchy improvement. "We tried to do too much, too fast", Fraser suggests. "I remember why we did it, I was arguing for it. We wanted to cover all the teaching and learning principles in a term, and we didn't want it to feel basic. I think we assumed too much existing knowledge. And that staff would be able to change much more quickly than they actually could."

"What are we going to do?" Manthan asked. "We've planned next term already".

"We can't stick with it, it's not working", Fraser said.

"Fraser's right", Charlotte said reluctantly. "A single session to cover something like feedback isn't enough. We can introduce the key ideas. But we want teachers to understand them, practise, and change how they give feedback - forever. Then the next week, we ask them to do something else! They need more time and help - we can't cover so many topics so quickly. Let's go through the plan for next term and pick out the two most important skills. We'll do half a term on each, and give ourselves time to do each step properly."

We set out ambitiously, assuming we'll cover ground quickly. But learning and change take longer than we expect. Teachers need time and opportunities to work through ideas and their implications. We come to "cover" far less, but in more depth - making teachers more likely to actually improve.

h) How can we keep improving?

We must also lead our own improvement, by:

- **Building a team within school**
- **Visiting other schools**
- **Building a team outside school**
- **Carefully checking the impact of professional development**
- **Reading**

Maths and languages are different, but heads of department can share ways to manage staff and get exam entries done. We are in the scary position of being *the* experts on professional development; we lack immediate peers who can push us to get better. This means we must lead our own improvement.

Build a team within school

We can build a team of teacher educators within the school (as we discussed in Section 8a). They will be our sounding boards, advocates, session leaders - and successors.

Visit other schools

We don't spend enough time in other schools. Visiting another head of teaching and learning should offer new ideas about everything - from formal structures, such as when to do training, to small tweaks to make sessions run better.

Build a team outside school

Better than a single visit is ongoing collaboration with other teacher educators. We face similar challenges - but working in different schools, we can be honest about problems and relationships. Often, this allows them to articulate our issues, and possible solutions, better than we can. Within a group of schools, building a team should be easy. Otherwise, we may want to find a sustained course for teacher educators, in which we spend lots of time working with peers.

Carefully check the impact of professional development

Assessing the impact of professional development is important (as we discussed in Chapter 7). It's particularly important as a way to hold ourselves to account. Sharing progress and what we've learned with colleagues helps us stay focused and keep improving.

Read

The best writing on professional development can be eye-opening. Here are a few suggestions which have transformed my thinking.

- Berliner, D. (2001). *The development of expertise in pedagogy*. American Association of Colleges for Teacher Education.

David Berliner reviews how teachers go from novice to expert. His research suggests experts see differently, and work fluidly and eventually "arationally". He offers suggestions for teacher educators, including specific guidance on how to help novices improve.

- Ericsson, A., & Pool, R. (2016). *Peak: Secrets from the new science of expertise*. Bodley Head.

Anders Ericsson describes the research on expertise and explains what makes deliberate practice special: focus, feedback, and sequencing. Practice is more complicated (and more limited) than he perhaps suggests, but it's a thought-provoking book offering valuable ideas for training design.

- Grossman, P., Compton, C., Igra, D., Ronfeldt, M., Shahan, E., & Williamson, P. W. (2009). Teaching practice: A cross-professional perspective. *Teachers College Record, 111*(9), 2055–2100.

Comparing the preparation of priests, teachers, and clinical psychologists, Pam Grossman and her colleagues identified three key aspects: representations revealing elements of practice, decomposition of that practice into smaller units, and approximations - activities which can be practised by trainees. They also noted that teachers tend to practise planning, rather than interactions like discussion and classroom management. This article offers a theory and structure for using practice in training.

- Kennedy, M. (2016a). Parsing the practice of teaching. *Journal of Teacher Education, 67*(1), 6–17.

To improve teaching, we need a model of what teachers do. Mary Kennedy suggests their actions address five universal challenges, such as managing behaviour and understanding student thinking. Her model helps us understand teacher practice and choose professional development goals.

- Menzes, A., & Maier, A. (2014). *Fast start: Training better teachers faster, with focus, practice and feedback*. The New Teacher Project.

The New Teacher Project found their approach to training new teachers wasn't working. Teachers who don't master basic skills early, never do. They redesigned their programme to focus on a few crucial skills, and to develop them through practice and coaching. Their approach illustrates ways we can help newer teachers improve rapidly.

- Sims, S., Fletcher-Wood, H., O'Mara-Eves, A., Cottingham, S., Stansfield, C., Van Herwegen, J., & Anders, J. (2021). *What are the characteristics of effective teacher professional development? A systematic review and meta-analysis*. Education Endowment Foundation.

In this paper, we developed a theory for why professional development might work and tested how well it explained the success of over 100 professional development programmes. Chapters 2 and 4 draw on these ideas - here you can examine their source.

Finally, my two previous books inform many of the ideas in this book about what effective teaching looks like, and how we can help people to change.

> Fletcher-Wood, H. (2018). *Responsive teaching: Cognitive science and formative assessment in practice*. Routledge.

In this book, I tried to offer a usable summary of the evidence around cognitive science and formative assessment, helping teachers to plan, check understanding, and respond to student needs more easily.

> Fletcher-Wood, H. (2021). *Habits of success: Getting every student learning*. Routledge.

This book addresses the challenges of student behaviour and motivation, applying behavioural science to show how we can help students - and teachers - make lasting changes.

i) How can we gauge our programme?

We've discussed ways to assess improvements in teaching and learning (in Chapter 7). These survey questions are a way to gauge the programme overall. We might use them when we first take on leadership of professional development, then perhaps annually. It reflects the ideas in the rest of the book; I have added notes in italics to explain some of the questions. They need not all be asked at once - even a small selection might give a useful indication of what's working and what's needed.

1) I am...
    a) In my first three years teaching
    b) A classroom teacher
    c) A middle leader
    d) A senior leader

I much prefer to offer respondents anonymity. We could ask other demographic questions, but if we know a teacher's subject, gender, and experience, we can often identify them immediately. The most important dimension affecting their needs is their experience.

Overall impressions

2) The time and resource the school spends on professional development improves teaching.
    a) Strongly disagree
    b) Disagree
    c) Neutral
    d) Agree
    e) Strongly agree

In England, Teacher Tapp found 41% of teachers agreed or strongly agreed, 32% were neutral and 26% disagreed or strongly disagreed.

3) Professional development at the school is part of a coherent programme
    a) Strongly disagree
    b) Disagree
    c) Neutral
    d) Agree
    e) Strongly agree

What does professional development focus on?

4) We get time to improve our... (tick all that apply)
    a) Planning and assessment

  b) Subject knowledge
  c) Understanding of how students learn
  d) Classroom management
  e) We don't get time for any of these
5) I am challenged and supported to improve my. . . (tick all that apply)
  a) Planning and assessment
  b) Subject knowledge
  c) Understanding of how students learn
  d) Classroom management
  e) We don't get time for any of these
6) I use what we learn about ______ in my teaching (tick all that apply).
  a) Planning and assessment
  b) Subject knowledge
  c) Understanding of how students learn
  d) Classroom management.
  e) I don't use any of these
  f) I don't learn about any of these
7) When we learn something about teaching/learning in general (across subject/phase), we get time to apply it to our subject/phase.
  a) Strongly disagree
  b) Disagree
  c) Neutral
  d) Agree
  e) Strongly agree

How does professional development work?

8) The school provides time dedicated to improving our teaching.
  a) Weekly
  b) Fortnightly
  c) Half-termly
  d) Termly
  e) Never
9) There are colleagues I can go and observe who are highly effective teachers.
  a) Strongly disagree
  b) Disagree
  c) Neutral
  d) Agree
  e) Strongly agree
10) When we learn new teaching skills, we practise them outside the classroom before using them inside the classroom.
  a) Never
  b) Occasionally

c) Sometimes
d) Always

11) In the last half-term, I received feedback on my teaching _ times.
12) In the last half-term, I went to see _ colleagues teach (you intended to observe, not to give them a message, ask them something, etc.).
13) I have a current objective to improve my teaching.
    a) Yes
    b) No
    c) Not applicable
15) I will be challenged and supported to meet my objective.
    a) Strongly disagree
    b) Disagree
    c) Neutral
    d) Agree
    e) Strongly agree

The next four questions test the four essential components of professional development discussed in Chapter 2.

16) In the last year, I have come to see teaching/my teaching differently as a result of our professional development programme.
    a) Strongly disagree
    b) Disagree
    c) Neutral
    d) Agree
    e) Strongly agree
17) In the last year, I have set new goals as a result of our professional development programme.
    a) Strongly disagree
    b) Disagree
    c) Neutral
    d) Agree
    e) Strongly agree
18) In the last year, I have gained new skills I can use in the classroom through our professional development programme.
    a) Strongly disagree
    b) Disagree
    c) Neutral
    d) Agree
    e) Strongly agree
19) In the last year, I have made lasting changes to my practice as a result of our professional development programme.
    a) Strongly disagree

b) Disagree
c) Neutral
d) Agree
e) Strongly agree

20) Can you give a specific example of a change you've made due to professional development?
21) In the last year, I have changed my teaching as a result of observation feedback.
    a) Strongly disagree
    b) Disagree
    c) Neutral
    d) Agree
    e) Strongly agree
22) Can you give a specific example of a change you've made due to feedback?
23) The best thing about our professional development programme is. . .
24) Professional development would be better if. . .

Conclusion

I have spent fifteen years studying how best to improve teaching: reading, writing, training, and learning from teacher educators. It has been time well spent – it's a complex, fascinating, valuable task. Complex because we are seeking to influence so many dimensions at once: students' thinking and actions, teachers' thinking and actions, school policies and politics; teaching and learning; habits and interactions. Fascinating, because improving teaching means understanding each of these elements: what are students really thinking? How can teachers plan better? What can we do to gain leaders' support? Valuable, because improving teaching can make students' and teachers' lives better.

I imagine you are on a similar journey. I hope you find the work of improving teaching similarly meaningful and rewarding – and that this book helps you do it better.

DOI: 10.4324/9781003439622-12

Notes

Introduction

1 These statements come from teacher educators I have worked with across a range of contexts, when asked to describe the biggest problem they face currently.
2 See, for example, Slater, H., Davies, N.M., & Burgess, S. (2012). Do teachers matter? Measuring the variation in teacher effectiveness in England. *Oxford Bulletin of Economics and Statistics*, *74*(5), 629–645.
3 Jackson, C.K., Rockoff, J.E., & Staiger, D.O. (2014). Teacher effects and teacher-related policies. *Annual Review of Economics*, 6(1), 801–825.
4 Allen, R., Mian, E., & Sims, S. (2016). *Social inequalities in access to teachers*. Social Market Foundation Commission on Inequality in Education: Briefing 2.
5 Allen et al. (2016).
6 Elmore, R. (1996). Getting to scale with good educational practice. *Harvard Educational Review*, 66(1), 3.
7 Kini, T., & Podolsky, A. (2016). *Does teaching experience increase teacher effectiveness? A review of the research*. Learning Policy Institute. I cite US data here, first, because multiple studies have been conducted; second, because these studies draw on two kinds of data we tend to lack in England: data linking teachers to the learning of the individual students they teach, and external assessments across consecutive years, which show growth in learning.
8 The New Teacher Project (2015). *The mirage: Confronting the hard truth about our quest for teacher development*, 13.
9 Teacher Tapp survey of 7593 teachers, 29 October 2022; 5% strongly agree (that time and resource spent on professional development improves teaching), 36% agree, 32% neutral, 20% disagree, 6% strongly disagree,
10 Teacher Tapp survey of 8883 teachers, 10 September 2023; 18% expected no impact as their important development happens in the classroom; 17% expected to stay the same; 41% expected a slight negative impact; 19% expected a significant negative impact; 5% were unsure.
11 Teacher Tapp survey of 9056 teachers, 24 July 2023: 49% wanted the extra free period; 15% of teachers wanted no cover lessons, 6% a tablet.
12 Teacher Tapp survey of 7593 teachers, 29 October 2022; 68% of headteachers and 59% of senior leaders believe time and resources spent on professional development improves teaching; just 33% of classroom teachers concur.
13 Sims, S., & Fletcher-Wood, H. (2021). Identifying the characteristics of effective teacher professional development: A critical review. *School Effectiveness and School Improvement*, *32*(1), 47–63.
14 Fletcher-Wood, H., & Zuccollo, J. (2020). *The effects of high-quality professional development on teachers and students: A rapid review and meta-analysis*. Education Policy Institute.
15 This arose in at least two programmes. Hanley, P., Böhnke, J., Slavin, B., Elliott, L., & Croudace, T. (2016). *Let's think secondary science: Evaluation report and executive summary*. Education Endowment Foundation. See 6 for a description of the approach, 25–26 for teacher non-intervention and the problems it caused. Humphrey, N., Hennessey, A., Ashworth, E., Frearson, K., Black, L., Petersen, K., Wo, L., Panayiotou, M., Lendrum, A., Wigelsworth, M., Birchinall, L., Squires, G., & Pampaka, M. (2018). *Good behaviour game: Evaluation report and executive summary*. Education Endowment

Foundation. See 9 for a description of the approach, as part of it, "teacher does not interact with pupils", while they are learning. See 43 for teachers' concerns about the impact on students.

16 McNally, S. (2014). *Hampshire hundreds: Evaluation report and executive summary*. Education Endowment Foundation.

17 This is a problem facing almost all professional development programmes; for a particularly marked example, see Wiggins, M., Parrao, C., Austerberry, H., & Ingold, A. (2017). *Foreign language learning in primary school: Evaluation report and executive summary*. Education Endowment Foundation.

18 See, for example, Biggart, A. (2015). *Quest: Evaluation report and executive summary*. Education Endowment Foundation.

19 Sims, S., Fletcher-Wood, H., O'Mara-Eves, A., Cottingham, S., Stansfield, C., Van Herwegen, J., & Anders, J. (2021). *What are the characteristics of effective teacher professional development? A systematic review and meta-analysis*. Education Endowment Foundation.

20 I am indebted to Brent Maddin for this insight.

1 How can we build a coherent professional development programme?

1 Teacher Tapp survey of 7340 teachers, 21 March 2021.

2 84% of teachers had heard of cognitive load theory; Teacher Tapp survey of 7340 teachers, 21 March 2021. Given a list of eight types of cognitive load, and invited to tick three, 65% of teachers chose intrinsic and 67% extraneous. The highest incorrect answer was overload, at 40%, while 6% said none of the above. Teacher Tapp survey of 5,195 teachers, 25 February 2024. For a publicly accessible summary of some of this data, but with older data, see Teacher Tapp (2019, 4 June), So . . . you've heard of Cognitive Load Theory . . .? https://teachertapp.co.uk/articles/so-youve-heard-of-cognitive-load-theory/.

3 Lemov, D., Woolway, E., & Yezzi, K. (2012) *Practice perfect: 42 rules for getting better at getting better*. Jossey-Bass, 66–68.

4 For one such objection, see Claxton, G. (2022, 15 August). Cognitive load theory: Just brain gym for traditionalists? https://www.guyclaxton.net/post/cognitive-load-theory-just-brain-gym-for-traditionalists.

5 Futures 1 and 3, in his terms. Future 2 is less relevant here. Young, M., Lambert, D., Roberts, C., & Roberts, M. (2014). *Knowledge and the future school: Curriculum and social justice*. Bloomsbury, esp. 67.

6 Murre, J. M., & Dros, J. (2015). Replication and analysis of Ebbinghaus' forgetting curve. *PLOS One*, *10*(7), e0120644.

7 Contrast, for example, Burgoyne, A.P., Hambrick, D.Z., & Macnamara, B.N. (2020). How firm are the foundations of mind-set theory? The claims appear stronger than the evidence. *Psychological Science*, *31*(3), 258–267, with Yeager, D.S., Hanselman, P., Walton, G.M., Murray, J.S., Crosnoe, R., Muller, C., Tipton, E., Schneider, B., Hulleman, C.S., Hinojosa, C.P., & Paunesku, D. (2019). A national experiment reveals where a growth mindset improves achievement. *Nature*, *573*(7774), 364–369.

8 Bjork, E.L., & Bjork, R.A. (2011). Making things hard on yourself, but in a good way: Creating desirable difficulties to enhance learning. In Gernsbacher, M.A.E., Pew, R.W., Hough, L.M., & Pomerantz, J.R. (Eds.). *Psychology and the real world: Essays illustrating fundamental contributions to society*. Worth Publishers. Ch.5.

9 This idea derives from the persistent problems described by Kennedy (2016a); the challenges listed here follow the sequence adopted by Steplab, and are adapted slightly from those Kennedy suggests. See Goodrich, J. (2024). *Responsive coaching*. John Catt, 87.

10 There's an obvious link here to the limits of working memory; this limit was also suggested by Atul Gawande's experience looking at how to make a checklist useful and usable for professionals. Gawande, A. (2010). *The checklist manifesto: How to get things right*. Profile.

11 Fletcher-Wood, H., Bignall, B., Calvert, J., Goodrich, J., & McCrea, E. (2020). *The learning curriculum: Version 3.0*. Ambition Institute. https://improvingteaching.co.uk/wp-content/uploads/2024/04/The-Learning-Curriculum-3.0.pdf.

12 Fletcher-Wood et al. (2020), 13.

13 Teacher Tapp survey of 8850 teachers, 27 March 2024; 13% strongly agree their school has a shared language for talking about effective teaching, 57% agree, 25% disagree, 5% strongly disagree.

2 How can we lead effective training?

1 See, for example, Cordingley, P., Higgins, S., Greany, T., Buckler, N., Coles-Jordan, D., Crisp, B., Saunders, L. & Coe, R. (2015). *Developing great teaching: Lessons from the international reviews into effective professional development*. Teacher Development Trust; Darling-Hammond, L., Hyler, M.E., & Gardner, M. (2017). *Effective teacher professional development*. Learning Policy Institute; Timperley, H. (2008). Teacher professional learning and development. *Educational Practices, 18*. International Academy of Education.
2 Sims and Fletcher-Wood (2021).
3 Sims et al. (2021).
4 This formulation originally came from Josh Goodrich.
5 Ericsson, A., & Pool, R. (2016). *Peak: Secrets from the new science of expertise*. Bodley Head, 98.
6 Ericsson & Pool (2016), 99–100.
7 McGaghie, W.C., Issenberg, S.B., Cohen, E.R., Barsuk, J.H., & Wayne, D.B. (2011). Does simulation-based medical education with deliberate practice yield better results than traditional clinical education? A meta-analytic comparative review of the evidence. *Academic Medicine, 86*(6) 706–711.
8 See, for example, Lemov et al. (2012), 1-5.
9 Heath, C., & Heath, D. (2017). *The power of moments: Why certain experiences have extraordinary impact*. Simon and Schuster, Ch.9.
10 Duhigg, C. (2012) *The power of habit: Why we do what we do in life and business*. Random House, Ch.5.
11 Sims et al. (2021), 39.
12 Grossman, P., Compton, C., Igra, D., Ronfeldt, M., Shahan, E., & Williamson, P. W. (2009). Teaching practice: A cross-professional perspective. *Teachers College Record, 111*(9), 2094–5. Grossman et al. use the terms preactive and interactive practice to describe preparation for lessons (like planning) and lesson activities (like asking and answering questions).
13 Menzes, A., & Maier, A. (2014). *Fast start: Training better teachers faster, with focus, practice and feedback*. The New Teacher Project, 10.
14 In their seminal paper, Ericsson and colleagues stated, "We reject any important role for innate ability." However, they did accept a potential role for individual differences in motivation and thus improvement. Ericsson, K.A., Krampe, R.T., & Tesch-Römer, C. (1993). The role of deliberate practice in the acquisition of expert performance. *Psychological Review, 100*(3), 399.
15 For example, a careful and improved replication of Ericsson et al. (1993) on the role of practice in violin players' success found deliberate practice was not the key to the top performers' success; Macnamara, B., & Maitra, M. (2019). The role of deliberate practice in expert performance: Revisiting Ericsson, Krampe, & Tesch-Römer (1993). *Royal Society Open Science, 6*(8) 190327. For a thorough review, challenging Ericsson's claims, see Macnamara, B.N., Hambrick, D.Z., & Oswald, F.L. (2014). Deliberate practice and performance in music, games, sports, education, and professions: A meta-analysis. *Psychological Science, 25*(8), 1608-1618.
16 Macnamara, B.N., Hambrick, D.Z., Frank, D.J., King, M.J., Burgoyne, A.P., & Meinz, E.J. (2018). The deliberate practice view: An evaluation of definitions, claims, and empirical evidence. In Hambrick, D.Z., Campitelli, G., & Macnamara, B.N. *The science of expertise: Behavioral, neural, and genetic approaches to complex skill*. Routledge (Ch.9), 152.
17 Berliner, D. (2001). Learning about and learning from expert teachers. *International Journal of Educational Research, 35*, 463–482.
18 For a good example of this in sports, see Lemov et al. (2012), 37.
19 Ball, D., & Forzani, F. (2009). The work of teaching and the challenge for teacher education. *Journal of Teacher Education, 60*(5), 498.
20 Lampert, M. (2001). *Teaching problems and the problems of teaching*. Yale, 16.
21 Kennedy, M. (2016a). Parsing the practice of teaching. *Journal of Teacher Education, 67*(1), 6–17.
22 Hobbiss, M., Sims, S., & Allen, R. (2020). Habit formation limits growth in teacher effectiveness: A review of converging evidence from neuroscience and social science. *Review of Education, 9*(1), 3–23.
23 Lemov et al. (2012), 49, emphasis mine.
24 Microteaching is rehearsing a condensed lesson, or part of a lesson. Role play is rehearsing a specific situation.
25 Strictly, the question is what our lesson will make students think about. Willingham, D. (2009). *Why don't students like school? A cognitive scientist answers questions about how the mind works and what it means for the classroom*. Jossey-Bass, 79.

26 Sims et al. (2021); Sims, S., Fletcher-Wood, H., Godfrey-Faussett, T., Mccrea, P. & Meliss, S. (2023). *Modelling evidence-based practice in initial teacher training: causal effects on teachers' skills, knowledge and self-efficacy*. Centre for Education Policy and Equalising Opportunities, UCL.
27 Grossman et al. (2009).
28 See discussion of Radar and Strong Voice in Lemov, D. (2015). *Teach like a champion 2.0*. Jossey-Bass.
29 I'm eliding "insights" with "threshold concepts": Meyer, J., & Land, R. (2003). *Threshold concepts and troublesome knowledge: Linkages to ways of thinking and practising within the disciplines*. Enhancing Teaching-Learning Environments in Undergraduate Courses Project. The discussion of insights which follows owes a substantial debt to the work of Kennedy, M. (2016b). How does professional development improve teaching? *Review of Educational Research, 86*(4), 945–980.
30 Sims et al. (2021).
31 Sims et al. (2021). Julie Cohen and her colleagues suggest that reflecting on a problem - without being supported to solve it - can drive increasing negative perceptions of student behaviour. That is, an insight without the skill to address it makes things worse for a teacher. Cohen, J., Wong, V., Krishnamachari, A., & Berlin, R. (2020). Teacher coaching in a simulated environment. *Educational Evaluation and Policy Analysis, 42*(2), 208–231.
32 Kennedy (2016b), 955.
33 Heath and Heath (2017), Ch.5.
34 Lemov et al. (2012), 116–117.
35 See Fletcher-Wood, H. (2018). *Responsive teaching: Cognitive science and formative assessment in practice*. Routledge,19.
36 Berner, E.S., & Graber, M.L. (2008). Overconfidence as a cause of diagnostic error in medicine. *The American Journal of Medicine, 121*(5), S2–S23, cited in Kahneman, D. (2011). *Thinking, fast and slow*. Penguin, 263.
37 Wiliam, D. (2011). *Embedded formative assessment*. Solution Tree, 129.
38 Lemov et al. (2012), 26–29.

3 How can we coach individual teachers to improve?

1 Kraft, M., Blazar, D., & Hogan, D. (2018). The effect of teacher coaching on instruction and achievement: A meta-analysis of the causal evidence. *Review of Educational Research, 88*(4), 547–588.
2 Teacher Tapp survey of 8710 teachers, 9 January 2024. Only 38% of teachers described their observation process as helping them to improve. 19% said it was designed to help them improve - but didn't; 24% said it was designed purely to check compliance, and 12% said they had no observation process; 8% selected other.
3 Teacher Tapp survey of 9830 teachers, 14 August 2024. In the preceding academic year, teachers recalled being observed: never, 14%; once, 14%; twice, 20%; three times, 18%; four-six times, 20%; seven-ten times, 7%; eleven-twenty times, 3%; 21–39 times, 3%; forty or more, 1%.
4 Burgess, S., Rawal, S., & Taylor, E. S. (2021). Teacher peer observation and student test scores: Evidence from a field experiment in English secondary schools. *Journal of Labor Economics, 39*(4), 1155–1186.
5 Gollwitzer, P.M., & Sheeran, P. (2006). Implementation intentions and goal achievement: A meta-analysis of effects and processes. *Advances in Experimental Social Psychology, 38*, 69–119.
6 Kahneman (2011), 417.

4 How can we help teachers change?

1 Wood, W., Quinn, J., & Kashy, D. (2002). Habits in everyday life: Thought, emotion, and action. *Journal of Personality and Social Psychology, 83*(6), 1281–1297. For a good overview of habit research, see Wood, W., & Neal, D. (2016). Healthy through habit: Interventions for initiating and maintaining health behavior change. *Behavioral Science & Policy, 2*(1), 71–83.
2 Hobbiss et al. (2020).
3 Feldon, D.F. (2007). Cognitive load and classroom teaching: The double-edged sword of automaticity. *Educational Psychologist, 42*(3), 123–137.

4 Deutschman, A. (2005, 1 January). Change or die. *Fast company*. https://www.fastcompany.com/52717/change-or-die.
5 Sims et al. (2021)
6 Berliner (2001).
7 Sims et al. (2021).
8 Lavecchia, A.M., Liu, H., & Oreopoulos, P. (2016). Behavioral economics of education: Progress and possibilities. *Handbook of the economics of education* 5, 1-74. Elsevier.
9 For a detailed discussion of the nature of habits, see Fletcher-Wood, H. (2021). *Habits of success: Getting every student learning*. Routledge, especially the Introduction and Ch.1.
10 Collin, J., & Quigley, A. (2021). *Teacher feedback to improve pupil learning: guidance report*. Education Endowment Foundation.
11 Gollwitzer and Sheeran (2006).

5 How can we choose a focus for improvement?

1 These examples of diagnosis errors draw on Croskerry, P. (2003). The importance of cognitive errors in diagnosis and strategies to minimize them. *Academic Medicine, 78*(8), 775-780.
2 Cambridge Assessment (2017). *A Cambridge approach to improving education: Using international insights to manage complexity*.
3 This insight reflects the discussion of resilience and control factors in Cambridge Assessment (2017).
4 See the Introduction.
5 Teacher Tapp survey of 6,017 teachers, 15 November 2021; 95% of leaders believe leaders enforce the behaviour management policy consistently; 45% of teachers agree. See Teacher Tapp (2021, 23 November). What do you think of your school's behaviour policy? https://teachertapp.com/uk/articles/what-do-you-think-of-your-schools-behaviour-policy-this-and-more/. Teacher Tapp survey of 6760 teachers on 4 January 2022: 97% of headteachers believe leaders listen and respond to staff concerns most or all of the time; 50% of teachers agree. Teacher Tapp survey of 7242 teachers on 21 July 2022: 94% of headteachers agree staff are recognised for a job well done; 46% of teachers strongly or somewhat agree.
6 I have simplified the story told in Nonaka, I. (1991). The knowledge-creating company. *Harvard Business Review*. For a fuller description and model of this process, see Nonaka, I., Takeuchi, H., & Umemoto, K. (1996). A theory of organizational knowledge creation. *International Journal of Technology Management, Special Issue on Unlearning and Learning for Technological Innovation, 11*(718), 833-845; Nonaka, I., Toyama, R., & Konon, N. (2002). SECI, Ba and leadership: A unified model of dynamic knowledge creation. In S. Little, P. Quintas, and T. Ray (Eds.), *Managing knowledge*. Sage.
7 Menzes and Maier (2014).
8 McCrea, P. (2019). *Learning: What is it, and how might we catalyse it?* Ambition Institute. https://www.ambition.org.uk/research-and-insight/learning-what-is-it/.

6 How can we lead change?

1 Andrews, M., Pritchett, L., Samji, S., & Woolcock, M. (2015). Building capability by delivering results: Putting problem-driven iterative adaptation (PDIA) principles into practice. *A governance practitioner's notebook: Alternative ideas and approaches*. OECD, 129.
2 This chapter draws heavily on their work. I particularly recommend the PDIA Toolkit, Samji, S., Andrews, M., Pritchett, L., & Woolcock, M. (2018). *PDIA toolkit: A DIY approach to solving complex problems*. Building State Capability at Harvard, CC BY-NC-ND 4.0, from which many of these prompts are drawn.
3 Elmore (1996), 3.
4 Allen, B., & Sims, S. (2018). *The teacher gap*. Routledge, Ch.7.
5 Andrews et al. (2015), 123-124.
6 Andrews et al. (2015), 123-124, emphasis original.
7 Andrews et al. (2015), 123-124.

8 Hall, P. (1980). *Great planning disasters*. University of California Press.
9 Flyvbjerg, B., Ansar, A., Budzier, A., Buhl, S., Cantarelli, C., Garbuio, M., Glenting, C., Holm, M.S., Lovallo, D., Lunn, D., & Molin, E. (2018). Five things you should know about cost overrun. *Transportation Research Part A: Policy and Practice, 118*, 174–190.
10 Pritchett, L. (2014, 18 April) Selling solutions vs. Solving problems. Building state capability: PDIA in action [Video]. Vimeo. https://vimeo.com/92338009.
11 Andrews, M. (2014, 11 April). *Constructing problems that matter. Building state capability: PDIA in action* [Video]. Vimeo. https://vimeo.com/91733935.
12 Andrews, M. (2015, 20 October). Deconstructing sticky problems. Building state capability: PDIA in action [Video]. Vimeo. https://vimeo.com/91733930.
13 Womack, J., Jones, D., & Roos, D. (2007 [1990]). *The machine that changed the world: How lean production revolutionized the global car wars*. Simon & Schuster, 56–57.
14 Andrews, M. (2015, 2 November) *Problem-driven sequencing. Building state capability: PDIA in action* [Video]. Vimeo. https://vimeo.com/91733933.
15 Andrews, M. (2015, 2 November).

7 How can we assess improvement?

1 Guskey, T. (2002) Does it make a difference? Evaluating professional development. *Redesigning Professional Development*, 59(6) 45–51.
2 Grove, A. (2015 [1983]). *High output management*. Vintage Books, 21.
3 Wiliam, D. (2016) *Leadership for Teacher learning: Creating a culture where all teachers improve so that all students succeed*. Learning Sciences International, 220ff.
4 This is an adaptation of the model offered by Thomas Guskey: I've omitted a check on teachers' feelings and added a more precise break down of the process of teacher change, reflecting the ideas in Chapter 2, Guskey (2002).
5 Fletcher-Wood (2018), Ch.4.
6 (b) should give students the best chance of remembering.
7 Coe, R. (2013). *Improving education: A triumph of hope over experience*. Centre for Evaluation and Monitoring, vii.
8 Guskey (2002), 46.
9 Christodoulou, D. (2017). *Making good progress: The future of assessment for learning*. Oxford University Press, Ch.8.
10 Guskey (2002), 49.

8 How can we improve as teacher educators?

1 In the English school system, a TLR – Teaching and Learning Responsibility – is a role for which you receive additional payment, such as being a head of department. The nationally-recognised roles are TLRs 1, 2a, and 2b.
2 The English system provides for five training days per year. Leaders can break them up, providing training after school, rather than as a standalone day. The same principles – set aside time for training and break it up – apply wherever we are working. Leaders can direct what teachers do during certain hours, but we can meet volunteers outside these hours (for example, after school).
3 Grove (2015 [1983]), 53.

References

Allen, B., & Sims, S. (2018). *The teacher gap*. Routledge.

Allen, R., Mian, E., & Sims, S. (2016). *Social inequalities in access to teachers*. Social Market Foundation Commission on Inequality in Education: Briefing 2.

Andrews, M. (2014, 11 April). *Constructing problems that matter. Building state capability: PDIA in action* [Video]. Vimeo. https://vimeo.com/91733935.

Andrews, M. (2015, 20 October). *Deconstructing sticky problems. Building state capability: PDIA in action* [Video]. Vimeo. https://vimeo.com/91733930.

Andrews, M. (2015, 2 November) *Problem-driven sequencing. Building state capability: PDIA in action* [Video]. Vimeo. https://vimeo.com/91733933.

Andrews, M., Pritchett, L., Samji, S., & Woolcock, M. (2015). *Building capability by delivering results: Putting Problem-Driven Iterative Adaptation (PDIA) principles into practice. A governance practitioner's notebook: Alternative ideas and approaches*. OECD.

Ball, D., & Forzani, F. (2009). The work of teaching and the challenge for teacher education. *Journal of Teacher Education*, *60*(5), 497–511.

Berliner, D. (2001). Learning about and learning from expert teachers. *International Journal of Educational Research, 35*, 463–482.

Biggart, A. (2015). *Quest: Evaluation report and executive summary*. Education Endowment Foundation.

Bjork, E.L., & Bjork, R.A. (2011). Making things hard on yourself, but in a good way: Creating desirable difficulties to enhance learning. In Gernsbacher, M.A.E., Pew, R.W., Hough, L.M., & Pomerantz, J.R. (Eds.). *Psychology and the real world: Essays illustrating fundamental contributions to society* (Ch.5). Worth Publishers.

Burgess, S., Rawal, S., & Taylor, E.S. (2021). Teacher peer observation and student test scores: Evidence from a field experiment in English secondary schools. *Journal of Labor Economics*, *39*(4), 1155–1186.

Burgoyne, A.P., Hambrick, D.Z., & Macnamara, B.N. (2020). How firm are the foundations of mind-set theory? The claims appear stronger than the evidence. *Psychological Science*, *31*(3), 258–267.

Cambridge Assessment (2017). *A Cambridge approach to improving education: Using international insights to manage complexity*. Cambridge University Press

Christodoulou, D. (2017). *Making good progress: The future of assessment for learning*. Oxford University Press.

Claxton, G. (2022, 15 August). *Cognitive load theory: Just brain gym for traditionalists?* https://www.guyclaxton.net/post/cognitive-load-theory-just-brain-gym-for-traditionalists.

Coe, R. (2013). *Improving Education: A triumph of hope over experience*. Centre for Evaluation and Monitoring.

Cohen, J., Wong, V., Krishnamachari, A., & Berlin, R. (2020). Teacher coaching in a simulated environment. *Educational Evaluation and Policy Analysis*, *42*(2), 208–231.

Collin, J., & Quigley, A. (2021). *Teacher feedback to improve pupil learning: guidance report*. Education Endowment Foundation.

Cordingley, P., Higgins, S., Greany, T., Buckler, N., Coles-Jordan, D., Crisp, B., Saunders, L., & Coe, R. (2015). *Developing great teaching: Lessons from the international reviews into effective professional development*. Teacher Development Trust.

Croskerry, P. (2003). The importance of cognitive errors in diagnosis and strategies to minimize them. *Academic Medicine, 78*(8), 775–780.

Darling-Hammond, L., Hyler, M.E., & Gardner, M. (2017). *Effective teacher professional development*. Learning Policy Institute.

Deutschman, A. (2005, 1 January). Change or die. *Fast Company*. https://www.fastcompany.com/52717/change-or-die.

Duhigg, C. (2012). *The power of habit: Why we do what we do in life and business*. Random House.

Elmore, R. (1996). Getting to scale with good educational practice. *Harvard Educational Review, 66*(1), 1–26.

Ericsson, K.A., Krampe, R.T., & Tesch-Römer, C. (1993). The role of deliberate practice in the acquisition of expert performance. *Psychological Review, 100*(3), 363–406.

Ericsson, A., & Pool, R. (2016). *Peak: Secrets from the new science of expertise*. Bodley Head.

Feldon, D. F. (2007). Cognitive load and classroom teaching: The double-edged sword of automaticity. *Educational Psychologist, 42*(3), 123–137.

Fletcher-Wood, H. (2018). *Responsive teaching: Cognitive science and formative assessment in practice*. Routledge.

Fletcher-Wood, H. (2021). *Habits of success: Getting every student learning*. Routledge.

Fletcher-Wood, H., Bignall, B., Calvert, J., Goodrich, J., & McCrea, E. (2020). *The learning curriculum: Version 3.0*. Ambition Institute. https://improvingteaching.co.uk/wp-content/uploads/2024/04/The-Learning-Curriculum-3.0.pdf.

Fletcher-Wood, H., & Zuccollo, J., (2020). *The effects of high-quality professional development on teachers and students: a rapid review and meta-analysis*. Education Policy Institute.

Flyvbjerg, B., Ansar, A., Budzier, A., Buhl, S., Cantarelli, C., Garbuio, M., Glenting, C., Holm, M.S., Lovallo, D., Lunn, D., & Molin, E. (2018). Five things you should know about cost overrun. *Transportation Research Part A: Policy and Practice, 118*, 174–190.

Gawande, A. (2010). *The checklist manifesto: How to get things right*. Profile.

Gollwitzer, P.M., & Sheeran, P. (2006). Implementation intentions and goal achievement: A meta-analysis of effects and processes. *Advances in Experimental Social Psychology, 38*, 69–119.

Goodrich, J. (2024). *Responsive coaching*. John Catt.

Grossman, P., Compton, C., Igra, D., Ronfeldt, M., Shahan, E., & Williamson, P. W. (2009). Teaching practice: A cross-professional perspective. *Teachers College Record, 111*(9), 2055–2100.

Grove, A. (2015 [1983]). *High output management*. Vintage Books.

Guskey, T. (2002) Does it make a difference? Evaluating professional development. *Redesigning Professional Development, 59*(6) 45–51.

Hall, P. (1980). *Great planning disasters*. University of California Press.

Hanley, P., Böhnke, J., Slavin, B., Elliott, L., & Croudace, T. (2016). *Let's think secondary science: Evaluation report and executive summary*. Education Endowment Foundation.

Heath, C., & Heath, D. (2017). *The power of moments: Why certain experiences have extraordinary impact*. Simon and Schuster.

Hobbiss, M., Sims, S., & Allen, R. (2020). Habit formation limits growth in teacher effectiveness: A review of converging evidence from neuroscience and social science. *Review of Education, 9*(1), 3–23.

Humphrey, N., Hennessey, A., Ashworth, E., Frearson, K., Black, L., Petersen, K., Wo, L., Panayiotou, M., Lendrum, A., Wigelsworth, M., Birchinall, L., Squires, G., & Pampaka, M. (2018). *Good behaviour game: Evaluation report and executive summary*. Education Endowment Foundation.

Jackson, C.K., Rockoff, J.E., & Staiger, D.O. (2014). Teacher effects and teacher-related policies. *Annual Review of Economics, 6*(1), 801–825.

Kahneman, D. (2011). *Thinking, fast and slow*. Penguin.

Kennedy, M. (2016a). Parsing the practice of teaching. *Journal of Teacher Education, 67*(1), 6–17.

Kennedy, M. (2016b). How does professional development improve teaching? *Review of Educational Research, 86*(4), 945–980.

Kini, T., & Podolsky, A. (2016). *Does teaching experience increase teacher effectiveness? A review of the research*. Learning Policy Institute.

Kraft, M., Blazar, D., & Hogan, D. (2018). The effect of teacher coaching on instruction and achievement: A meta-analysis of the causal evidence. *Review of Educational Research, 88*(4), 547–588.

Lampert, M. (2001). *Teaching problems and the problems of teaching*. Yale

Lavecchia, A.M., Liu, H., & Oreopoulos, P. (2016). Behavioral economics of education: Progress and possibilities. *Handbook of the Economics of Education 5*, 1-74. Elsevier.

Lemov, D. (2015). *Teach like a champion 2.0*. Jossey-Bass.

Lemov, D., Woolway, E., & Yezzi, K. (2012) *Practice perfect: 42 rules for getting better at getting better*. Jossey-Bass.

Macnamara, B.N., Hambrick, D.Z., Frank, D.J., King, M.J., Burgoyne, A.P., & Meinz, E.J. (2018). The deliberate practice view: An evaluation of definitions, claims, and empirical evidence. In D.Z. Hambrick, G. Campitelli, & Macnamara, B.N. (Eds.), *The science of expertise: Behavioral, neural, and genetic approaches to complex skill*. Routledge.

Macnamara, B.N., Hambrick, D.Z., & Oswald, F.L. (2014). Deliberate practice and performance in music, games, sports, education, and professions: A meta-analysis. *Psychological Science*, *25*(8), 1608-1618.

Macnamara, B., & Maitra, M. (2019). The role of deliberate practice in expert performance: Revisiting Ericsson, Krampe, & Tesch-Römer (1993). *Royal Society Open Science*, 6(8) 190327.

McCrea, P. (2019). *Learning: What is it, and how might we catalyse it?* Ambition Institute.

McGaghie, W.C., Issenberg, S.B., Cohen, E.R., Barsuk, J.H., & Wayne, D.B. (2011). Does simulation-based medical education with deliberate practice yield better results than traditional clinical education? A meta-analytic comparative review of the evidence. *Academic Medicine*, *86*(6) 706-711.

McNally, S. (2014). *Hampshire hundreds: Evaluation report and executive summary*. Education Endowment Foundation.

Menzes, A., & Maier, A. (2014). *Fast start: Training better teachers faster, with focus, practice and feedback*. The New Teacher Project.

Meyer, J., & Land, R. (2003). *Threshold concepts and troublesome knowledge: Linkages to ways of thinking and practising within the disciplines*. Enhancing Teaching-Learning Environments in Undergraduate Courses Project.

Murre, J.M., & Dros, J. (2015). Replication and analysis of Ebbinghaus' forgetting curve. *PLOS One*, *10*(7), e0120644.

Nonaka, I. (1991). *The knowledge-creating company*. Harvard Business Review.

Nonaka, I., Takeuchi, H., & Umemoto, K. (1996). A theory of organizational knowledge creation. *International Journal of Technology Management, Special Issue on Unlearning and Learning for Technological Innovation*, *11*(718), 833-845.

Nonaka, I., Toyama, R., & Konon, N. (2002). SECI, Ba and Leadership: A unified model of dynamic knowledge creation. In S. Little, P. Quintas, & T. Ray (Eds.), *Managing Knowledge*. Sage.

Pritchett, L. (2014, 18 April) *Selling solutions vs. solving problems, building state capability: PDIA in action* [Video]. Vimeo. https://vimeo.com/92338009.

Samji, S., Andrews, M., Pritchett, L., & Woolcock, M. (2018). *PDIA toolkit: A DIY approach to solving complex problems*. Building State Capability at Harvard. CC BY-NC-ND 4.0.

Sims, S., & Fletcher-Wood, H. (2021). Identifying the characteristics of effective teacher professional development: A critical review. *School Effectiveness and School Improvement*, *32*(1), 47-63.

Sims, S., Fletcher-Wood, H., Godfrey-Faussett, T., McCrea, P., & Meliss, S. (2023). *Modelling evidence-based practice in initial teacher training: Causal effects on teachers' skills, knowledge and self-efficacy*. Centre for Education Policy and Equalising Opportunities, UCL.

Sims, S., Fletcher-Wood, H., O'Mara-Eves, A., Cottingham, S., Stansfield, C., Van Herwegen, J., & Anders, J. (2021). *What are the characteristics of effective teacher professional development? A systematic review and meta-analysis*. Education Endowment Foundation.

Slater, H., Davies, N.M., & Burgess, S. (2012). Do teachers matter? Measuring the variation in teacher effectiveness in England. *Oxford Bulletin of Economics and Statistics*, *74*(5), 629-645.

Teacher Tapp (2019, 4 June). So . . . you've heard of Cognitive Load Theory . . .? https://teachertapp.co.uk/articles/so-youve-heard-of-cognitive-load-theory/.

Teacher Tapp (2021, 23 November). What do you think of your school's behaviour policy? https://teachertapp.com/uk/articles/what-do-you-think-of-your-schools-behaviour-policy-this-and-more/

Timperley, H. (2008). *Teacher professional learning and development. Educational Practices*, *18*. International Academy of Education.

The New Teacher Project (2015). *The mirage: Confronting the hard truth about our quest for teacher development*.

Wiggins, M., Parrao, C., Austerberry, H., & Ingold, A. (2017). *Foreign language learning in primary school: Evaluation report and executive summary*. Education Endowment Foundation.

Wiliam, D. (2011). *Embedded formative assessment*. Solution Tree.

Wiliam, D. (2016). *Leadership for teacher learning: Creating a culture where all teachers improve so that all students succeed*. Learning Sciences International.

Willingham, D. (2009). *Why don't students like school? A cognitive scientist answers questions about how the mind works and what it means for the classroom*. Jossey-Bass.

Wood, W., & Neal, D. (2016). Healthy through habit: Interventions for initiating and maintaining health behavior change. *Behavioral Science & Policy, 2*(1), 71–83.

Wood, W., Quinn, J., & Kashy, D. (2002). Habits in everyday life: Thought, emotion, and action. *Journal of Personality and Social Psychology, 83*(6), 1281–1297.

Womack, J., Jones, D., & Roos, D. (2007 [1990]). *The machine that changed the world: How lean production revolutionized the global car wars*. Simon & Schuster.

Yeager, D.S., Hanselman, P., Walton, G.M., Murray, J.S., Crosnoe, R., Muller, C., Tipton, E., Schneider, B., Hulleman, C.S., Hinojosa, C.P., & Paunesku, D. (2019). A national experiment reveals where a growth mindset improves achievement. *Nature, 573*(7774), 364–369.

Young, M., Lambert, D., Roberts, C., & Roberts, M. (2014). *Knowledge and the future school: Curriculum and social justice*. Bloomsbury.

Index